T0243377

YEAR ZERO

MILLER CENTER STUDIES ON THE PRESIDENCY

Guian A. McKee and Marc J. Selverstone, Editors

YEAR ZERO

The Five-Year Presidency

CHRISTOPHER P. LIDDELL

University of Virginia Press

CHARLOTTESVILLE AND LONDON

Published in association with the University of
Virginia's Miller Center of Public Affairs

University of Virginia Press
© 2024 by Christopher P. Liddell
All rights reserved
Printed in the United States of America on acid-free paper

First published 2024

9 8 7 6 5 4 3 2 1

Library of Congress Cataloging-in-Publication Data

Names: Liddell, Christopher P., author.
Title: Year zero : the five-year presidency / Christopher P. Liddell.
Description: Charlottesville : University of Virginia Press, 2024. | Series: Miller center
    studies on the presidency | Includes bibliographical references and index.
Identifiers: LCCN 2023029003 (print) | LCCN 2023029004 (ebook) | ISBN 9780813951133
    (hardcover) | ISBN 9780813951140 (ebook)
Subjects: LCSH: Presidents—United States—Transition periods. | Presidents—United
    States—Transition periods—Planning. | Executive departments—United States—
    Management. | United States—Politics and government—21st century.
Classification: LCC JK516 .L38 2024 (print) | LCC JK516 (ebook) | DDC 352.23/70973—
    dc23/eng/20230728
LC record available at https://lccn.loc.gov/2023029003
LC ebook record available at https://lccn.loc.gov/2023029004

Cover art: Detail from the seal of the President of the United States

Contents

Acronyms

APs	assistants to the president
BoB	Bureau of the Budget
CEA	Council of Economic Advisers
CIA	Central Intelligence Agency
DACA	Deferred Action for Childhood Arrivals
DAPs	deputy assistants to the president
DC	Deputies Committee
DCoS	deputy chiefs of staff
DHS	Homeland Security Department
DPC	Domestic Policy Council
EEOB	Eisenhower Executive Office Building
EOP	Executive Office of the President
EPA	Environmental Protection Agency
FCC	Federal Communications Commission
FTC	Federal Trade Commission
GC	Office of the General Counsel
GPRA	Government Performance and Results Act of 1993
GSA	General Services Administration
HSC	Homeland Security Council
IMF	International Monetary Fund
NAFTA	North American Free Trade Agreement
NATO	North Atlantic Treaty Organization
NEA	National Emergencies Act of 1976
NEC	National Economic Council
NEPA	National Environmental Policy Act of 1970
NLRB	National Labor Relations Board
NSA	national security adviser
NSC	National Security Council
NSM	national security memoranda
OCA	Office of Cabinet Affairs
OECD	Organisation for Economic Co-operation and Development

OFFM	Office of Federal Financial Management
OFPP	Office of Federal Procurement Policy
OIA	Office of Intergovernmental Affairs
OIRA	Office of Information and Regulatory Affairs
OLA	Office of Legislative Affairs
OLC	Office of Legal Counsel
OMB	Office of Management and Budget
OPL	Office of Public Liaison
OPM	Office of Personnel Management
OPOTUS	Office of the President of the United States
OPPM	Office of Performance and Personnel Management
OSTP	Office of Science and Technology Policy
PADs	program associate directors
PAs	presidential appointments not subject to Senate confirmation
PASs	presidential appointments subject to Senate confirmation
PCAST	President's Council of Advisors on Science and Technology
PCC	Policy Coordinating Committee
PC	Principals Committee Process
PIAB	President's Intelligence Advisory Board
POTUS	President of the United States
PPO	Presidential Personnel Office
PPTE	Public-Private Talent Exchange
PTCC	Presidential Transition Coordinating Council
PTEA	Presidential Transition Enhancement Act of 2019
RMOs	Resource Management Offices
SAPs	special assistants to the president
SES	Senior Executive Service
SGEs	special government employees
TARP	Troubled Asset Relief Program
USDS	United States Digital Services
Y0LT	Year Zero leadership team

INTRODUCTION

I didn't turn off a light—not when I closed my office door in the West Wing for the last time, or as I walked through the White House a few minutes before the inauguration of Joe Biden as the country's forty-sixth president. Yet America's transition from one president to another resembles nothing so much as the flip of a switch: at noon on January 20, it's instantaneous.

The lights were shining brightly when I walked into the Oval Office, where I had attended so many meetings across four years. President Trump had left a few hours earlier to take his final trip on Air Force One, but I skipped the send-off at Joint Base Andrews in Maryland. As the operational head of the Transition Coordinating Council, a body created by Congress to ease the changeover from one administration to the next, I believed that it was my duty to stay on-site until 11:59 a.m., the very end of the Trump presidency.

Inside the Oval, workers scrambled to move chairs, couches, and paintings. The room was receiving a complete makeover in double time. President Trump's personal effects were gone. A portrait of Benjamin Franklin replaced that of Andrew Jackson. President Trump's yellow rug had been rolled up and vanished, and for a moment I watched the installation of the dark-blue rug chosen by his successor. Everything had to be ready for when President Biden arrived. It was like a scene on a home-renovation TV show, but with a hard deadline.

The frantic sight reminded me that no organization in the world aims to function in this manner, except, ironically, the one that may be the world's most important: the White House. Its lights never turn off, but the White House changes from one team to a totally new one with the metaphorical flick of a switch. There is 100 percent turnover of a large staff tasked with huge responsibilities, and the incoming staff often have little to no accumulated institutional knowledge. A poor start to White House management can hobble an entire presidency. And a suboptimal functioning of the West Wing is, in my view, a major contributor to the public crisis of confidence in the federal government and, because of that, American democracy itself.

Transitions of power are one of the great successes of American democracy, even when they happen amid controversy, as they did in the wake of the elections of 1800, 1876, 2000, and 2020. As President Reagan observed, "In the eyes of many in the world, this every-four-year ceremony we accept as normal is nothing less than a miracle."[1] However, very few institutional norms last for more than two hundred years, and nothing can be presumed to last forever. The chances of a future contested election and even a constitutional crisis over the transition period are unfortunately increasing. The proud record of successful transitions, and the security of the country, needs to be protected as well as admired.

Given the presidency's central role in the American political system, it is time to better prepare presidents and their staffs for the task of governing, and how we send them into office. Everyone from candidates to the voters who select them should see the job of the chief executive of the federal government not just as part of a constitutional four-year term but as a longer five-year journey. I call that journey the "Five-Year Presidency."

This novel concept launches at least a year before an election—what I've dubbed Year Zero—to help an aspiring president prepare for the task of managing the White House and, with it, one of the world's largest enterprises, the U.S. federal government.

THE CRISIS OF DEMOCRACY

The need to improve the functioning of the White House occurs against the decades-long backdrop of Americans questioning whether American democracy retains the potency to deliver for its citizens. Unfortunately, this doubt is also a global trend: citizens across most democracies are expressing increasing disapproval of their governments, even as global challenges requiring leadership and robust international cooperation are growing.

Hardly anyone expected this trend thirty years ago. With the collapse of the Soviet Union in the late twentieth century, it appeared democracy had emerged triumphant over both communism and fascism as the supreme form of governing. That historical moment prompted ideas such as Francis Fukuyama's famous theory that humanity was now living at the "end of history"[2]—a sense that democracy had won a permanent victory in the global battle of political ideologies.

Those halcyon days are over. Since the beginning of the twenty-first century, public opinion regarding the health and legitimacy of democracy has trended in a negative direction. Just 9 percent of U.S. adults think democracy is working "extremely" or "very well," according to an October 2022 poll by the Associated Press–NORC Center for Public Affairs Research.[3] The political scientist Andrew Heywood describes the apparent unraveling of confidence in democracy over the last few decades as a shift from "democratic triumph to democratic winter."[4]

The erosion of trust in democracy is also occurring simultaneously alongside the rise of authoritarian governments. China's multidecade economic growth and ascent to geopolitical power has led many across the world to wonder if Chinese-style autocracy is a superior model to democracy for driving stability, growth, development, and social progress. It is easy to believe that because authoritarian leaders are unconstrained by time-consuming legislative processes or accountability at the ballot box, they can more speedily implement their ideas and better deliver for their people than democratic leaders can. In light of this growing narrative, it is important that America and other liberal democracies exhibit a superior ability to achieve results for their citizens. It's time to improve how the greatest seat of power in America functions.

MANAGING LEVIATHAN

Even assuming the most qualified holder of the Oval Office, the size and complexity of the issues he or she is expected to confront, and the size and complexity of the organization over which the president must preside, makes effective governance extremely difficult.

In Federalist No. 51, James Madison wrote, "In framing a government which is to be administered by men over men, the great difficulty lies in this: you must first enable the government to control the governed; and in the next place oblige it to control itself."[5] Since he wrote those early words, the size of the U.S. federal government has grown dramatically both in dollars of expenditure and as a percentage of gross domestic product.

More recent expenditure has risen in waves. In the 1930s and 1940s, President Franklin Delano Roosevelt (FDR) grew spending as he attempted to fix a depression-ravaged America through the New Deal. Defeating the Axis powers in World War II also meant dramatic expenditures. During the Cold War, the federal government scaled up an international military, diplomatic, intelligence, and foreign aid apparatus to protect the American homeland and contain communism. In the 1960s, the Great Society expanded expenditures on entitlement programs, and the creation of regulatory agencies in the 1970s such as the Environmental Protection Agency and the U.S. Department of Education tacked on to the budget further.

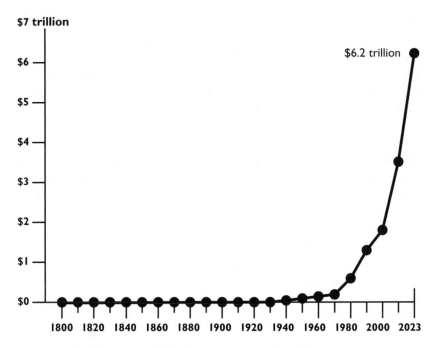

FIGURE 1. Leviathan grows: Federal government outlays, 1800–2023

After the terrorist attacks of September 11, 2001, came the Department of Homeland Security and foreign wars.

It's not just the size of government that has grown but the number of people working in it. The number of federal employees, including members of the military, has grown from 699,000 in 1940[6] to more than 4.2 million in 2022.[7] That number has been augmented in recent decades by several million additional federal government contractors.

Government interventions in the nation's economic affairs have also increased. For example, the U.S. federal government took a very active role in trying to mitigate the economic destruction from the 2008–9 financial crisis and the 2020 COVID-19 pandemic. On the foreign stage, the United States has taken a massively increased role since World War II. It was instrumental in designing and implementing the geopolitical architecture of the postwar world, helping to create international organizations such as the United Nations (UN), North Atlantic Treaty Organization (NATO), the World Bank, and the International Monetary Fund (IMF). A robust diplomatic, military, and humanitarian presence around the world consumes high levels of ongoing resources.

While this book does not seek to answer the question of the appropriate size of government, it's clear that the size of government is outstripping the ability of any one person, the president, to adequately manage it. A modern president has the task of implementing an agenda through the vast machine of the federal government in the face of oppositional political forces, and the complexities of managing the White House itself.

In an attempt to manage a sprawling federal government, staff levels within the White House itself have also increased dramatically throughout the years. In 1939 FDR created what we now know as the Executive Office of the President (EOP), a cluster of offices whose total head count was probably only modestly above the 37 staffers he started with in 1933.[8] The EOP now numbers some 2,000 people.[9]

Despite the roughly fiftyfold growth in the size of the EOP from the Roosevelt administration to today, a larger White House hasn't necessarily helped to better deliver on citizen expectations. Even the hardest-working staffers within the White House struggle to accurately track and influence all of the activities of a federal government that had a budget of $6.2 trillion in 2023.[10] Additionally, the EOP has reached a diseconomy of scale: adding more people can make it less effective, not more. As a result, the size of the EOP has plateaued, even while the size of the leviathan it seeks to control has grown.

Ultimately, the White House's capability has reached its limits at a time when citizens expect more success than ever from their presidents. Thus, as Terry Moe has stated succinctly, "the expectations surrounding presidential performance far outstrip the institutional capacity of presidents to perform."[11] Since legitimacy is derived from competent performance, there is diminishing faith in the federal government to deliver on its promises.[12] A 2021 Gallup poll revealed that a record-low 39 percent of Americans trusted the federal government to handle domestic problems, down from an average of 53 percent from 1997 to 2021.[13]

INCREASED EXPECTATIONS

The inability of any president to properly manage the federal government has, ironically, occurred at a time when campaign messaging has inflated citizens' expectations of what a president can and will do to solve their problems once in office. Candidates have always made grand promises on the campaign trail—think of Woodrow Wilson's mantra, "He kept us out of war," during his 1916 reelection campaign, or Warren G. Harding's promise of a "return to normalcy" in 1920. But candidates have arguably projected a more aggressive image of omnipotence on the trail in recent decades, from President Obama's iconographic "Hope" posters to Donald Trump's vow of "I alone can fix it." Additionally, as candidates compete for loyalty (and money) from various interest groups, the list of promises a would-be president is forced to make—and deliver on—has grown.

As the realization sets in that presidents aren't all-powerful and that they struggle to deliver everything that they promised on the campaign trail, their popularity decreases over the course of their administration. This diminishing popularity is often fueled by the same media apparatus that did much to increase expectations during the campaign period. Low popularity ratings in turn weaken the presidential bargaining position in delivering promised outcomes.

Though political mud fights can capture eyeballs and drive clicks, research indicates that Americans overwhelmingly want a functional government that delivers services in an effective fashion. An October 2022 NBC News poll, for instance, asked the question, "If you could send one message with your vote this year so the people who win the election know what you mean with your vote, in a short phrase, what would that message be?" The most common response was "Be More Effective/Productive/Do More."[14]

WE NEED TO FIX THE "HOW" OF GOVERNMENT, NOT JUST THE "WHAT"

Margaret Thatcher was known to quip to her advisers, "Don't tell me what. I know what. Tell me how."[15] This remark captures the subject of this book: refining the "how" of the White House. It's a topic that few books have addressed. Political philosophers have for centuries pondered *why* government exists. Still more political scientists have written on *what* policies a president or other public officials should institute while in office. And there is a seemingly insatiable appetite for memoirs that cover *who* was "in the room."

My contention is that there needs to be equal attention paid to the operational effectiveness of the institutions of government. The reality is that if an organization can't deliver an effective "how," it's unlikely to get much "what" done, and therefore will fail in its "why."

Furthermore, academic literature on the presidency has generally examined what presidents did with a descriptive focus. These studies review past action, mostly leaving the reader to surmise the lessons for future action. My approach is to focus on prescriptions for the future—and in particular how a small entity composed of a few thousand people can better run a government that employs several million people, delivers services to some 330 million people, and crafts policies that impact not only them but billions of people around the world.

This book is novel in postulating how to create a more effective White

House by improving structures and processes, in particular those that are (to a very large extent) inside the president's control, even as the executive's overall power is hemmed in by forces inside and outside government.

The best approach to refining the "how" is an interdisciplinary one. Some commentators have approached the topic of how government should work simply by advocating for the application of private sector management techniques. That is not my purpose in this book. My view is that the federal government, including the White House, is simply too different from any private sector organization to superimpose blanket principles of private sector management on it with any expectation of success. It is more appropriate to apply first principles of organization design. There are some concepts that apply to any organization regardless of size or purpose. The challenge is to decide which apply to an entity as unique as the White House, and which don't.

History brings useful perspectives for analyzing how to improve the "how." What has been tried before, what has worked well, and what hasn't? Yet one disadvantage of history as a guide is the small sample size of presidential administrations to survey: in 234 years, there have been forty-six U.S. presidents. That number shrinks to fourteen in the modern age of the presidency (since the creation of the EOP in 1939). Over that time every dimension of the U.S. government has ballooned. Very different individuals, very different size of government, very different circumstances.

Last, there is a psychological level of analysis in this work. Perhaps what is unique about the White House—the pressures of globally significant decisions, the intense media focus on it, the almost limitless power of its resources, and the intrigue of court politics—makes it the world's most interesting petri dish of human interaction. Static organization charts massively oversimplify the reality of having hundreds of human beings—many of them brilliant, ambitious, and at odds with one another—coexisting in one of the most high-pressure work environments in the world. Solutions require carefully considering the behavioral characteristics of both presidents and the teams around them.

MEASURING THE DRAPES

I come to this problem as a former senior aide inside the White House and a participant in three presidential election cycles. In 2012, as the executive director of Mitt Romney's transition team, I saw it from the perspective of an unsuccessful challenger.[16] In 2016, I was appointed to President Trump's transition team after his election and helped the candidate move into office. And in 2020—following four years of public service, including as assistant to the president and deputy White House chief of staff—I worked from the inside, preparing initially for a possible second Trump term, and then overseeing efforts to transition to the incoming Biden administration. In my time at the White House, I immersed myself in presidential biographies and since 2021 have reread a number with a new interest in how they dealt with the issues raised here.

My most important takeaway from my experiences and research is that a standard bit of D.C.'s conventional wisdom is wrong: I believe that it is never too soon to "measure the drapes." This metaphor is widely used to describe an attitude of entitlement on the part of would-be officeholders: they "measure the drapes" of the physical space they seek to inhabit but have not yet earned. The critics' implication is that, rather than tending to the fundamentals of an election, candidates distract themselves with dreams of authority before the voters have awarded them public office. The idea of "measuring the drapes" has become something of a clichéd synonym for brazen overconfidence. In a feat of presumption, the candidates are thinking too much about what should happen after their election.

However, underpreparing for leadership in the Oval Office is, in my view, a larger blunder for an aspiring president than anticipating what he or she will do once there. I prefer the phrase "measuring the drapes" to mean undertaking the necessary and comprehensive work of preparing to command the most powerful office on earth.

At its heart, this book is a call to assist future presidents by transforming the connotations surrounding the "measuring the drapes" metaphor from pejorative ones to positive ones. Instead of regarding early activity as a sign of arrogance, political insiders and the larger American voting public should see it as a sign of competence. It shows voters a candidate preparing to effectively govern. And that, in governing well, a would-be president can help restore faith in the American system.

Moreover, I recommend that candidates not only do more preparation but that they also highlight it to the voting public and make it part of their election pitch. By showcasing their activities, they will demystify the process of governance, and convince skeptical voters of their ability to not just create a policy platform but deliver on it.

THE FIVE-YEAR PRESIDENCY

In 1939, a government-commissioned panel of experts called the Brownlow Committee found that "the President needs help," leading to the creation of the Executive Office of the President.[17] I now believe that it is the *presidency* that needs help. Preparations for governance of the White House have failed to keep pace with the growth and complexity of White House operations. The advent of primaries and the decrease in importance of party conventions have swung the initial selection criteria for presidential candidates toward media and fundraising skills and away from bargaining and managerial ones. Voters in more recent general elections have seldom used as a criterion for selection of a president the skills and experience necessary for managing anything as complex as the White House—let alone the enormous federal government.

And polarization in our politics has made the task even more challenging. At a practical level, candidates need to embrace the potential for significantly shortened transition periods. Whether because of a contested election, the need to involve the Supreme Court in some aspect of the election, or even a need for the House of Representatives to decide the winner (perhaps because of a third-party candidate successful enough that no one candidate gains an electoral college majority), the time between certainty of result and the inauguration of the president could be dramatically reduced. Not only might the management of the transition be impacted but also the national security of the country, which is particularly exposed over this period.

The book introduces a new concept: the Five-Year Presidency. That term clearly does not mean a change to the length of the president's term of office but, rather, a change in the paradigm of how would-be presidents prepare for the responsibilities of governing in the White House. My proposals accept the reality of the turbulent world that we inhabit and make practical suggestions about how to design, build, and operate a more effective White House and, by extension, the executive branch of the U.S. federal government. Even more specifically, my recommendations entail the addition of what I describe as "Year Zero"—a prepresidency year of consciously designing what will happen at 1600 Pennsylvania Avenue and how it will be done.

The concepts presented here also apply to a second-term president. The reelection is a perfect opportunity for a major reset to reinvigorate the institution, lock in the actions from the first term, and be even more ambitious for the second. Presidents can use the fourth year of their first term as a new "Year Zero" that plans for a major restructuring and "rebooting" to be rolled out in the postelection period.

It is important to emphasize, given my own roles within one party, that my argument is nonpartisan. With this book, I wish to help future presidents of any party assume the responsibility of running a vast and complicated government.

The book is structured in two parts. The first consists of two chapters that provide a contextual understanding of the presidency by describing the instruments of power available to the president, and an overview of the modern White House. The second part outlines in eight chapters the essence of the Five-Year Presidency, in particular the seven tasks and fifty proposals that should be incorporated into Year One. Knowledgeable observers of presidential politics may wish to go straight to part 2, whereas the general reader is almost sure to find some useful nuggets of background in the first two chapters.

In my work overseeing the White House's role in the 2020 transition, I saw the strength of our institutions pressure-tested and hold in the wake of a contested election. My goal now is to ensure that future presidents can harness the strength and power of the White House for future good. If successfully executed, the Five-Year Presidency approach can make for a significantly more effective White House, lessen the impact of contested elections, and in so doing, enhance trust in democracy.

I

PRESIDENTIAL POWER AND IMPACT

Although American presidents have vast powers at their disposal, even the most strategic and charismatic chief executives will encounter constraints on their ability to accomplish their objectives. President Reagan's unsuccessful nomination of Judge Robert Bork provides us with an example.

On the strength of his résumé alone, Bork was one of the most qualified people to ever be nominated to the U.S. Supreme Court. As a former solicitor general, Yale Law School professor, and judge on the prestigious D.C. Circuit Court of Appeals, he had spent his career at the summit of the mountain of American law. These qualifications would seem to ensure a smooth confirmation—especially in an era when Supreme Court justice Antonin Scalia could be confirmed by a vote of 98–0 in 1986. But when President Reagan submitted Bork's name to replace the retiring associate justice Lewis F. Powell on July 1, 1987, Bork became the target of an intense political backlash. Civil rights groups and Senate Democrats mounted ferocious opposition to him, believing that he would roll back legal protections of civil rights secured during the 1960s. He was also unpopular because of his role in the "Saturday night massacre," when President Richard Nixon ordered the firing of Watergate special prosecutor Archibald Cox. Senator Ted Kennedy of Massachusetts commented, "President Reagan is . . . our president. But he should not be able to reach out from the muck of Irangate, reach into the muck of Watergate and impose his reactionary vision of the Constitution on the Supreme Court and the next generation of Americans. No justice would be better than this injustice."[1]

After months of drama, the Senate rejected Bork's nomination in a 58–42 vote, and the Reagan administration withdrew Bork's name from consideration. Eventually, Anthony Kennedy was confirmed by a vote of 97–0.

The Bork nomination is an illustration of the dimensions of presidential power—and, specifically, its limits. Despite President Reagan's *institutional* power to nominate Bork and his *personal* power to lobby senators to confirm him, the president's power within this specific political environment—his *situational power*—was insufficient for achieving his goal. The moment was not right.

DIMENSIONS OF PRESIDENTIAL POWER

Power is the ability to direct or influence the behavior of others or of events. Presidential power, therefore, is the ability to shape the course of national policy and influence the necessary political actors to achieve desired ends.

There are three dimensions to presidential power. The first is *institutional power*—that which arises from the legal powers given to the president by the Constitution, either initially as set out in Article II or through subsequent precedent and interpretation. Institutional power is the traditional lens through which the presidency has been studied.[2]

In 1960, Richard Neustadt published the first edition of his influential book *Presidential Power*, which studied the behavioral aspects of a president's power—what could be categorized as *personal power*. This book, and subsequent editions over the years, was a revelation to the understanding of how presidents use their office, and it has informed generations of observers and experts ever since (it has even influenced presidents themselves—by all accounts, it greatly influenced John F. Kennedy when he became president).

The third aspect of presidential power is that of *situational power*. It is not possible to fully consider the use of the first two types of power without the context within which they operate. For example, the external economic environment, the size of the governing mandate that presidents perceive they have through their margin of electoral victory, broader societal trends, and the political makeup of the Congress that they must work with all influence how they can exercise their institutional and personal power.

Institutional Power

The Constitution sets the framework of the president's institutional power. However, the totality of Article II is only a little more than one thousand words, leaving considerable scope for interpretation. Article II states, "The executive power shall be vested in a President." Even though the Framers spent a significant amount of time on how a president should be chosen, they spent relatively little time defining what "executive power" actually entailed. That lack of specificity on presidential power set up a debate that goes on today. Does the Constitution define the *maximum level* of a president's powers or the *minimum level*?

An argument claiming that it sets the maximum level means that the president only has powers directly referenced or implied by the Constitution (the position taken by most presidents in the eighteenth and nineteenth centuries). These would include such powers as are clearly spelled out in the Constitution, such as the right to veto federal legislation or appoint federal judges and ambassadors. President William Howard Taft, who governed from 1909 to 1913, took that approach in writing: "the true view of the Executive function is, as I conceive it, that the President can exercise no power which cannot be fairly and reasonably traced to some specific grant of power . . . either in the Federal Constitution or in an act of Congress passed in pursuance thereof."[3]

Other presidents, including both Roosevelts, and most post–World War II presidents, have viewed the Constitution as defining the minimum level of their power. For them, the president is the only elected official with a national constituency, and as Thomas Jefferson observed, the inhabitant of the only U.S. government office capable of commanding "a view of the whole ground."[4] Thus the president's view of national issues necessitated an expansive approach to presidential power. Progressive Teddy Roosevelt's belief on presidential power was "that it was not only [the president's] right but his duty to do anything that the needs of the Nation demanded unless such action was forbidden by the Constitution or by the laws."[5]

Presidents have often claimed expanded presidential power during times of war. Abraham Lincoln's suspension of habeas corpus during the Civil War, Woodrow Wilson's crackdown on dissenters during World War I, Roosevelt's "destroyers for bases" deal before entering World War II, and George W. Bush's use of domestic surveillance as part of the "War on Terror" are just a few examples. These presidents believed that the protection of national interest justified presidential powers that, many claimed, exceeded those defined in the Constitution. In Lincoln's words, "measures, otherwise unconstitutional, might become lawful, by becoming indispensable to the preservation of the constitution, through the preservation of the nation."[6] This expansive view finds intellectual roots in the writings of the seventeenth-century philosopher John Locke, who described the concept of executive prerogative as "to act according to discretion, for the public good, without the prescription of the Law, and sometimes even against it."[7]

More recently, there has been the development under various presidents of the concept of a "unitary executive," that is, one that is fully unconstrained by Congress. As former White House counsel John Dean has written, "In its most extreme form unitary executive theory can mean that neither Congress nor the federal courts can tell the president what to do or how to do it, particularly regarding national security matters."[8] Presidents

Reagan, George H. W. Bush, and George W. Bush all invoked some concept of the unitary executive to justify unilateral action.

Fearing that presidents' views of power could become so expansive as to become unconstitutional and destructive to the republic, Congress and the federal courts have over the years passed and upheld legislation limiting them. The Twenty-Second Amendment, passed in the wake of the death of four-termer FDR, limited presidents to two terms only. The War Powers Resolution of 1973 attempted to limit the president's ability to enter into armed conflict without the consent of Congress. In response to President Nixon's decisions to refuse to release congressionally appropriated funds for various budget items, Congress passed the Congressional Budget Act to force presidential compliance. And the Founders bequeathed to Congress the ultimate sanction on a president's perceived abuses of power: impeachment. Although that power has seldom been used, and a president has never been impeached and removed from office, Congress has initiated attempts against Andrew Johnson, Richard Nixon, Bill Clinton, and Donald Trump.

In spite of constitutional strictures and laws passed down the centuries, federal law has increasingly accommodated a more expansive view of presidential power, and presidents have generally taken advantage of the opportunity to expand it where they can.

Personal Power

Richard Neustadt was the first observer, and remains perhaps still the best known, to study the personal and behavioral aspects of presidential power in his 1960 book of that name. He revised the book over the decades but came to the same overall conclusion in the preface to the 1990 second edition: "Presidential weakness . . . remains my theme. Weakness is still what I see: weakness in the sense of a great gap between what is expected of a man (or someday woman) and assured capacity to carry through. Expectations rise and clerkly tasks increase, while prospects for sustained support from any quarter worsen as foreign alliances loosen and political parties wane."[9]

Neustadt made the central point that American government is "separate institutions sharing each other's power."[10] Neustadt's work was critical in pointing out the limits of the president's institutional power and countering the impression of the president as an all-powerful individual. This led to the famous line, "Presidential power is the power to persuade," and from that, "The essence of a President's persuasive task, with congressmen and everybody else, is to induce them to believe that what he wants of them is what their own appraisal of their own responsibilities requires them to do in their interest, not his."[11] He recommended an active presidency, suggesting that a president who simply carries out the legislature's wishes is nothing more than a "clerk."

President Obama lamented his own relative lack of power within the federal system when he remarked, "What I didn't fully appreciate, and nobody can appreciate until they're in the position, is how decentralized power is in this system. . . . A lot of the work is not just identifying the right policy but now constantly building these ever shifting coalitions to be able to actually implement and execute and get it done."[12]

Another influential study of presidential personal traits was James David Barber's 1972 book *The Presidential Character: Predicting Performance in the White House*.[13] He measured and categorized each president on two dimensions—his "activity level" in office and whether he "gives the impression he enjoys his political life." By combining these two factors, he came up with four "types" of presidents:

Active-positive: ambitious and exuberant (e.g., FDR, JFK)
Passive-positive: compliant, affection-seeking (e.g., Taft, Reagan, Harding)
Passive-negative: dutiful, self-denying (e.g., Coolidge, Eisenhower)
Active-negative: (the least desirable): power-seeking, ambitious out of anxiety (e.g., Nixon)

The other aspect of personal power, which writers such as Fred I. Greenstein have examined, is "skill." The combination of some mixture of skills such as vision, cognitive style, political skill, communicative ability, organizational capacity, plus emotional strength, was thought to explain a lot of the desire and ability of an individual president to place himself along the minimalist-maximalist spectrum, and then to be able deliver on an agenda.[14]

We can see in the psychological approach to evaluating the presidency the echoes of the Great Man Theory of history, what Paul Quirk describes as "the view that critical events and major transformations result from the actions of extraordinary leaders rather than broad impersonal forces."[15] Woodrow Wilson embraced the notion of a president injecting the force of his particular personality into the office, writing, "The President is at liberty, both in law and in conscience, to be as big a man as he can. His capacity will set the limit."[16] Certainly, presidents such as Theodore Roosevelt, Lyndon Johnson, and Donald Trump were comfortable throwing their political weight around in accordance with their belief in their personal ability to effectuate action (with varying degrees of success). But less charismatic presidents such as Gerald Ford or Jimmy Carter, while having certain political gifts, do not seem to have put as much confidence in their own personal charisma to drive outcomes. Consequently, any inhabitant of the Oval Office must demonstrate a keen self-awareness in assessing their own personal power to cajole, or even coerce, the outcomes they are seeking.

Situational Power

The third aspect of presidential power is the context that presidents inherit during their time in office. In an anecdote that may be apocryphal, Harold Macmillan was asked what was the biggest problem he faced as Britain's prime minister. His answer was, "Events, dear boy, events."[17] Forces far beyond presidents' control will routinely impact their power.

For example, eight presidents—John Adams, Martin Van Buren, James Buchanan, Abraham Lincoln, Grover Cleveland, Herbert Hoover, Franklin Roosevelt, and Barack Obama—all faced financial crises in the first year of their presidencies, and more recently Joe Biden had to deal with the COVID-19 pandemic.

Another major determinant of situational power is the size of the electoral mandate that the president receives, which translates into a president's level of political capital at the starting gate. Since World War II, the average margin of a president's victory as a percentage of the popular vote has progressively shrunk. Combined with the ongoing polarization of American democracy, lesser quantities of political support have severely constrained presidents' ability to get things done. Two recent presidents, George W. Bush and Donald Trump, were even elected with a minority of the popular vote, leading some to perceive that their governing mandates were quite small, or even nonexistent. Hence, future presidents and their staffs will have to seek out creative new methods of accomplishing their goals, since they may often have little political capital to expend in pursuing them.

The most specific determinative situational factor impacting a president's ability to achieve domestic goals is the Congress that the White House has to work with. Since World War II, American government has featured every different combination of Republican and Democratic control of the presidency, the House, and the Senate. The president has enjoyed party support from both houses of Congress in a minority of years (sixteen of the last fifty) and very seldom filibuster-proof (six out of fifty). Based on historical norms, over a complete term a president typically will have to navigate a split or hostile Congress, and in almost all situations because of the filibuster will have to deal with a Senate where the opposition party has an effective veto.

A less obvious but equally important situational factor for a president to navigate is the composition of the federal courts, and specifically, the

Supreme Court. Controversial legislation or other presidential actions are likely to find their way into the court system and hence be subject to judicial review, often at the Supreme Court. Franklin Delano Roosevelt tried to get around what he saw as the Supreme Court's obstruction of New Deal legislation by putting forward an ill-fated proposal to expand the size of the Court. Its failure became one of his few significant defeats. In the famous 1952 *Youngstown* case, which became a landmark ruling on the limits of presidential power, the Supreme Court restricted the power of the president—in this case, Harry S. Truman—to seize private property, even during wartime. Presidents today routinely face challenges to their power from federal courts.

More generally presidents are impacted by what the political scientist Stephen Skowronek describes as "political time," which "measures the years that unfold between periodic resets of the nation's ideological trajectory. It tells of the political movements contesting power, or the expectations of the mobilized polity."[18] In other words, is the nation ready for the degree of change consistent with the president's agenda, and were they elected to be a guardian of the status quo or a disrupter of it?

Balancing the Dimensions of Power

All three elements of presidential power are continuously at play. Institutional rules and context set upper and lower bounds, and within those bounds different presidents have judged their situational circumstances and personal capabilities and played their hands better or worse than others. In the postwar era, presidents have accumulated more institutional power, but, ironically, a more complex political environment has constrained its use. Presidents who are most successful in accomplishing their agenda, such as FDR, are the ones who both protected and utilized their power. The more they utilized it successfully, the more it grew.

In the modern presidency, it is increasingly not just the president but also the structure and personnel of the White House that enhance power or diminish it. The actions of everyone that presidents appoint impacts their power. Presidents need not only a plan for how to use and protect their power to make a more effective democracy but an institution around them that does the same.

THE TOOLS OF PRESIDENTIAL POWER

American presidents have many ways of utilizing their power to effect action. These generally fall into three categories. The first is general policy actions, which entail influencing and signing legislation (including the use of veto power), implementing regulations pertaining to that legislation, and issuing executive orders, presidential memoranda, and proclamations.

The second major category of presidential power is actions centered on foreign affairs: conducting diplomacy, negotiating treaties and signing executive agreements with foreign nations, using military force, and using economic power and other means of engaging with other nations.

The third major category of presidential power is any other actions within their remit, especially those that are domestically focused. These include making personnel appointments, granting pardons, declaring national emergencies, engaging in public messaging activities, and producing a federal budget that promotes the president's priorities.

Based on the sheer number of tools that presidents have at their disposal, presidential ability to create change unilaterally would seem significant. But few of these authorities are truly unilateral in practice. Those tools that are relatively unconstrained have less potency in their ability to achieve impact and establish outcomes that survive beyond any presidency. Executive orders, for example, cannot institute the long-term, sweeping changes of legislation on the scale of the Affordable Care Act or the Tax Cuts and Jobs Act. Achieving action is therefore a balance between deploying the tools available and understanding (and counteracting) the forces that constrain them.

Shaping Federal Legislation

In terms of achieving outcomes, legislation is the most significant federal tool for creating permanent impact. Article I of the U.S. Constitution grants "all legislative powers" to Congress, but presidents do have the ability to significantly influence what they see as desirable policy. Though they cannot force Congress to pass anything, they can shape legislation by setting out priorities, suggesting specific legislation, negotiating with Congress, and choosing to sign a bill—or veto it.

Article I, Section 3, states, "He shall from time to time give to Congress information on the State of the Union, and recommend to the consideration such measures as he shall judge necessary and expedient."

The original drafting of this clause had the words "He may" rather than "He shall." The change to "shall" allowed a more active role for the president, with them able to interpret the clause as meaning they should introduce a legislative agenda for Congress to consider.

Presidents then have the power to influence specific legislation by lobbying members of Congress. They and their staff can do this privately by engaging with members of Congress, or through public campaigns of speechmaking and other activities.

Modern-day presidents have also often found creative ways to exercise power by using provisions in legislation passed years or even decades prior for new ends.

An additional tool for presidents in the legislative process is their right to veto a bill. As Article I, Section 7, of the Constitution states, "Every Bill which shall have passed the House of Representatives and the Senate, shall, before it become a Law, be presented to the President of the United States; If he approve he shall sign it, but if not he shall return it." Presidents have gotten more comfortable with veto power over time. Although George Washington did issue the first veto, he only did so four years into his presidency. President Andrew Jackson was the first to employ the veto power with any real frequency, using it more than the previous six presidents combined. He was also the first to use it for explicitly political reasons (as opposed to rejecting a law purely as a defense of constitutional orthodoxy). Since then, presidents have used it frequently, albeit not at the rate of President Franklin D. Roosevelt, whose 635 vetoes—the highest of any president—reflect both the length of his presidency and his activist approach to governing.

Congress is not without its own powers to fight back against a veto. If the president vetoes a bill, the Constitution gives Congress the right to overturn the veto if two-thirds of both chambers vote to do so. But there are very few issues that can command that degree of unanimity, especially in the polarized twenty-first century, meaning that presidential vetoes are very powerful instruments of influence. The difficulty of securing a two-thirds override vote means that Congress must anticipate the president's support before drafting legislation. The president does not have to veto a bill to influence the outcome of the legislative process—merely threatening one can shape the drafting of legislation in the first place.

Unlike individual state governors, presidents do not have "line-item veto" power, the ability to veto some components of a bill and pass others—it is all or nothing. But they can make their views clear with a signing statement that sets out how they intend to interpret or enforce aspects of the bill, if at all. Signing statements are also intended to guide agency rule-making associated with the bill, and/or influence judicial interpretation. It then becomes a matter of debate about whether the president's interpretation of a bill is lawful and enforceable. President Obama was clear in his view: "No one doubts that it is appropriate to use signing statements to protect a president's constitutional prerogatives."[19]

Issuing Executive Orders, Presidential Memoranda, and Proclamations

The president can direct the federal bureaucracy to take certain actions through the issuance of an executive order. Executive orders, which must be published in the *Federal Register,* have the force of law if the topic is "founded on the authority of the President derived from the Constitution or statute," according to a widely cited 1957 House of Representatives Government Operations Committee characterization.[20] Roughly 14,000 of them have been issued since 1907, when the U.S. government began a numbering system (retrospectively numbered to start with EO1 in 1862), with likely thousands more issued prior to then. Executive orders vary enormously in scope, for example, the desegregation of the U.S. military in 1948 and the mass incarceration of Japanese during World War II through to the reestablishment of the National Space Council in 2017 and clarifying COVID-19 vaccination requirements for federal workers in 2023.

This form of lawmaking is the president's most flexible unilateral tool for achieving some action. It allows the president to move quickly in creating policy, obtain sole credit for what the order achieves, and dispense with the compromises that attend passing a bill through the legislature. As one Bill Clinton aide commented, "Stroke of the pen, law of the land. Kind of cool."[21] President George W. Bush expressed the presidential authority captured in an executive order when he remarked, "Congress wouldn't act. . . . I signed an executive order. That means I did it on my own."[22] President Obama likewise viewed executive orders as a convenient policymaking tool that eschewed the laborious process of maneuvering legislation through Congress. "I've got a pen, and I've got a phone," he told his cabinet at the beginning of 2014.[23] Recent presidents have used executive orders extensively, issuing them at an average rate of nearly one per week for their entire presidency.

In theory, while executive actions such as executive orders and presidential memoranda can be issued unilaterally, presidents in practice are still subject to constraint. During the drafting process, they are subject to revisions by various offices within the White House and federal agencies, and there is seldom any document that survives in its original form. There is also an extensive legal review process by the Department of Justice's Office of Legal Counsel, which ensures that an order is legally enforceable, which can have the impact of removing or significantly modifying aspects of the original policy intention. All of these processes happen at a staff level, with limited direct presidential input, given the practicality of time and focus.

Once signed, executive orders can take time to implement, with a general principle holding that the greater the policy scope, the longer the implementation process. Often, they will require multiple stages of implementation. The president can sign an executive order asking for a report and recommendations on an issue from an agency or collection of agencies. These recommendations will then go through a subsequent process of review and legal sign-off. Then the policy will need to be turned into regulations or programs, which in turn require time. Thus, the period between the germination of an initial policy idea and actual change on the ground can be months or even years. The constitutionality and legality of specific executive orders are frequently litigated in court, often resulting in overturning them or slowing their implementation.

Administrations are also able to revoke executive orders from previous administrations, significantly limiting their long-term viability and impact. Incoming presidents typically target the previous president's most politically salient executive orders in a package of their own presidential directives that they sign on Inauguration Day. The issuance of many other executive orders will follow within the first one hundred days of a presidency, as presidents signal their broader policy agenda to come. Sometimes the rules made by executive order can be instantiated, suspended, and then reinstated between successive administrations. For example, President Obama instituted some auto emission rules that President Trump then overturned, only for President Biden to reinstate them.

Presidential memoranda are similar in effect to executive orders but have some stylistic differences and do not need to be published in the *Federal Register*. Generally, memoranda, which also have the force of law, are used to direct the federal government to initiate a plan or take certain actions under the president's authority. The National Security Council issues a special type of memoranda called national security memoranda (NSM), a variant of presidential memoranda that has also had many different names down the years, and many of which are classified based on their topic and content, and hence not made public. A notable example of a public NSM would be NSM-1 of January 21, 2021, "United States Global Leadership to Strengthen the International COVID-19 Response and to Advance Global Health Security and Biological Preparedness."

In keeping with their intent to direct action outside of the machinery of the executive branch, presidential proclamations, which also have the force of law, are today mostly ceremonial in nature and are commonly used to announce certain events such as Black History Month and Veterans Day. But in keeping with their usefulness as presidential directives for action, they are also still used for substantive matters such as presidential pardons, restrictions on use of federal land, and visa restrictions on individuals entering the United States. In the past they have had much more significance, with the Emancipation Proclamation being the most famous presidential proclamation in U.S. history.

Implementing Legislation and Presidential Directives via Federal Agencies

Congress passes laws, and presidents issue directives, but the work of implementing the policies they create is left to federal agencies. This process is not without controversy due to the high level of interpretation involved. Executive branch officials must often spend time parsing language in a passed bill to determine what Congress intended. Once that meaning is determined, the White House provides the guidance necessary for the relevant agencies to take action.

The initial cabinet agencies—the Departments of the Navy, State, the Treasury, and War—were created in 1789, with many federal agencies added progressively over time. Federal agencies now range from the very large (the Department of Homeland Security claims more than 260,000 employees)[24] to the relatively small (the Marine Mammal Commission has only about two dozen).[25]

Remarkably, because of various definitional criteria, there is no consensus on the question of how many federal agencies there are: the *Federal Register*, for example, listed more than 430 of them in 2015, but the 2012 Administrative Conference of the United States' *Sourcebook of United States Executive Agencies* listed 115 in its appendix. The *Sourcebook*'s authors even commented, "There is no authoritative list of government agencies."[26] What is known is that there are fifteen executive cabinet agencies, and some number of statutorily independent federal agencies—such as the Federal Reserve, the Central Intelligence Agency, the Federal Communications Commission, the Federal Trade Commission, the Consumer Financial Protection Bureau, NASA, the National Labor Relations Board, and the United States Postal Service—over which the president has some control.

How the executive branch interprets new laws can be significant. For example, as Andrew Rudalevige has noted, testing and accountability requirements in the 2002 No Child Left Behind Act were written in a vague way; the U.S. Department of Education then promulgated regulations dictating the types of tests and how states would set standards for pupil performance.[27] The Tax Cuts and Jobs Act of 2017 created Opportunity Zones—geographic areas with special tax incentives—and in 2019 the Department of the Treasury issued guidance on when taxpayers can claim certain tax benefits the Opportunity Zones promised. The recent Inflation Reduction Act permits the distribution of significant subsidies, leaving agencies such as Treasury to determine qualifications for receipt. One of the federal agencies routinely involved in controversies over its interpretations of federal laws is the U.S. Environmental Protection Agency.

The great majority of people who work in the agencies are career civil servants—ostensibly nonpartisan career officials who turn the gears in the machine of American government. The federal civil service itself was created in 1883 by the Pendleton Act. Prior to its passage, government employees were all appointed through political patronage, a process fraught with corruption. The Pendleton Act, seeking to increase the professionalism, competency, and integrity of federal government employees, determined that merit should be the primary factor for selection. Today, while the president will appoint the senior ranks of the agencies, political appointees represent less than 0.01 percent of the total federal government workforce of approximately 2 million nonmilitary personnel. So, although political appointees such as cabinet secretaries are often identified as the most visible and senior government officials, they are minuscule in number.

Every White House faces the challenge of making sure federal agencies—or, more accurately, federal civil servants—properly implement the sitting administration's policies. There are multiple reasons why civil servants cannot (or choose not to) honor presidential directives or implement them in a slower way than an administration hopes for.

First, civil servants have an inherent potential conflict in either having to act as part of a professionalized bureaucracy that provides policy stability over time, or following political directives, often controversial ones, that can oscillate between administrations. Second, civil servants often work on multiple (sometimes conflicting) priorities, and with limited resources. Adding another item from the White House onto the to-do list may be beneficial in its own right, but without a plan to implement and resource it, it simply adds another task onto an already overfull agenda. Third, change takes time. Changing a program, or adding another one, requires setting up all the processes and procedures (through Statements of Operating Procedures) at the "street level." In some cases, that can mean impacting several million people. Even with sufficient resources, change of that scale is difficult and needs to be rolled out carefully. Fourth, civil servants are aware of the potential for executive orders to be overturned by subsequent administrations. They are not highly motivated to carry out a program of significant change if the expectation is that it will have a very short life. Fifth, sometimes civil servants do have personal agendas. A government badge cannot erase human nature.

With these factors in mind, it is not surprising that civil servants can find convenient excuses for not implementing the president's agenda. As far back as the 1930s President Franklin Roosevelt said:

> The Treasury is so large and far-flung and ingrained in its practices that I find it is almost impossible to get the actions and results I want. . . . But the Treasury is not to be compared with the State Department. You should go through the experience of trying to get any changes in the thinking, policy, and action of the career diplomats and then you'd know what a real problem was. But the Treasury and the State Department put together are nothing as compared with the Na-a-vy. . . . To change anything in the Na-a-vy is like punching a feather bed. You punch it with your right and you punch it with your left until you are finally exhausted, and then you find the damn bed just as it was before you started punching.[28]

Equally challenging is stopping civil servants from implementing policies that are contrary to the president's vision. Agencies have significant ability to initiate regulations through rule-making authorities delegated to them. This bottom-up policy creation may or may not be consistent with presidential wishes, and without active oversight the results can be rolled out in a way that is invisible to the White House review process.

Presidents have addressed concerns about how to control this misalignment through a process called "regulatory review." President Nixon was the first to try to control the agencies' regulatory process through the creation of the "Quality of Lifetime Review." This program, which forced agencies to submit to a White House review of regulations before implementing them, was carried out by the Office of Management and Budget (OMB). President Carter built on this concept with Executive Order 12044, which created the Office of Information and Regulatory Affairs (OIRA), an office inside OMB dedicated to regulatory review. President Reagan's Executive Order 12291 reflected his overall philosophy: "Regulatory action shall not be undertaken unless the potential benefits to society for the regulation outweigh the potential costs to society."[29]

Successive presidents have kept the same overall approach of evaluating every federal regulation but have done so according to their own definition of costs and benefits. OIRA's role as a central hub of review of every executive branch regulation makes it one of the most influential and important parts of the White House, albeit also one of the most anonymous, given its somewhat technical approach.

The difficulty of pushing policies aligned with the president's vision through the federal bureaucracy highlights the need for political appointees, who generally occupy positions in which they give direction to career officials. But there are factors particular to political appointees that constrain action, even if they themselves are entirely aligned with the president's policy agenda. Generally, they are at an informational disadvantage—they are newcomers working with people who have been doing tasks for many years and understand every aspect of their role and issue area. Sometimes the appointees are campaign staff or others who are being rewarded for loyalty but have little subject domain expertise. In total, the presidential appointees on average only serve at their agencies for approximately 2.5 years,[30] compared to 7.5 years for all federal workers.[31] A variety of factors explains their short tenure: long delays in achieving Senate confirmation, difficulty in obtaining security clearances or White House approval, and long hours, overwhelming stress, and absences from family life that attend their duties, causing them to suffer burnout.

Independent Agencies

Independent agencies are those that are constitutionally part of the executive branch but retain a degree of independence from it, mainly because of the way in which their leaders are chosen. Major ones include the Federal Reserve, the Central Intelligence Agency, NASA, the Federal Communications Commission, and the Federal Trade Commission (FTC). The extent of presidential control over them varies and is a matter of long-running dispute. Presidents effect some degree of control through their ability to nominate their heads and other senior officials, who are subject to Senate confirmation.

Many independent agencies are not controlled by a single person but by a board of five to seven people. These people frequently serve defined but staggered terms that normally last longer than four years. Although presidents appoint some of them, they seldom appoint them all, and these boards often have a mixed political composition. Presidents are limited in how easily they can dismiss members of the board—generally only for cause, not for political reasons. The Supreme Court's ruling in *Humphrey's Executor v. United States,* decided in 1935, held that President Roosevelt did not have the authority to remove an FTC member for reasons other than "inefficiency, neglect of duty, or malfeasance in office."[32] That ruling is still seen today as a bellwether affirming the independence of certain agencies on matters of policy. The net effect is that there are very large parts of the regulatory landscape and executive branch where presidents have some influence, but their true control is limited.

Conducting Diplomacy, Negotiating Treaties, and Signing Executive Agreements with Foreign Nations

In perhaps no area does the president have a greater level of unilateral powers than in foreign affairs. Alexis de Tocqueville wrote, "It is chiefly in the realm of foreign relations that the executive power of a nation finds occasion to demonstrate its skill and strength."[33] As the executive in charge of the State Department and other federal agencies that liaise with foreign governments, the president is the de facto leader of American diplomacy. The Constitution spelled out specific powers concerning international relations. The president, according to Article II, Section 3, "shall receive Ambassadors and other public ministers." This clause has become almost universally interpreted to mean that the president is the primary conductor of foreign affairs, including meeting with foreign heads of state. To some extent this is a practical necessity—there is only one president, and there are many members of Congress, none of whom are individually elected by the whole country or can plausibly claim to best represent the country in meetings with a singular foreign head of government.

The president's authority in the diplomatic domain has become even more important since World War II, as the United States has taken a greater leadership role in the world. The president now typically meets with heads of other states dozens of times per year, including collectively once a year at the annual G7 summit (the world's seven wealthiest liberal democracies: the United States, the United Kingdom, France, Germany, Italy, Canada, and Japan), the annual G20 summit (which consists of the twenty wealthiest countries by GDP), and the annual NATO leaders' summit. These meetings have a ceremonial element, but they can be substantive opportunities to address shared problems. Diplomats below the presidential level do significant policy work ahead of time, and the leaders announce at the meeting initiatives that have been previously agreed to. The meetings can also announce policy intentions setting the framework for future work to be carried out by the countries' executives.

Not all the president's diplomatic power is unilateral. While Article II, Section 2, gives the president the "Power . . . to make Treaties," those treaties must be entered into "by and with the Advice and Consent of the Senate." Treaties are the most significant and binding agreements between countries. As such, they require two-thirds of the Senate to vote in favor of their ratification if they are to become law. Significant treaties involving the United States include the Treaty of Paris, which ended the Revolutionary War, and the 1949 Washington Treaty, which established NATO. In recent decades, owing to the difficulty of securing a two-thirds Senate majority to ratify a diplomatic agreement, treaties have become a less common form of diplomatic agreement. Only relatively uncontroversial treaties pass easily through the Senate, such as an amendment to the multination Montreal Protocol on Substances That Deplete the Ozone Layer that passed in September 2022.

Instead, presidents have opted to embrace other forms of agreements governing relations between the United States and another country. These executive agreements do not have the force of law unless Congress subsequently passes a law to support them. As with domestically focused executive orders, until they become law, they lack permanence and are subject to being overturned by successive presidents. Key examples of such turnover would include the Paris Agreement detailing U.S. commitment to climate change action, and the Joint Comprehensive Plan of Action (the Iran nuclear deal) forged by the Obama administration. President Trump dispatched both, just as President Biden overturned Trump's decision to exit the World Health Organization.

Use of Military Force

The Constitution gives Congress the right to declare war, and it has exercised that right five times, declaring war with England in 1812, Mexico in 1846, Spain in 1898, and the two world wars in 1917 and 1941. But the presidency also has a role in executing U.S. military action. Article II, Section 2, stipulates that the president "shall be Commander in Chief of the Army and Navy of the United States." This was an action on the part of the American Founders, who both established civilian control of the military and realized the advantages of unilateral decision-making in times of national security crises.

Declarations of war are not the only legal mechanisms by which the United States can authorize military actions against its foes. Congress has authorized "Use of Force" against enemies considerably more often. For example, the legislature passed resolutions authorizing use of force against Iraq in 1990 and 2002, both times prior to U.S. military action against the country. Use of Force resolutions often give presidents considerable discretion on when they can exercise military power, and although they don't constitute the technical definition of a declaration of war, sometimes the effect can be very similar. After the 9/11 attacks, Congress resolved that the president could use "all necessary and appropriate force against those nations, organizations, or persons he determines planned, authorized, committed, or aided the terrorist attacks that occurred on September 11, 2001, or harbored such organizations or persons."[34]

Sometimes the president has used military force unilaterally, claiming the right to do so independent of Congress. For example, FDR implemented a deal with the United Kingdom to swap American naval destroyers for the right to base U.S. troops on British territories before the United States had formally entered the Second World War. Truman sent troops to Korea in 1950 under the auspices of a United Nations Security Council resolution. More recently, there have been a number of instances of presidentially di-rected use of force carried out under the banner of national interest, such as President Obama's expanded use of drone strikes to kill al-Qaeda terrorists, and President Trump's action to kill Iranian general Qasem Soleimani. In such cases, presidents often point to broad authorities to justify unilateral military action not authorized by Congress, and those justifications are frequently controversial as a matter of law and public opinion. President George W. Bush's Justice Department, for instance, claimed that "the Con-stitution grants the president unilateral power to take military action to protect the national security interests of the United States. . . . This indepen-dent authority is *supplemented* by congressional authorization."[35]

The president's ability to use force has grown commensurate with the size of the U.S. military. In the United States' earliest military conflicts, the armed forces were built up quickly but then dismantled after the military action was completed. With the onset of sustained international compe-tition with the Soviet Union after World War II, the military expanded in accordance with the need to defend the homeland and project force across the world, leading to quasi-permanent presence for the American military overseas. In inflation-adjusted real dollars the defense budget has risen from about $9 billion after World War II to nearly $800 billion today.[36] This figure is significantly higher than in any other country, and ten times higher than in any other large liberal democracy. The U.S. Department of Defense is the largest employer in the nation, with 1.3 million active-duty service members, 750,000 civilian personnel, and more than 811,000 Na-tional Guard and Reserve service members.[37] Including active-duty person-nel, its 3-million-strong workforce dwarfs the federal agency with the next-largest staffing levels—the U.S. Postal Service, with more than 500,000 employees.[38] Today the American president retains power over a vast and formidable military apparatus.

Use of Economic and Soft Power

The president can use other means short of direct military force to achieve foreign policy and national security goals. Military aid is commonly used to reinforce American national security interests by enabling allies and partners to use their own capabilities and signaling American resolve to confront bad actors in the international system. Throughout 2022, for example, the United States disbursed some $46 billion in military aid to Ukraine, coming in the form of weapons and other equipment, training, logistics support, and grants and loans for additional gear.[39] Two American allies in the Middle East, Jordan and Israel, each receive more than $1 billion per year in U.S. security assistance.

In addition to military aid, the U.S. government often distributes foreign aid directly though the U.S. Agency for International Development, or through multilateral organizations such as the United Nations Refugee Agency or the World Food Program. Programs run or supported by the federal government, such as the Peace Corps or the State Department's Youth Leadership programs, also project American "soft" power—nonmilitary power—across the world. Given the vast resources that the United States commits globally, the president's ability to add or subtract American funds or determine participation in various humanitarian and soft power initiatives can have a major impact on relations with other nations.

Economic sanctions (the prohibition of economic activity with designated entities) and export controls (restrictions on the export of American products, and in particular technologies that can be leveraged for military use) are important tools in presidents' arsenal for coercing the foreign policy outcomes they seek. Sanctions cause economic pain by cutting off state and nonstate actors from global financial and business networks, of which America and its businesses are at the center. Given the punishing impact they can have—witness the condition of the ever-sanctioned North Korean economy—sanctions have likewise increased in popularity as a foreign policy tool useful for imposing costs on adversaries without resorting to costly military action. More recently, export controls targeting Russia in retaliation for its invasion of Ukraine, and the curtailment of Russian oil imports into the United States, have been utilized to damage the Russian economy.

Presidential Appointments

The Constitution gives presidents a powerful tool in their ability to seed the federal government with personnel of their choosing. Per Article II, Section 2, "he shall nominate, and by and with the Advice and Consent of the Senate, shall appoint Ambassadors, other public Ministers and Consuls, Judges of the Supreme Court, and all other Officers of the United States." The number of politically appointed leaders inside the federal government has grown over time, and now constitutes some 8,000 people. Of these, approximately 3,500–4,000 are full-time political appointee positions eligible to be filled by the president, and 4,000 are officials serving part-time on various boards and commissions. Some of these positions require Senate confirmation, but the majority don't. The commissions for most of these appointments expire at the end of the president's term.

Approximately 1,000 of the appointees occupy the highest echelons of leadership within their various government agencies. These include the secretary and deputy secretary of each agency, and generally the top two or three ranks within that agency: undersecretaries, assistant secretaries, and deputy assistant secretaries. Not only do presidents appoint these people, but the appointees also serve at the presidents' pleasure, meaning that presidents can fire them at any time and for any reason. The Senate did contest that concept in 1867, when it passed the Tenure of Office Act, which held that any political appointee confirmed by the Senate could also only be fired with Senate approval. This led to the first impeachment of a president, when Congress accused President Andrew Johnson of violating the act by firing Secretary of War Edwin M. Stanton. Johnson narrowly survived the conviction of the impeachment charges. Congress repealed the act in 1887, and the Supreme Court confirmed it as unconstitutional in 1926. All subsequent presidents have therefore been free to dismiss appointees, whether Senate-confirmed or otherwise, at their discretion. The only exceptions are certain appointees to independent agencies.

It is reasonable to assume that, by virtue of being appointed by the president, political appointees would do exactly what the president wants and directs, either verbally or through official directives. While this is generally the case, it is not always so, for a variety of reasons.

First, senior agency officials must be responsive to the reality that Congress can make their jobs either easier or considerably harder. Congress confirms their personnel, appropriates their budget, has the power to call them to testify, and can investigate both them as individuals and their agency. Second, political appointees can also feel responsibility to the agency's constituents—the citizens whom their policies impact. These constituents have influence because they are the beneficiaries of the agencies' actions and are generally represented by special interest groups, lobbyists, or vocal issue advocacy organizations.

Third, the officials themselves can have mixed motivations for being in their roles. While they are primarily there, presumably, out of a desire to serve the president, it is likely they have some additional personal objectives that they believe will be well-served by executive branch experience, often a lifetime commitment to a policy cause.

Fourth, they may be influenced by past or future employment prospects. It is not uncommon for the appointees to have worked for industry participants and to expect to do so again in the future. While past industry or agency expertise is useful in carrying out their role, the expectation of returning to the same company or industry from which they came can influence the decisions that a political appointee makes.

Last, the heads of agencies can feel a natural affinity, which grows over time, to the agency itself and its staff. Presidential directives that aren't necessarily beneficial to the agency (for example, budget or program cuts) cause a split loyalty, and agency officials can protect the status of existing agency rights rather than executing presidential directives. Generally, these split loyalties and competing priorities are not significant, but they can frustrate presidents and slow down their agendas.

Appointing Federal Judges

The United States Constitution grants the federal judiciary independence from the executive and legislative branches, and federal courts often issue rulings that constrain executive power. The president does have some power to influence the federal judiciary through the nomination of federal judges, who must be confirmed with the "advice and consent" of the Senate. Modern presidents have varied in how much "advice" they have sought from the Senate as opposed to just "consent." They are often willing to consult with senators in the selection of nominees for district and appeals courts but tend to retain the primary initiative in driving nominations for Supreme Court nominees.

Every presidential administration will find itself entangled in litigation at the Supreme Court, and the solicitor general, or someone from that office, will usually lead the effort to argue for the administration's position at the Court. But even if an administration is not a direct party in a Supreme Court proceeding, the Court also frequently makes decisions that can dramatically shape the national policy and political landscape, such as its ruling in *Dobbs v. Jackson Women's Health Organization* in 2022, which overturned a woman's constitutional right to an abortion. Thus, the Supreme Court's pronouncements have major potential to impact a presidency.

Typically, presidents' choices of judges will reflect their ideological leanings, and they presume that the nominated judge will reflect some common degree of ideology in their rulings. But this is not a guarantee—judges retain independence to rule as they see fit, and even the president's own choices of judges can frustrate their agenda by deeming their policies unconstitutional. The most notable of the judgeships a president is authorized to fill are the nine who make up the Supreme Court. However, equally important, given the breadth of their rulings, are the 673 who serve on district courts, 179 serving on appeals courts, and, to a lesser extent, the 9 on the Court of International Trade. While the president may nominate potentially hundreds of federal judges, the majority of the 870 federal judges serving under a president at any given time will have been appointed by previous administrations.

Federal judges hold lifetime tenure. Other than through death, slots can open up through resignations, voluntary retirements, promotions to higher courts, or, very rarely, impeachment. Historical trends indicate that up to 25 percent of federal judgeships will become vacant and need to be filled over the course of a presidential term, and hence up to 50 percent over a two-term presidency. This equates to roughly one opening to be filled per week. President George W. Bush appointed 327 judges over eight years, President Obama 329, and President Trump 234 in his four years.

The rapidity with which judicial spots are filled depends on the speed not only of the president but also the Senate. Given judges' power to influence law, as well as their length of service, the political party in opposition to the president frequently works hard to slow or stop confirmations. In recent years, leaders in the Senate have started using the filibuster (a procedural delay tactic) to slow down nominations. In 2013, Democratic Senate Majority Leader Harry Reid, frustrated at Republicans' refusal to confirm President Obama's judicial nominees, eliminated the filibuster for nominees below the Supreme Court level, paving the way for confirmations. But in a characteristic Washington "tit-for-tat" payback, Republican Senate Majority Leader Mitch McConnell kept the change in place, and in 2017 even expanded it to prevent the filibustering of Supreme Court judges, easing Justice Neil Gorsuch's confirmation.

Though judges must preside in a politically neutral manner, courts can demonstrate patterns of rulings that may be either favorable or contrary to the president's own policy agenda. Thus, opponents of administration policy often choose to file appeals in jurisdictions with judges whom they believe are likely to rule in their favor. The appeals process can take months, or even years, to move through the court system, thereby slowing down policy implementation and jeopardizing its long-term prospects if a future administration decides not to continue it.

Pardons

The right to pardon is one of the president's least-constrained powers as well as, in modern presidencies, one of the more controversial ones. Article II, Section 2, of the Constitution states, "he shall have Power to grant Reprieves and Pardons for Offences against the United States, except in

Cases of Impeachment." The original intention can be captured in Hamilton's words in Federalist No. 74: "In seasons of insurrection or rebellion, there are often critical moments, when a well-timed offer at a pardon to the insurgents or rebels may restore the tranquility of the commonwealth." Washington's pardons during the Whiskey Rebellion, Lincoln's amnesty for two hundred thousand Civil War soldiers, and Carter's and Ford's clemency for Vietnam draft dodgers illustrate how presidents have subscribed to this view.

The great bulk of the approximately thirty thousand individual pardons issued by presidents over the years have been without much fanfare or controversy, but certain ones have been criticized as purely political in nature. President George H. W. Bush pardoned Reagan's secretary of defense, Caspar Weinberger, and in doing so negated the chance that he himself would have to testify at Weinberger's trial on the Iran-Contra affair. Bill Clinton pardoned Marc Rich, a fugitive who had donated to Clinton's presidential library. And perhaps the most famous was Ford's pardon of President Nixon for any crimes associated with Watergate, which was extremely controversial at the time. Because pardons are often issued at the end of administrations, when the president will face less political accountability for a controversial action, they often impact perceptions of the president's legacy.

Public Messaging

Presidents also have the power to persuade through their leadership platform. The term "bully pulpit" has frequently been used in connection with the presidency. The term was coined by President Theodore Roosevelt, who, bucking a tradition of presidential reticence, resolved to use his "bully" (i.e., terrific) platform to advocate for his agenda. Today, through a constant stream of speeches, television interviews, campaign appearances, social media outreach, and other forms of communication, presidents can get their message across to various constituencies, thus attempting to galvanize support for their policies or their political agenda, including their reelection.

But there is no guarantee that what the president has to say will be reported—and hence received—favorably. Virtually every president has felt unfairly treated by the media. Even those who saw the media as a useful tool for their communication complained about them. President Kennedy said, "When we don't have to go through you bastards, we can really get our story over to the American people."[40] President Reagan described them as "sharks."[41] Presidents are bound to be frustrated with coverage of "palace intrigues" or other topics they see as irrelevant to the American people.

President Carter observed, "I would really like for you all as people who relay Washington events to the world to take a look at the substantive questions I have to face as a president and quit dealing almost exclusively with personalities."[42] President Reagan commented, "For eight years the press called me the 'Great Communicator.' Well, one of my greatest frustrations during those eight years was my inability to communicate to the American people . . . the seriousness of the threat we faced in Central America."[43] In sum, by virtue of their editorial choices, the media can play a decisive role in either hindering or helping accomplish a president's goals.

Article II, Section 3, states that the president "shall from time to time give to the Congress Information of the State of the Union." Presidents Washington and Adams delivered the message in person to joint sessions of Congress. The transmission of the "Information of the State of the Union" was done in writing from 1801 to 1913, until President Woodrow Wilson revived the practice of addressing Congress in person. This set of remarks is now observed as the annual "State of the Union" address. The address sets out, among other things, the president's priorities for the year ahead. If carried out well, a State of the Union address can guide the legislative agenda. When combined with the power of threatening a veto, the State of the Union address gives presidents a significant opportunity to influence Congress to adopt their agenda, or elements of it.

However, the State of the Union address is often a wish list of policy agenda items they want accomplished, without respect to the likelihood of them coming to fruition (and indeed, they usually don't). More than anything, it has become an exercise in political messaging—a chance for presidents to sell their past accomplishments and their vision to the nation.

One thing the State of the Union does *not* seem useful for is generating good public opinion for the president. The Gallup polling agency has found that State of the Union addresses coincided with an average improvement in a president's approval rating of just 0.4 percentage points.[44]

CONCLUSION

Richard Neustadt wrote, "When we inaugurate a President of the United States, we give a man the powers of our highest public office. From the moment he is sworn the man confronts a personal problem: how to make those powers work for him."[45]

The president has a wide array of tools to achieve impact—whether by way of legislative, executive, economic, military, or other actions. These tools may be short-term or long-term in duration, domestic or international in focus.

But presidents are not as all-powerful as is popularly imagined. They operate in a system that severely constrains action, and their ability to achieve action depends on their ability to successfully mobilize these tools in the face of the forces that constrain them. How they navigate that tension determines their effectiveness.

Furthermore, in the modern presidency it is increasingly not just the president but the whole White House that either enhances executive power or diminishes it. Presidents may be the decision-makers, but their staff generate the options and implement the actions. Hence, it has become even more important for presidents to have an effective organization around them.

2
THE MODERN WHITE HOUSE

To understand how best to design the White House of the future we must first understand its past and current state.

In the earliest iterations of the White House, the staff was tiny. Early presidents, who often employed family members or friends, had to pay for personal staff out of their own salary—Congress only first appropriated money for an assistant to help the president in 1857. Very often the household staff working in the Executive Mansion also performed official functions. Through most of the 1800s all the staff could fit into the second floor of the White House itself, which, until the creation of the West Wing, was the presidential working area. (Today the second floor contains the residence where the president's family lives.)

The West Wing of the White House is a separate structure and was built in 1902 on the site of the White House stables. It was constructed at the insistence of Theodore Roosevelt, who felt that there was simply not enough workspace in the White House for a president with a wife and six children. A series of renovations and expansions of the West Wing occurred throughout the early twentieth century. Notable changes included the first "Oval Office," under President Taft, which mimicked the shape of some of the main White House rooms and was originally located in the center of the West Wing. Franklin Roosevelt created the current configuration with a basement and second level and shifted the Oval Office to the side of the building closest to the Executive Residence, allowing him to access it along the colonnade in a wheelchair without public attention. Despite the massive increase in the staff size, the West Wing today is essentially the one that he created, leading to the intimate and energetic environment that visitors find today. Viewers of the television show *The West Wing* would be surprised to find the actual one is even smaller than that portrayed, but similarly kinetic.

With respect to its early inhabitants, Joseph Alsop, a famous columnist of the 1940s and 1950s, wrote that, in FDR's day,

There literally was no White House staff of the modern type, with policy-making functions. Two extremely pleasant, unassuming, and efficient men, Steve Early and Marvin McIntyre, handled the president's day-to-day schedule and routine, the donkeywork of his press relations, and such like. There was a secretarial camilla of highly competent and dedicated ladies who were led by "Missy" LeHand. . . . There were also lesser figures to handle travel arrangements, the enormous flow of correspondence, and the like. But that was that; and national policy was strictly a problem for the president, his advisers of the moment (who had constant access to the president's office but no office of their own in the White House), and his chosen chiefs of departments and agencies.[1]

A BRIEF HISTORY OF THE EOP

Faced with the complexities of managing the New Deal programs, in 1936 President Roosevelt commissioned the Brownlow Committee, a panel of experts charged with delivering recommendations for reorganizing the executive branch. A year later, the three-man committee produced a fifty-three-page report stating, "The President needs help." It continued: "His immediate staff assistance is entirely inadequate. He should be given a small number of executive assistants who would be his direct aides in dealing with the managerial agencies and administrative departments of the government. These assistants, probably not exceeding six in number, would be in addition to the present secretaries, who deal with the public, with the Congress, and with the press and radio."[2]

The Brownlow Committee's recommendations led Congress and the president to create the institution of the modern White House via the Reorganization Act of 1939. A signature element of that legislation was the creation of the Executive Office of the President (EOP), the constellation of offices that support the president's work. With the birth of the EOP in 1939 came the White House Office (responsible for overall administration), the Bureau of the Budget (previously housed inside the Treasury Department since 1921, and later renamed the Office of Management and Budget), Personnel (the forerunner to the Office of Presidential Personnel), the Office of Government Reports (the forerunner to the White House staff secretary, which began under President Eisenhower), and the National Resources Planning Board (the forerunner to the modern policy offices).

World War II accelerated growth of the White House staff to manage new government agencies and the multiplicity of war-related programs they were overseeing—in 1945 defense spending was a mind-boggling 33.8 percent of GDP.[3] After the war, numerous offices were added to the

White House, some congressionally created, some created unilaterally by the president. Noteworthy among these, and that have endured until the present day, were the Council of Economic Advisers, created in 1946, and the National Security Council, created in 1947.

The creation of these offices, plus their subsequent expansion of scope and personnel, led to a significant increase in the number of people in the EOP. Indeed, Louis Brownlow remarked in his 1958 autobiography that he was "quite certain that FDR, when creating the Executive Office, 'had not in his wildest dreams' envisioned the expansion that later occurred."[4] Today, for example, in a far cry from Brownlow's prescribed staff of six, the Executive Office of the President in the Biden White House employs approximately 2,000 people across fifteen main offices and multiple suboffices.[5]

The Decreasing Role of the Cabinet

Long-term trends also indicate that the growth of the EOP has contributed to the diminishing importance of cabinet officers as advisers to the president—or at least their exclusive roles as presidential advisers on given subject matter areas. Until roughly World War II, members of the cabinet served almost exclusively as the president's principal advisers on policy. Of course, there were some exceptions, such as Woodrow Wilson's right-hand man Edward House, who became President Wilson's key foreign policy staffer and was even granted living space inside the White House. But on the whole, because the president had no staff, he relied on his cabinet for advice and counsel.

With the creation of the EOP in 1939, the approach of relying entirely on the cabinet progressively fell out of favor, for several reasons. First, as the size of the EOP grew, and specific offices that had a policymaking role were created, the staff that worked there changed from being generalist administrators and managers to being issue-area specialists. This meant that more White House staffers had the ability to substitute for cabinet members in furnishing information and recommendations to the president. Issue experts working within the White House complex also enjoyed the simple advantage of proximity. The original agencies of the government, such as the War Department, the Department of the Navy, Department of the Treasury, and the Department of State, were in buildings located within walking distance from the White House, such as the Old Executive Office Building on the White House grounds, originally constructed during the presidency of Ulysses S. Grant. But the increase in the size and number of cabinet agencies meant that their locations became spread out around the city of

Washington, D.C. Meanwhile, EOP staff still occupied the West Wing, seconds away from the Oval Office.

Moreover, the duties of members of the cabinet were in some ways more complex than those performed by EOP staff. Cabinet members have split loyalties: although their first allegiance is to the president who appointed them, they are also beholden to Congress (for funding and personnel authorization) and to the workforces they lead. Some presidents, such as Richard Nixon, grew to deeply distrust the agencies that the cabinet represented, and in some cases the secretaries themselves. He wanted to centralize power in people whom he unilaterally appointed with no Senate confirmation. We see this in Nixon's total reliance on National Security Adviser Henry Kissinger for foreign policy strategy, with Secretary of State William P. Rogers being almost a total nonfactor in shaping Nixon's views. Eventually, Kissinger took on the unprecedented role of serving as national security adviser and secretary of state simultaneously.

Where Franklin Delano Roosevelt had ten executive departments headed by a secretary, today there are fifteen cabinet departments headed by a secretary, and hundreds of other agencies The increase in federal outlays from less than $100 billion in 1945 to $6.2 trillion in 2022 is a proxy indicator for the growth in the number of agencies and their responsibilities, and thus also reflects that the cabinet is an increasingly cumbersome decision-making body.[6] Cabinet members also tended to become more specialized in the fields of their agencies, and hence some members of the cabinet became less useful for unrelated policy decisions.

THE STRUCTURE OF THE EOP

The structure of the EOP reveals it to be a cluster of offices and offices within offices, each with a mixture of various discrete and overlapping responsibilities. The largest office is the Office of Management and Budget, with a staff of more than 500. Other offices vary in size from modest (e.g., the Office of Science and Technology Policy at around 40) to large (e.g., the U.S. Trade Representative, with close to 300).

Terminology for describing the White House can be confusing. The Executive Office of the President encompasses all the offices and people above. The White House Office is, technically, inside the EOP. In turn, inside of the White House Office are many key offices, such as the Office of the Chief of Staff, the Presidential Personnel Office, the Press Office, and various senior advisers. Depending on the context, when commentators refer to "the White House," they can mean the president as the decision-maker, the White House Office, or the whole EOP.

I will now detail the nature and responsibilities of several offices, some of which are stand-alone units with their own budget requests, and some of which are encompassed within the White House Office.

The Office of the Vice President

The Constitution created the role of the vice president with a view toward the leadership of the Senate, and as a replacement for the president in a time of incapacitation, death, or impeachment. It was also created as a result of the Electoral College system. In order to stop each state simply voting for a presidential candidate hailing from within its own borders, the election rules stated that they had to cast two votes, with at least one being for a candidate from another state. The vice president was then to be the candidate with the second-most votes. The passage of the Twelfth Amendment in 1803 changed this system such that the electorate cast one vote for the president and one for the vice president. With the advent of political parties around the same time, the modern system developed where the two roles are effectively "tied" together.

Through most of the 1800s and up to World War II, the role of vice president was largely irrelevant. As John Adams said, "my Country has in its Wisdom contrived for me the most insignificant Office that ever the Invention of Man contrived or his Imagination conceived."[7] More recently, and certainly more vividly, FDR's first vice president, John Nance Garner, described it as "hardly worth a pitcher of spit."[8] Yet on occasions throughout American history, the death of a president has catapulted vice presidents from obscure figureheads to indispensable leaders. Eight times in history has the vice president replaced a sitting president: four times by natural causes, four times by assassination. William Henry Harrison was the first to die in office, succumbing to pneumonia after only thirty-one days as president. John Tyler replaced him. At the time, there was some ambiguity in the Constitution as to whether in doing so the vice president became president or simply took over the president's responsibilities. Those concerns notwithstanding, Tyler took the initiative and declared himself president. The informal understanding that the vice president assumed the presidency, not just its powers *pro tempore*, was not formalized until the passage of the Twenty-Fifth Amendment in 1967, which was itself a response to the question of presidential succession triggered by the assassination of President Kennedy in 1963.

The vice presidency started to have more significance in the modern era. At the invitation of President Eisenhower, Vice President Nixon became the first to be part of the cabinet. President Carter gave his vice president,

Walter Mondale, an office in the West Wing—a departure from the historical pattern of assigning the vice president an office in the Executive Office Building located alongside those of other presidential staff. Vice presidents also began to assume a role in leading various presidential policy initiatives. President Bill Clinton, for instance, gave Vice President Al Gore several important duties, including the leadership of an effort called the National Partnership for Reinventing Government. Dick Cheney was perhaps the most powerful of all vice presidents, with significant influence on policy. And President Trump tapped Vice President Pence to lead the White House's Coronavirus Task Force.

The president is also able to rely upon his or her vice president to perform ceremonial roles. These functions are not just important in their own right. They also allow the vice president to substitute for, and hence free up time for, the president. Commensurate with the transformation of the vice presidency into an important office for both policy action and political messaging, the modern vice president has a staff of his or her own that largely mirrors the presidents in the functions performed. Some of these staff are technically commissioned as an "Assistant to the President," causing some degree of confusion as to where their primary loyalty lies. In theory there should be no difference between the president and the vice president, but in practice there are occasional mixed priorities.

The Office of the Chief of Staff (White House Office)

The chief of staff, the highest-profile political appointee in the White House, competes with the vice president for the role of the second-most-important member of the White House, and yet the position is a relatively recent invention. Though most of the first thirty-one presidents had some form of chief aide, there was no formal Office of the Chief of Staff. Nor was one terribly necessary; their staffs were small, and each staffer could report directly to the president without an intermediate layer. It was John Steelman, under President Truman, who became the first modern equivalent of a chief of staff. He was given the title of assistant to the president and was charged with helping to keep order as the size of the executive branch swelled in the immediate wake of World War II. The role became truly formalized under Eisenhower in 1953, when the White House chief of staff title came into use. His first chief of staff, Sherman Adams, shaped the position into one that was more than clerical and became one of the most powerful gatekeepers in Washington.

Since the 1980s, the role has been a fixture of every White House and is generally the first appointment that presidents make after their election.

It has become responsible for a variety of functions: managing the flow of people and information to the president, organizing staff processes, hiring and firing some staff, shaping the policy agenda, acting as a surrogate for the president in negotiations with Congress, being his personal adviser and confidant, talking to the press, and even making some minor policy decisions on behalf of the president, simply checking in later to endorse the decision.

Despite its importance, chief of staffs' formal authorities are surprisingly vague. The title suggests all staff report to them, but this is only partially true. Presidents commission officers of varying rank (assistants to the president, deputy assistants to the president, and special assistants to the president), and, as their names suggest, in concept they are all there to serve the presidents directly. Chiefs of staff may have some implicit seniority over them, but it is seldom explicit, and their authority over staff is often shaped according to the specific personnel dynamics of a given White House. I personally observed during my White House service some members of staff (e.g., John Bolton, the head of the National Security Council) bristling at the suggestion that they did not have a direct line to the president and were obligated to obtain authorization to access the president through the chief of staff.

The importance of the role therefore mainly derives from the relationship between the president and the chief of staff: how much the president defers to that person and his or her decision-making abilities. He or she can be exceptionally powerful if people perceive that the chief of staff is close to the president, or very weak if seen as irrelevant. He or she can dominate the White House or just be a conduit. A quintessential example of a domineering chief of staff was George H. W. Bush's chief of staff, John Sununu, who fiercely guarded access to the president, to the point that Bush was forced to set up a post office box near his vacation home in Kennebunkport, Maine, as a means of unmediated communication with top advisers.

Several deputy chiefs of staff also form part of the office supporting the chief in the multiplicity of tasks needed to be carried out. Different White Houses have had different configurations of deputies, but the most common is to have one who covers policy coordination, and one who runs the operations of the White House.

National Security Council

The National Security Council (NSC) was created by statute under the National Security Act of 1947, the same law that also established the Central Intelligence Agency and the Joint Chiefs of Staff. The act intended for the

NSC to be a coordinating body: "The function of the Council shall be to advise the President with respect to the integration of domestic, foreign, and military policies relating to the national security so as to enable the Armed Forces and the other departments and agencies of the Government to cooperate more effectively in matters involving the national security."[9]

Comprised of the president (who serves as chairman), the vice president, and the heads of the State Department, the Defense Department, the CIA, the Joint Chiefs, and other agencies with responsibility for national security, the NSC was initially (and occasionally still is) an actual council where those members meet to plan strategy and coordinate lines of effort. Different presidents have utilized the NSC as a convening mechanism to varying extents.

The main influence the NSC enjoys today comes through the national security adviser and his or her staff, who are not formal members of the Council but do the work associated with it. The National Security Act stipulated that "the Council shall have a staff to be headed by a civilian executive secretary," a position originally meant to be mainly clerical. The national security adviser (NSA) has since become one of the most powerful roles in the U.S. government. Not only does this person, appointed by the president and not subject to Senate confirmation, have an office in the West Wing and (presumed) direct access to the president, but he or she sits over a large group of foreign policy experts. The size of the NSC has ebbed and flowed according to each administration, but it generally contains at least 150 to 300 staff. President Obama's NSC numbered around 450 individuals, indicating the primacy of his national security advisers and their staffs in the creation of foreign and national security policy.

The size of the Obama NSC also reflected the supplanting of cabinet functions by EOP staff. Prior to the NSC's inception, the secretaries of state and war (later renamed the secretary of defense) were the main advisers to the president in matters of foreign affairs and military action. Anticipating the loss of control that would follow the introduction of White House cooks in the national security kitchen, originally the State Department and Department of Defense lobbied to have the NSC housed within their organizations. However, President Truman placed it in the EOP, where he would have greater access and control. The NSC's inception triggered a still-ongoing tension between the NSC, the State Department, and the Defense Department over which actors in the national security space will lead policy formulation. At various times, the national security adviser's proximity to the president, and the strength of his or her personality, has allowed him or her to become the top influence over the president on national security policy. The quintessential example of Henry Kissinger looms large in this respect. Zbigniew Brzezinski also overshadowed Secretary of State Cyrus Vance in the Carter administration and became Carter's most trusted aide on national security.

The NSC has a number of positive features, including its ability to ensure that sprawling government agencies can coordinate in the execution of variously complementary and competing military, diplomatic, and economic lines of effort. But the NSC has also been the source of problems throughout its history. Because it has no congressional or regulatory oversight outside of the White House, there are opportunities for national security advisers and their staffs to stray from their core missions of coordinating policies and developing recommendations and to assume an operational role. They frequently hold diplomatic meetings with heads of state. President Kennedy's national security adviser, McGeorge Bundy, went from being an adviser to an operator, being directly involved in fact-finding missions to Vietnam. Less benignly, and much more infamously, in 1985, U.S. Army Colonel Oliver North, then a military aide on the NSC, began to direct a scheme by which the United States sold arms to Iran (at the time subject to an arms embargo) and redistributed the profits to Nicaraguan Contras—a rebel group for which Congress had prohibited U.S. funding. Once this arrangement was discovered, the Iran-Contra scandal led to the indictment of many administration officials, including North and Secretary of Defense Caspar Weinberger.

The Iran-Contra scandal led to President Reagan establishing a special board of review known as the Tower Commission, which, according to its own report, was directed by the president to "examine the proper role of the National Security Council staff in national security operations, including the arms transfers to Iran."[10] The Tower Commission included former Nixon and Ford deputy national security adviser Brent Scowcroft, who would become NSA in 1991 under President George H. W. Bush. Scowcroft helped to develop an NSC model that emphasized the Council's role as a coordinating body, one that would neither be the personal fiefdom of the national security adviser nor an instrument for operationalizing foreign policy. That model mostly survives today.

Homeland Security Council

In response to the terrorist attacks of September 11, 2001, Congress created the Homeland Security Council (HSC), an office within the EOP. The assistant to the president for homeland security "shall be the individual primarily responsible for coordinating the domestic response efforts of all departments and agencies in the event of an imminent terrorist threat and during and in the immediate aftermath of a terrorist attack within the United States and shall be the principal point of contact for and to the President with respect to coordination of such efforts."[11]

Like the NSC, the HSC has a council chaired by the president, but, as with all White House councils, the staff work is generally more impactful than the actual council meetings. The NSC can contain the Homeland Security Council within it, or the HSC can be an entity in its own right— different White Houses have treated it differently, and it is often the focus of a power struggle between the NSC and other parts of the White House. The HSC is also noteworthy as a White House office in that it was created by statute, which makes it one of the few at 1600 Pennsylvania Avenue with that legal status.

The same legislation that created the HSC also created a new cabinet agency: the Department of Homeland Security (DHS). Its creation entailed the combination of twenty-two offices disbursed throughout the federal government into the new agency. Congress's decision to create the DHS was in large part the result of a belief (notably articulated in the *9/11 Commission Report*) that turf wars and breakdowns in communications between various federal agencies contributed to the success of the 9/11 plot.

As is the case with the creation of any office inside the White House that overlaps with the functions of a cabinet agency, the coexistence of the HSC and the DHS has produced conflicts and management challenges. The secretary of the DHS is charged with being "responsible for coordinating federal operations within the United States to prepare for, respond to, and recover from terrorist attacks, major disasters, and other emergencies," a very similar description to the assistant to the president for homeland security.[12]

Office of Management and Budget

Originally known as the Bureau of the Budget, the Office of Management and Budget (OMB) traces its roots back to 1921, with its creation by statute in reaction to the then-significant growth in federal spending. Until that time, spending had been uncoordinated, with each agency essentially pitching its own budget request to Congress. Congress needed a coordinating entity to remedy this headache, and OMB's primary purpose then was—and is still to some extent—to produce a proposed consolidated federal budget each year. Concerned to not give the president too much control over spending, Congress housed the Bureau of the Budget inside the Treasury Department rather than inside the White House, implying a joint control. President Roosevelt changed that structure as part of his broader push for control over the administrative state, moving it in 1939 into the newly created EOP, and renaming it the Office of the Budget. In 1974, President Nixon added the "M"—"management"—duties. This move reflected a desire to have greater control over a number of managerial issues within federal agencies but was also part of Nixon's broader transfer of power away from agencies to the White House.

By head count, OMB is the largest unit within the EOP, with some 500 people and 7 Senate-confirmable senior staff. Parts of OMB have little external visibility, but significant scope, and include the Office of Performance and Personnel Management (OPPM), the Office of Federal Financial Management (OFFM), the Office of Federal Procurement Policy (OFPP), and the Office of E-Government and Information Technology. One of the most important parts of OMB is perhaps the least known—the Office of Information and Regulatory Affairs (pronounced "O-I-Ra"). This innocuous name hides the fact that this office has developed under successive presidents to take a very active role in monitoring, adjusting, and in some cases stopping agency-written regulations. It therefore has a very significant impact on the president's regulatory approach.

National Economic Council (White House Office)

The National Economic Council (NEC) was established in 1993 to advise the president on economic policy and to coordinate policymaking on domestic and international economic policy issues. Unlike the NSC or the HSC, it was created by an executive order and therefore has no statutory standing. However, because economic issues permeate virtually all decisions and are critical to the president's actual and perceived performance, it has become one of the most influential parts of the White House.

The NEC works closely with the other major economic arms of the federal government: the Department of the Treasury and the Council of Economic Advisers (CEA). The Treasury is an agency with a much broader role, and depending on the personality of the leaders, the secretary of the Treasury and the head of the NEC can vie to be the most important economic adviser to the president. The chairman of the CEA is the third component of the economic troika and can likewise have more or less weight in policy debates, depending on its leader and his or her relationships with the president and other economic policy leaders. Though the CEA was created much earlier (1946) by statute and was significantly more influential in policymaking debates before the creation of the NEC, today the NEC has supplanted it in importance, mainly because the NEC has focused on policy, whereas the CEA tends to focus on researching the overall economic environment.

Domestic Policy Council (White House Office)

The Domestic Policy Council (DPC) coordinates and advises the president on education, healthcare, and other domestic policy issues deemed to be "noneconomic." Versions of the DPC have existed since the 1960s, but the current version came about in 1993, when President Clinton split the erstwhile Office of Policy Development into the NEC and DPC. As with the NSC and HSC, turf battles can occur between these councils, as virtually every domestic issue has some economic component and vice versa. Like the NSC and the NEC, the DPC was initially set up as a true council, chaired by the president and consisting of a number of senior White House officials. However, it seldom meets that way, and most of its work is done by DPC staff.

Similar tensions and role ambiguities can exist between White House offices and multiple agencies, say, the head of the Domestic Policy Council and the secretaries of education or health and human services.

Presidential Personnel Office (White House Office)

The Presidential Personnel Office (PPO) plays an outsized role in most White Houses, as it is the funnel through which most presidential appointments flow. The president has the power to appoint up to several thousand people to positions across the federal government, and these positions are generally the most senior, influential, and sought after.

There are two types of appointees. The first are presidential appointees, requiring Senate confirmation (senior agency roles such as secretary, deputy secretary, undersecretary, assistant secretary, and ambassador). The second type are presidential appointees who do not require confirmation (most White House staffers, deputy assistant secretaries at federal agencies, and other advisers within the agencies such as chiefs of staff, communications aides, executive assistants, and so on).

Presidential appointees who require Senate confirmation can expect to wait months, or even more than a year, before they gain the green light to serve in the positions for which they are nominated. This process has become progressively more politicized over time, and hence the speed with which Senate-confirmable appointees reach office has slowed. The average time to confirm a position has lengthened from an average of 56 days during President Reagan's time, to 81 days under Bill Clinton's presidency, to 112 days during President Obama's term in office, to 115 days when Donald Trump was president. The Center for Presidential Transition reports that "In 2019 alone, the Senate took an average of 136 days to confirm appointees."[13]

The process of making presidential appointments is continuous through-out the life of an administration. It may take an administration weeks or months to identify a nominee willing and qualified to serve (many either decline to serve or withdraw their nomination during the confirmation pro-cess because of a disqualifying factor). Senate confirmations can then drag out almost interminably. Once in office, owing to the difficulty of their jobs, the often highly political environment that they exist in, and the opportu-nities that open up when positions turn over, the average length of service for an agency appointee is two and a half years.[14] Consequently, filling all political appointee slots takes years, and many are filled two, three, or even four times in the course of an eight-year administration.

There is an ongoing tension as to who controls the appointment of politi-cal personnel inside agencies below the level of secretary. The secretary of an agency naturally wants total discretion to choose his or her team, while the White House wants to ensure agency leaders choose people who it be-lieves are loyal to the president (they are, after all, "presidential" appoint-ments). Loyalty and competence, however, are not always found in equal measures in one appointee, resulting in a tug-of-war between an agency and the White House that the PPO must often referee.

Communications and Press (White House Office)

The White House has had a press secretary since 1929, when George Aker-son first served in the role under President Hoover. Initially the press secre-tary's focus was dealing with a relatively small (by today's standards) group of newspaper reporters. The various types of media outlets covering the White House have grown considerably with the successive advent of broad-cast television, cable, and the internet. So too has intense interest increased in every aspect of the president's agenda from within the United States and around the world. Outside of the president, the press secretary is the most visible continuous spokesperson, giving a series of regular and semi-regular press briefings. President Kennedy was the first to introduce a live televised press briefing, and its broadcast is now a regular and accepted practice.

The Communications Office works closely with the Press Office. Whereas the press secretary and his or her team is concerned with addressing daily, or even momentary media concerns, the Communications Office is pre-occupied with setting a long-term, strategic direction for the president's communications: What should the president's messaging focus on next month, next week, and in the next few days? It needs to not only decide on the messaging angle but then coordinate all the relevant people within an administration who will serve as spokespeople—whether they are cabinet secretaries, White House senior staff, or surrogates outside of government employment who are willing to advance the president's messaging. As with most aspects of the relationship between the White House and agencies, there can be inherent tensions between messaging objectives. The Communications Office has a network of communications offices inside each of the agencies to manage this tension. They need to provide incoming information and also ensure that their individual messaging is consistent with that of the White House.

Other Offices

The list above enumerates only some of the main offices. There are dozens of others within the Executive Office of the President, each with an important role. Some are "offices" in their own right (with a specific mandate and led generally by an assistant to the president) and some nested inside larger offices (and often led by a deputy assistant to the president). Some of the other notable ones are as follows:

The White House Counsel's office, nested in the White House Office, provides presidents with in-house legal advice, although it is important to note that this is not advice to presidents as individuals but to them in their capacity as the leader of the institution of the presidency. The White House Counsel's role and its advice are in addition to that which comes from the attorney general and the Department of Justice. A specialist office like the White House Counsel is justified because of its small scale (the Department of Justice has, by contrast, more than 100,000 employees), its focus on serving the president's interests only, and the practical benefit of physical proximity to the president.[15] As with other components of the White House that have an agency counterpart, the overlap can cause some confusion and tension unless the respective leaders have a good working relationship. The White House counsel is more than just a lawyer—he or she is consistently looking at issues through a combined legal and policy framework. He or she should be a person who, consistent with a commitment to serve a president's agenda, looks for positive solutions within the context of what is lawful. He or she must also be able to say "no" when appropriate. The White House Counsel team also interfaces with the Office of Legal Counsel in the Department of Justice, which legally clears all presidential documents, oversees ethics rules and record management, and supervises the legal clearance of nominees.

The White House Counsel's office also has a strong role in the selection of judges and, in particular, a Supreme Court nominee, meaning that once every few years it has a role, largely invisible to the public, that can define the legacy of the president and impact policy for decades.

Although presidential administration aides have liaised with Congress since the earliest administrations, the Office of Legislative Affairs was created to formally handle day-to-day interactions with Congress. Depending on the seniority and skill of its leader, it can be an exceptionally influential office, representing the president and influencing the shape of federal legislation.

The Office of Intergovernmental Affairs was started by President Eisenhower and coordinates the White House's relationships with state and local governments. The small staff of the Office of Intergovernmental Affairs is another example of having the potential for an outsized role given that they interface with a broad constituency of fifty states, tens of thousands of local and municipal government entities, and numerous collective D.C.-based groups such as the National Governors Association.

The Office of Public Liaison carries out a similar role as the Office of Intergovernmental Affairs, but with a focus on the thousands of nongovernmental civil society, nonprofit, and private-sector groups that require some form of relationship management. Successfully managing these relationships can involve understanding and representing internally their view of policy matters, but, more importantly, selling the president's policies to the public. The Office of Public Liaison can also have an impact by organizing events at the White House—everything from veterans' events to Iftar dinners—and for the president on the road. These events are small in number and can either be impactful or inconsequential depending on how well they are carried out.

The great majority of other people in the White House are in offices that can been described under the banner of "care and feeding of the president." Generally, personnel in these offices only experience public scrutiny when something goes wrong. These offices include those responsible for the logistics of the president's day and travel, as well as information technology, financial management, and operations. The total personnel in these offices number in the hundreds of people, and generally they are grouped together to report to a deputy chief of staff for operations.

The White House Military Office, too, has the all-important oversight of Air Force One, Camp David, and the White House Mess—the matchbox-sized basement dining room run by the U.S. Navy, which is still one of the most sought-after invitations in Washington, D.C., given who else may be in the room.

Special Advisers, Czars, and Task Forces (White House Office)

Each president has created roles with titles such as "special adviser." These are generally personal advisers with whom the president has a close pre-existing relationship. They often occupy a "floating" role, with ambiguous responsibilities. For example, President Obama made his longtime adviser Valerie Jarret senior adviser to the president concurrent with her service as assistant to the president for intergovernmental relations. Donald Trump made both his daughter Ivanka and her husband, Jared Kushner, senior advisers. And Joe Biden tapped longtime political aide Mike Donilon for the same role.

The president can also add individuals or task forces to deal with temporary issues. Presidents Kennedy and Johnson used task forces extensively. President Obama also created a series of czars who were tasked with specific mandates. New York financier Steven Rattner, for instance, was the lead adviser on the Presidential Task Force on the Auto Industry (you may know him better as Obama's "Car Czar"). President Biden appointed John Kerry an envoy to lead cross-government efforts on climate change.

Task forces can be brought together quickly to deal with crises or other short-term imperatives, such as those set up by both President Trump and President Biden to deal with the COVID-19 pandemic. In the cases of special advisers, czars, and task forces, the new entities provide a focus, but they can also create some confusion if their mandate is not clear, or if they cut across existing entities' mandates. The potential for turf wars increases exponentially to the power of the number of people who think they are in charge of an issue.

OTHER FACTORS SHAPING THE DYNAMICS OF THE EOP

Ranks and Span of Control

The president commissions senior personnel in the EOP as a means of creating hierarchy according to rank. Commissions from the president are denoted with the following ranks: assistant to the president (AP), deputy assistant to the president (DAP), and special assistant to the president (SAP).

An assistant to the president ranks in the highest echelon of staff. Typically, there are now approximately 25 of them in a modern White House. APs typically run one of the main offices or other components of the EOP (NSC, NEC, DPC, Press, etc.). Thus the "assistant to the president" title denotes the individual's rank, and the "director" or other title of a specific office denotes his or her official duty. AP is a coveted rank and comes with an even bigger prize for most—an office in the West Wing and a parking spot on West Executive Avenue.

DAPs (of which there are also generally around 25) report to APs and are generally the deputies to not only the president, but to each of the APs. SAPs (of whom there are roughly 50 to 75) report to DAPs. They also follow the useful rule of thumb that the larger the title in government, the less senior the role. SAPs are often the frontline and specialist worker bees churning out memos and executive orders, and generally assuming responsibility for the details of any issue.

While the rank system is a useful dimension of organization (there must be some hierarchy), it does little to mitigate the complications of managing a large span of control. The presence of 25 or so APs implies that 25 people notionally report directly to the president. After tacking on an additional 20 or so cabinet members who also report directly to the president, the result is a direct span of control for the president of close to 50 people. That's not to mention other heads of noncabinet agencies, ambassadors, and other appointees who believe they have a direct report to the president. No other organization would ever design a span of control this large, especially when the person in charge additionally has all-encompassing external responsibilities.

In practice, it is clearly impossible for the president to effectively manage fifty-plus direct reports. Consequently, chiefs of staff act to some extent as span breakers, although they often don't have total clarity as to how and when to insert themselves between the president and one of the president's direct reports.

The reality of any White House is that some cabinet members or APs only meet very occasionally with the president, or only in groups, so opportunities to meet with the president in one-on-one settings are coveted.

Physical Proximity to the President and West Wing Access Rights

The West Wing is a small building to the west of the main White House residence. It is a cramped and aging structure, unimpressive but for the fact that it contains the Oval Office and some of the most important offices in the world.

In my four years in the West Wing, I was privileged to be able to occasionally show visitors around the hallways of the West Wing. The walk took all of five minutes, but the overwhelming and universal reaction was one of humility at its history and mission.

The West Wing is mostly occupied by the people with the rank of assistant to the president, and their direct support staff (executive assistants). Its main purpose is to ensure that selected people are literally seconds away from the president.

The building has three levels. The lowest floor houses support offices and the White House Situation Room. The middle level contains the Oval Office, and the physical offices of the vice president, the chief of staff, the national security adviser, the special advisers, and the heads of Press and Communications. The topmost level houses physical offices for the heads of most of the DPC, the NEC, and other key roles such as the White House counsel.

Proximity to the president is the most critical and sought-after staff privilege. The ability to walk into the Oval Office—potentially without an appointment—gives a staff member an unrivaled opportunity to influence the president. Some of the offices within the EOP (e.g., the chief of staff's) have remained located in the same physical space from one administration to another. Other offices are afforded space in a process keenly watched by all White House staff, with each office's location within the West Wing signaling to a large extent the importance of that office and its leader's role in the particular administration.

Badges of varying colors issued by the Secret Service indicate corresponding levels of access rights. A blue badge allows free access to the West Wing and is only issued to senior staff. It generally comes with other privileges, such as being able to dine in the Navy Mess Hall. The main benefit of a blue badge is not just convenience regarding movement around the West Wing; it is also incredibly useful for being part of the informal flow of information among senior staff that is often equally or more important than the formal flow. Walking the corridors and having discussions with others in the hallways, dropping by West Wing offices, and seeing who is dining with whom can be extremely useful.

The great bulk of the remaining White House staff are housed in the very large building to the west of the West Wing, the Eisenhower Executive Office Building (EEOB). The EEOB is many times the size of the West Wing and was originally known as the State, War, and Navy Building. When the Department of Defense and the State Department shifted to their current dedicated buildings in the 1940s and 1950s (the Pentagon in Northern Virginia and the Harry S. Truman Building in Foggy Bottom, respectively), the EEOB became exclusively used for EOP staff. Its main benefit is that it sits inside the White House compound, so staff can quickly access the West Wing without having to go through an additional security check. This relocation of some of the most important cabinet departments also had the effect of increasing the impact of various EOP policy staffers by virtue of proximity.

Culture

The culture of the White House—the professional atmosphere that either drives or hinders achievements—varies from administration to administration. In every instance, there are bound to be big egos, type-A personalities, and competing policy views. How presidents and their staff overcome these impediments is key to driving impact.

Staff who have the honor of serving at the White House are thrust into one of the most intense work environments in the world. Staffers must pass security background checks and a political vetting process to determine their suitability for service. Once on the job, they are expected to display the highest level of competence and an ability to maintain poise and productivity under pressure. Long hours are standard, and the idea of work-life balance is an oxymoron. The staff's loyalty to the president and alignment on policy goals is a massive determinant of productivity.

Expecting political appointees to work in harmony is enough of a tall order. But the culture of any White House is also shaped by the interplay between the president's politically appointed team members and the career civil service staffers who populate the lower ranks of EOP offices such as the Office of Administration, the NSC, and OMB. Where political appointees will factor political considerations into a decision-making process, civil service employees are intended to be politically nonpartisan, performing what is asked of them by politically appointed leaders. This dichotomy can create a tension that also permeates the federal agencies—political appointees often grumble that career civil servants are insufficiently on board with the mission, or, in the worst cases, a force for subverting the sitting presidential administration's agenda. Meanwhile, civil servants are often keen to not appear to be giving one administration or another preferential treatment, lest they face accusations from their civil service colleagues of being too political.

Cadence

While there is no such thing as a standard day at the White House, there are certain operational rhythms that guide how every staffer spends his or her time. Above all, the president's activities drive each staffer's daily, weekly, and monthly duties. A solar system with the president at the center and a series of planets and smaller moons all operating (at least in concept) in a coordinated fashion around the sun is as good an analogy as any.

Formulating policy, implementing it, and creating a public message to accompany the action is a time-consuming process that involves the coordination of many different offices within the EOP, other agencies in the executive branch, and various outside groups. The Office of the Staff Secretary is indispensable for tracking and managing the flow of paper—information on policy developments, scheduling, public announcements, executive orders, and all other documents—coming to and leaving the president's desk. "Staff Sec" can also act as a liaison to other agencies in cases when various offices within the EOP wish to review various agency policy actions or communications before they are deployed.

The president's daily schedule is usually determined by the chief of staff's office and approved by the president. The public aspects are communicated to the outside world. No one day is the same, and any given day will consist of a mix of meetings with external leaders and internal teams on policy and other decisions. There are few gaps in the schedule, and those that do exist are filled quickly by ad hoc meetings around issues of the day. A "typical" day in the White House could look something like

8:00 a.m.: Daily intelligence briefing
9:00: Policy discussion
10:30: Greet the nation's governors for their annual White House meeting
12:00: Internal lunch with chief of staff
1:30: Meet with press secretary ahead of her press briefing
3:00: Meet with foreign leader in Oval Office
4:30 onward: Calls to congressional members
7:00: Dinner with family
8:00 onward: Review briefing book for next day

The schedule of these meetings will inevitably be impacted by events of the day and interspersed with ad hoc but important meetings with staff on issues that arise outside of the White House's control. Few meetings, other than those with external parties such as foreign heads of state, are "locked in" immovably on the schedule. Travel days are even less structured (except for the centerpiece meetings and events themselves), and meetings with advisers happen continually as the president travels on Air Force One.

PROBLEMS WITH THE DESIGN AND PROCESS OF THE EOP

The above sections cover the ways in which the EOP is organized and certain ways in which it *should* work. But there are a number of complications inhibiting the ideal functioning of the EOP, several of which are discussed below.

Given the array of offices that make up the EOP, and the way that they must interface with various parts of the executive branch, running it has always been a challenge, and even more so as it has grown. Everyone who works in the EOP should be there to serve the president. They have no statutory power to make policy in their own right. They also have no operational capability (at least they should not have—and problems such as the Iran-Contra affair indicate why) and no right to direct any agency to do anything, other than through the president's explicit direction.

Common wisdom holds that the White House should be designed to suit the president. That is true to an extent, but it is not exactly a strong basis for addressing the question of how to improve the functioning of the White House to make democratic government more effective. Presidents may have a White House perfectly crafted around their working style, and the results may be subpar, or nonexistent.

The titles of the offices can also suggest little about how the White House actually runs. Who is responsible for what? What hierarchy, if any, exists? How is each office's head count determined? How do offices relate to each other? How are disputes resolved? The primary answer to all these questions is, frustratingly, "It depends." Presidents have no constraints in the way they choose to organize the people who report to them. The only constraint is the White House's overall budget, which to some extent limits the number of people (although even that is somewhat flexible). The NSC, for example, can expand considerably by "detailing" in people from federal agencies, a resource that many White House teams have adopted with enthusiasm, since the home agencies, not the White House, continue to pay the detailees' salaries.

Additional issues are as follows: First, major problems can crop up when senior staffers transform from viewpoint-neutral coordinators into advocates for specific policies. Bodies such as the NSC and the DPC were originally intended to be strictly coordinating entities—bringing together agency officials and White House officers to formulate options for the president's decision. Roles such as the national security adviser were intended to be filled by "honest brokers" who would not favor one policy or another. Over time, however, there have arisen several exceptions to that model, mainly owing to the person who inhabits the role and the willingness of the president to accept their actions. Several NSAs have been more "principals"—decision-makers—than strictly conveners of the NSC or consensus-builders. While they may still suggest they are there to coordinate others' views, they either explicitly or implicitly tip the scales to shape the policy options proposed to the president and, hence, the result.

Second, the volume of decisions that could flow to the president is enormous and beyond the scope of any one person to process. Therefore, a system needs to be in place to organize which ones go to them, when, and with how much background. Different White Houses have been variously better or worse at filtering the decisions in a conscious and coordinated fashion, and trading off urgency for importance.

Third, the structure of the EOP little resembles any traditional concept of organization design. There are supposed to be formal lines of access to the president, and clear rules for accessing them either in person in the Oval Office, by phone, or by other means. However, these rules are made up from administration to administration. The lack of explicit rules can often create genuine ambiguity. Some rules are codified, but often they are just assumed by precedent, or even left deliberately vague. For example, while the title "chief of staff" would suggest all staff report to that person, that is only partially true. All staff, especially those titled "assistant to the president," report to the president, and the nature of their responsibility to the chief of staff is somewhat arbitrary. Some staff roles, for example, the national security adviser, who might claim that any national security issue is important enough to not have to go through a filter, seldom believe they have anything other than a direct line to the president. This exceptional procedure often causes friction inside the White House. The NSC lives by one set of rules and procedures, the rest of the staff by another.

Moreover, there is a strong history of "free agents" arising—people who feel that they have a strong enough relationship with the president that they can bypass formal channels and go directly to the president whenever it suits them. This breakdown in the process can arise for several reasons. If someone believes the system is not operating properly and, for example, is not giving their views strong enough airing, they can feel justified in "righting the wrong." Or if a system doesn't exist at all, they may feel the need and the right to interject their views into a discussion from which they have been absent. At times, direct access to a president outside established channels may be the result of a direct outreach they received from the president, who can either explicitly or implicitly open a channel. Or, a staffer can simply be a personality type that doesn't believe that any system of rules and guidelines needs to be followed.

Fourth, leaks are a commonplace problem in most White Houses. Although some leaks are intentional, made to informally shape the media coverage on an issue, the great bulk aren't. Leaks can cause numerous hardships for a president and their teams. They can contradict official communication, occasionally forcing the White House to make decisions on an earlier timeline than was intended. The motivation for leakers varies from personal (self-aggrandizement, vendettas) to policy-related (trying to strategically shape outcomes by raising the issue in the press, thus galvanizing public pressure for or against something).

Fifth, there are overlapping jurisdictions inside the EOP itself (in addition to their overlap with agencies) that have a tendency to create inefficiencies, turf battles, and frustrations. For example, aspects of technology policy are shared by the White House Office of Science and Technology Policy (OSTP), the technology component of the NEC, the NSC, and parts of the DPC that have "equities"—to use a common word inside government—in a policy. Sometimes structural solutions are used (NSC and NEC have a position that reports to both of them to address international economic issues), sometimes there are shared responsibilities, and sometimes there is a coordinator (say, the deputy chief of staff for policy). But turf battles are numerous and can lead to a breakdown in the process, and/or free agents and leaks.

Sixth, most of the people hired into the policy councils are policy experts in various issue areas. Therefore, they are often not particularly strong at duties that require managerial skills—such as running large-scale policy processes (including simple skills such as how to run an effective meeting)—which can lead to ineffectiveness or failure. They can be champions of certain policies, having worked in a particular field for many years, and therefore approach a problem with a very immovable view. They are also generally very interested in the decision but less interested in its implementation, assuming that once it is made, the machinery of government will midwife the desired end state. This is not a safe assumption—implementation is challenging and requires conscious management, especially as employees of various agencies within the federal government may work against an administration's directive for various reasons. However, if they overcompensate by taking "operational" matters into their own hands, it can cause issues of another kind, as the Iran-Contra scandal exhibited. The skill required is to coordinate implementation, which is basic management.

Seventh, bottom-up policymaking can be an issue in terms of overloading the policy system. Staff on the various policy councils can see their time at the White House as the peak of their career and the best opportunity to implement policy that they are passionate about, not necessarily what the president has identified as a priority. Policy suggestions can appear because of general council staff activity, proposals linked to campaign promises, lines slipped into presidential speeches, or other initiatives. Without a clear system for determining which proposals are or are not priorities, momentum can make them into White House policy by default.

CONCLUSION

Over the course of more than two hundred years, the White House has grown from a family office to a conglomerate of multiple offices. Staff have grown materially in number and specialization. However, that growth hasn't solved the fundamental problem of how to better deliver on citizen expectations, mainly because the White House has also grown exponentially more complicated to run, just as the federal government has.

One of the main barriers to effective operations is that there is no consistent overarching concept to the design of the Executive Office of the President. The building blocks of the current EOP do not fit into any traditional framework of organization design. Roles and responsibilities are often ambiguous, and a lack of structure is exacerbated by unclear reporting lines and strong personalities with their own agendas. Leaks and staffers freelancing on their own pet projects have the potential to further frustrate the mission.

These are all headwinds on presidents' ability to accomplish their agenda. They all point to a need for a new strategy, designed well before the responsibilities of governance consume an administration.

3
YEAR ZERO

In the final scene of the film *The Candidate,* Robert Redford's character, having just won his Senate race, turns to his main adviser and says, "What do we do now ?"[1] The film was made in 1972 and is obviously fictional, but it does have a truth buried in it—candidates have historically not needed to consider how they govern until the victory was secured.

In previous chapters I have surveyed the responsibilities, organization, and tools of power a president will assume. Citizen expectations are higher than ever, domestic and international challenges continue to mount, and the political environment has made fostering and translating bipartisan agreement into transformational legislation increasingly difficult. In light of such headwinds, a poor start can permanently damage a president's ability to get things done.

The good news is that the federal government and most campaigns have taken some efforts over the years to ensure that a new president can get off to a running start, and to try to minimize the disruption to the continuity of government operations. We have come a long way from the days when President-elect Eisenhower, having just won the election, headed off for a ten-day golfing vacation. But more must be done—and be done earlier—to get presidents of either party off on the right foot.

I have had the honor of being involved in three presidential transition processes, each of quite differing character. In 2012, I was executive director of candidate Romney's transition planning organization. Former governor Mike Leavitt of Utah, the chairman of the effort, described it by saying, "We built a fine ship. Unfortunately, it did not sail."[2] In other words, the Romney transition team's highly organized effort set new standards for detailed preparation, but the work output was never implemented. In 2016, I joined the Trump transition team after the election, coming aboard a team that had been rebooted after the firing of transition leader Chris Christie, and was trying to do months of work in a span of mere weeks. In 2020, I led the

White House efforts to prepare for the transition to a possible second term, and then took the reins of what turned out to be perhaps the most challenging transition of one presidency to another in modern times. Each of these experiences has reinforced the need to not only follow best practices (which the Romney and Biden teams did, with the latter actually testing them in the fire of a disputed election, and which the Trump team struggled to do) but also to continually push the boundaries of developing new ideas.

Given the president's control over the vast federal government, the time has come for a reconsideration of how they can better wield the tools at their disposal to deliver good outcomes for the country. Now is the time for a fresh (Year Zero) approach to the presidency—significantly front-loading the work of establishing an administration to a much earlier point, so that a new president can accomplish more, and faster.

TRANSITION PLANNING HAS DEVELOPED TO MEET THE CHALLENGES, BUT NEEDS TO KEEP EVOLVING

Until the 1930s, the presidential inauguration did not take place until the March following a November election, giving the incoming president four months to transition. Given the relatively small number of staff to be appointed and organized, the limited scope of government, and the generally slow nature of federal activities, incoming presidents didn't need to start thinking about governing until after their election.

However, during the "secession winter" of 1861, the outgoing president, James Buchanan, stood by as secessionists from the Union took control of U.S. government forts and arsenals. The newly elected president, Abraham Lincoln, watched helplessly. The problem with a four-month interregnum was evident again in 1932, when the banking system collapsed after the election of Franklin D. Roosevelt and the country headed toward the Great Depression with a lame duck government. As a result, the Twentieth Amendment was passed in 1933, bringing the inauguration of the president forward to its current date of January 20. This change meant that there are now only approximately seventy-five days in the transition period between the election and Inauguration Day.

That seventy-five-day period may be useful for reducing presidential paralysis in a time of crisis. But it is not an adequate time span in which a president-elect can prepare to commandeer the most powerful office in the world. Establishing a new White House has become exponentially more complicated since the days when people and information moved across the country at a glacial pace, and the federal government was less than 1 percent of its present size. Today presidents must appoint dozens of senior White

House staff and nominate (and persuade the Senate to confirm) their key cabinet members and appoint hundreds of others. They must start turning campaign promises into an actual legislative program. They must carry out reviews of more than one hundred federal agencies, begin contingency planning for any immediate crises, and start significant outreach to important players such as Congress. Presidents and their key staff must be ready to govern at 12:01 p.m. on January 20. Getting a presidency off to a strong start is wildly difficult in the best of circumstances.

The concept of the presidential transition period is familiar to Americans today, reinforced by TV cameras covering both the president and the president-elect meeting at the White House on the morning of a presidential inauguration (in a normal circumstance). But the concept of one presidential administration assisting another in taking the reins was completely nonexistent until the 1950s, when President Truman brought both presidential nominees—Dwight Eisenhower and Adlai Stevenson—to the White House in the summer of 1952 for national security briefings. The presidency had also come to a point when more connective tissue between one president and another was necessary—the White House staff by that point numbered hundreds of people, and the nation was on high alert for a potential Soviet nuclear attack. Still, Truman's attempt to facilitate a smooth transition was volitional. At the time, there was no federal funding or other resources available to an incoming administration, nor guidelines around how the outgoing administration should help facilitate a transition.

Fortunately, in tandem with legislative developments, transition planning has become progressively more professional and organized.

Congress formalized the idea of an operational framework to support the peaceful transfer of power from one president to another through the Presidential Transition Act (PTA) of 1963. Passing the act just months after Kennedy's assassination, Congress explained its reasoning for the bill by saying, "Any disruption occasioned by the transfer of the executive power could produce results detrimental to the safety and well-being of the United States and its people."[3] The act directed the General Services Administration (GSA) to supply office space and funding to the president-elect and vice president–elect for use in preparing for their official duties. It also gave the head of the GSA the authority to "ascertain" the "apparent successful candidates" as a prerequisite for disbursing transition resources. However, it did not establish the criteria on which the GSA administrator should ascertain the winner, which is normally a simple and automatic procedure, but which became an issue in the 2020 transition.

Since that first piece of legislation, the act has been modified and updated several times. The 1988 Presidential Transition Effectiveness Act responded to the growth of the federal government, and a chronic shortage of funding for transition activities, by growing the amount of public funds appropriated to the president-elect and vice president-elect. It also allowed their campaigns to supplement government resources by accepting private funding from any person, organization, or other entity for transition purposes.

Despite the passing of the PTA of 1963 and its first emendation in 1988, there was little initial formality to transition planning from candidates. It is only in the last twenty years that a well-defined process and organization for a transition has emerged. In 2000, with Vice President Al Gore poised to upgrade his office in the West Wing, President Clinton issued Executive Order 13176, creating the Presidential Transition Coordinating Council, a body comprised of officials from various federal entities and chaired by the president's chief of staff. The executive order also directed the federal government to create and furnish to the president-elect's team a transition directory with information on "the officers, organization, and statutory and administrative authorities, functions, duties, responsibilities, and mission of each department and agency."[4] It ordered the creation of a catalogue of all the positions across the federal government eligible to be filled by political appointees—today a publication known as the Plum Book. The executive order also directed the agencies to prepare orientation materials for each appointee. An updated version of the Presidential Transition Act in 2000 also then directed the GSA to develop a plan to transition the candidate's computer and communications systems.

The terrorist attacks of September 11, 2001, motivated a new set of reforms under President George W. Bush. On the day of the 9/11 attacks, almost a year after the 2000 election, only 57 percent of Senate-confirmable positions of national security importance at the Pentagon, Justice Department, and State Department were filled.[5] The 9/11 Commission found that a slow presidential transition "hampered the new administration in identifying, recruiting, clearing, and obtaining Senate confirmation of key appointees."[6] Consequently, the Intelligence Reform and Terrorism Prevention Act of 2004 expedited security clearances for key national security positions, recommended that administrations submit nominations for national security positions by Inauguration Day, and encouraged the full Senate to vote on these positions within thirty days of nomination. The act also emended the Presidential Transition Act to ensure that the president-elect received a classified briefing on "specific operational threats to national security; major military or covert operations; and pending decisions on possible uses of military force."[7]

In 2008, President Bush directed his chief of staff, Josh Bolten, to execute what he desired to be a comprehensive and cooperative transition, in large part to ensure the continuity of government operations amid the wars in Iraq and Afghanistan. As he wrote in his memoir *Decision Points,* "Months before the 2008 election, I had decided to make it a priority to conduct a thorough, organized transition."[8] Under Executive Order 13476, President Bush, as Clinton had done, created a Presidential Transition Coordinating Council (PTCC) and directed it to "assist the major party candidates and the President-elect by making every reasonable effort to facilitate the transition between administrations."[9]

By every account, the Bush team did this, with White House chief of staff Bolten and Obama transition co-chair John Podesta formalizing their terms of cooperation in a memorandum of understanding. It wasn't just a ceremonial document. As the financial markets crumbled in the fall of 2008, treasury secretary Hank Paulson spoke regularly with Obama's team, and the White House coordinated with Obama's team to help move the Troubled Asset Relief Program bill through Congress. Bush's team directed the FBI to speed up processing times for security clearances, and ultimately more than 100 members of Team Obama were able to get them before the election. On January 13, 2009, Bush and Obama officials joined one another in a national security exercise testing the government's response to a terrorist attack. That exercise would prove more valuable than they knew—on the morning of January 20, as Bush and Obama and their wives sipped coffee in the Blue Room of the White House, national security officials from both teams met in the White House Situation Room to respond to credible intelligence about an Inauguration Day attack on the National Mall.

Many of the features of the smooth Bush-Obama transition were formalized into law in subsequent years. The 2010 Pre-Election Presidential Transition Act brought forward the provision of support by tying the timing of the GSA's distribution of resources to the naming of both parties' presidential nominees. These are generally known at the time of the nominating conventions in the summer preceding the election. In other words, the federal government was now helping facilitate a smooth transition months *before* the election. The 2010 legislation also afforded more services to the incumbent administration to help prepare the incoming president.

In 2015, the Edward "Ted" Kaufman and Michael Leavitt Presidential Transitions Improvements Act mandated what had become customary—the establishment of a White House transition coordinating council. It also mandated an agency transition director's council and set down timing for both to be established no later than six months before a presidential election. It mandated as well that the GSA and each federal agency appoint a senior career appointee to lead transition coordination activities.

A few years later, the Presidential Transition Enhancement Act (PTEA) of 2019 ensured that the GSA entered into a memorandum of understanding with each presidential campaign by September 1 of a presidential election year. A condition of each memorandum of understanding held that each campaign will "implement and enforce an ethics plan to guide the conduct of the transition beginning on the date on which such candidate becomes President-elect."[10] It also called for each agency to develop a succession plan for each senior noncareer agency employee—in other words, to have a plan in place for a civil servant to take over each job filled by a political appointee, even temporarily, before a new politically appointed official filled it. Finally, the PTEA also directed the GSA to provide support for the president-elect and vice president–elect for up to sixty days after an election.

As a result of subsequent legislation, supplemented in some cases by executive orders, transition planning has become an increasingly elongated and formalized process—a far cry from the new president showing up at the White House on Inauguration Day. However, the legislation is still mainly the mere framework of a transition and leaves considerable flexibility and interpretation to the incoming (and outgoing) administrations. Cooperation and efficiency are presumed, but not guaranteed.

On the candidates' side, over recent election cycles, transition teams have started being formed earlier, and with increasing structure and formality. In early modern presidencies, for instance Kennedy's, the transition team did not really come together until after the election. More recently, most candidates have put together a skeleton transition team some months before the election and have started to scale it up in earnest after the nominating conventions, approximately four months before the election. This group then runs parallel to, and separate from, the main campaign, which needs to be focused on winning the election. It generally operates very quietly as it conducts various preparatory activities.

The head of a presidential transition team must be someone the candidate can trust completely—longtime Democrat powerbroker John Podesta and veteran Obama adviser Valerie Jarrett co-chaired Obama's transition team, and Mike Leavitt, the former governor of Utah, was likewise a longtime confidant of 2012 Republican nominee Mitt Romney when he accepted the job of chairing the transition. An ironclad bond of trust was not in place when Donald Trump originally selected Chris Christie to run his transition team, and days after the election, on November 11, 2016, Trump replaced him with Vice President–elect Mike Pence, causing the transition process to have to restart.

Transition staff generally start with no more than a handful of individuals. By Election Day the transition staff can increase to as many as 500 to

600 people, with another 500 or so waiting in the wings for deployment. They are all organized around key activities such as selecting personnel, forming agency review teams, building out president-elects' policy machinery, and managing their new daily life. I have described the Romney transition team formation in David Marchick's book *The Peaceful Transfer of Power* as "a startup on steroids."[11] Nevertheless, our team displayed a high degree of professionalism, and though we did not win the election, we put together an operation that prepared for the peaceful transfer of power in a near-exemplary way. Congress agreed, as Mike Leavitt was in part the namesake for the Edward "Ted" Kaufman and Michael Leavitt 2015 Presidential Transitions Improvements Act. Notably, the other individual honored in the name of that bill, Ted Kaufman, chaired the 2020 Biden transition team.

Believing that the lessons we learned would be useful to future transition teams, Daniel Kroese, Clark Campbell, and I wrote *The Romney Readiness Project* in early 2013. The book is a complete manual on how to run the logistics of a transition, based on the most advanced knowledge of such an undertaking at the time. It provides more detail than this book does on the execution of a transition team's day-to-day activities. But many of its key recommendations based on our experience still apply: "Develop a systematic approach," "Clearly define and delineate responsibilities," and "Focus energy narrow and deep" among them. But no conclusion we drew from the 2012 transition was more important than this: "Start early. Advanced preparation is prudent, not presumptuous."[12]

In summary, America is fortunate that the federal legislation passed since 1963 has established an increasing number of measures to facilitate a smooth transition. And the vast majority of people working on transition teams for presidential nominees of either party do the hard work of preparing candidates and their teams to assume the most powerful office in the world. But given the increasing scale of the challenges, transition planning needs to evolve again.

YEAR ZERO: A NEW PARADIGM OF MORE, EARLIER, AND VISIBLE

The scope of the problems a president must confront means he or she has no time to waste in getting things done—especially in the critical first year, when political capital is high and the looming midterm elections do not yet influence an administration's decision-making. As former White House chief of staff James Baker stated succinctly, "Prior preparation prevents poor performance."[13]

In the course of studying and planning transitions, I observed that a poorly run one could set back a presidency by months. If a transition team undertook slow or half-baked preparation regarding staffing an administration, designing and implementing policy, and structuring White House processes, then that work would still have to be carried out, but it would just happen once the president was in office. The *Romney Readiness Project* was so named for a reason—we wanted to do as much of the work of setting up an administration as possible during the pre-inauguration period, so that a future president Romney would not waste precious time on crafting new plans and selecting personnel in his first two hundred days. He would instead be left to do the presidential work of making and implementing policy. He would focus on delivering on the promises he had made during the campaign while his precious political capital was still high.

On the whole, I believe we put Governor Romney in position to do this well had he been elected president. But there were still gaps. Despite our efforts, Governor Leavitt could still acknowledge in the introduction to the *Romney Readiness Project 2012*, "I simply want to reflect that we mistakenly left the organization of President-elect support too long before we initiated serious planning." He also acknowledged, "We should have launched our communications efforts sooner."[14] Moreover, the planning was never tested. Looking back with the benefit of two other transitions and actual experience in the White House, I am sure that, had we won, we would have learned of other gaps.

There is also the little-contemplated reality that much can go wrong during a transition. America has already seen one postelection period in which the peaceful transition of power was threatened—and the Biden team was put on its back foot in its ability to prepare to assume the reins of leadership. Now imagine a scenario even more contentious than that which played out in 2020–21, perhaps involving challenges at the Supreme Court. Beginning transition activities sooner can mitigate the potential of unforeseen disruptive events in the postelection period to hamstring a presidency's early days and weeks.

As a result, aspirants to the presidency, their teams, and federal officials who help coordinate transitions should embrace the concept of "Year Zero." What I mean by Year Zero is a significant expansion of a presidential campaign's preelection activities, on a much earlier timeline, and with much more external visibility. Anyone who is serious about a run for president prepares for the race far in advance. Nowadays, campaigning can begin as early as the immediate days after midterm elections, a full two years before a presidential election. Planning how to govern, however, is rarely part of this process, which is instead dominated by fundraising, speeches, debates, and photo-ops. But preparing to govern should be much more than a secondary activity, and it should begin a year before the presidential election, not the typical six months or so before. My contention is that it is never too early to "measure the drapes"—not to become enamored with the trappings of power, but to plan for doing the work of holding presidential office.

A Year Zero approach—functionally, adding a year's worth of planning and design work to a four-year presidential term—will allow new presidents to enact their campaign promises faster, thus delivering outcomes more effectively, in particular in their first year. When the American people see the chief executive of the federal government getting things done, it will, I hope, help restore the public's faith in a democracy whose legitimacy is beleaguered at home and abroad. It will also pay dividends in the midterm elections and eventually presidential reelection. Lack of early years' results is one explanation for the poor performance of the president's party in recent midterm elections. By losing at least one of the two chambers of Congress, a president's ability to deliver substantial change over their whole four years is severely compromised. So Year Zero is not only crucial for a good start to the first year, but it flows on to all subsequent years.

The Year Zero approach also inverts how most transition teams have thought about operationalizing action in the White House. Usually, work processes are designed around the historical organizational blocks—the various offices and tools of power at a president's disposal, such as the chief of staff, the National Security Council, and so on. But those features are only means to an end—implementing the president's agenda. They ought not be the immovable centerpieces of White House organizational design. The better approach is to identify the would-be president's highest priorities and build a system that achieves them.

THE PHASES AND TASKS OF YEAR ZERO

The practical adoption of the Year Zero approach means undertaking its proposed activities across a logical sequence of phases: a Design Phase, Planning Phase, and Execution Phase. Ideally, the Design Phase should commence roughly a year before the election, or even earlier, so that the candidate can participate in the early Design Phase activities before he or she is totally consumed by the business of campaigning. The three-phased approach is designed in careful sequence.

The Design Phase, which could begin as a soon as a candidate declares for president, consists of four tasks:

Task 1: Assemble a Year Zero Leadership Team.
Task 2: Develop a strategy and operating model.
Task 3: Design core processes to achieve action.
Task 4: Design a coherent White House structure.

The Planning Phase has one main task:

Task 5: Plan for the first two hundred days.

The Execution Phase has two main (parallel) tasks:

Task 6: Build a policy pipeline.
Task 7: Build a people pipeline.

The phases and tasks are shown in figure 2 and discussed in detail in the following chapters.

The Design Phase, in particular, is much more comprehensive than modern transition teams currently conceive of, and it has not often been a significant part of the early planning. To the extent there has been a component for the design of the White House, it is often at the end of the transition, not the beginning, even as late as after the election or during the early days of the administration. Furthermore, it typically keys off the old organization charts, using them as a starting point rather than taking a clean-sheet approach. The design can also be influenced by early people hires who then seek to negotiate resources. This is the reverse of what should happen. The better approach is to hire the right people after determining the operating structure that best fulfills the expectations of the design.

Sitting presidents contemplating their possible second term can take much the same approach, adjusted for the benefit and knowledge of incumbency. Some of the timing will be different, but the concept is the same.

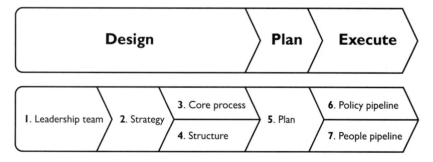

FIGURE 2. Year Zero: Phases and tasks

The Design Phase will need to address which aspects of the first term are retained and which are to be discarded and replaced.

CONCLUSION

Executing a comprehensive strategy in the year leading up to governing (Year Zero) is the key to establishing an effective presidency. Overall, Year Zero is a new paradigm that emphasizes the imperatives of more, earlier, and more visible. A well-structured Year Zero will give candidates a way to prepare for the hardest job they will ever have. In a White House and world of divided powers, the seven tasks constitute a rare combination of actions totally under the would-be president's control.

Setting up the White House has become more complicated because of more appointments to be made, more policy items to be prepared, more media scrutiny, and a transition period that is shorter than that which the early presidents enjoyed. Transition planning has developed to meet the challenges but needs to keep evolving. Outstanding execution of a transition can be the main differentiator between presidents who are successful in enacting their campaign promises, and ones who are not.

In the private sector, effective planning can marginally improve the effectiveness of the organization. In the White House, it can make the first year up to 100 percent more effective by not wasting the first six months learning how to govern. What would otherwise take a year can be done in the first two hundred days. The tasks will create the preconditions for policy achievements and effective government as well as building momentum for a successful presidency. Early success is self-reinforcing, leading to greater political capital, better prospects for midterm elections, and the building over time of a legacy.

Asking busy candidates to devote time, focus, and funds to preparing to govern before they have even won a primary is a tall order. But the task is worth doing—not just as a matter of serving the country well if they should win office, but as a signal to the electorate of their competency and seriousness of purpose. Quality of preparation should become a consideration in how voters select candidates, judging them not only for what they hope to accomplish and how they seek to lead, but whether they can build the infrastructure to do so. It is a leading indicator of their ability to run the most important political organization in the world.

4

TASK ONE

Assemble a Year Zero Leadership Team

Start at least twelve months before the inauguration.

In December 2009, Ed Whitacre, the newly elected chairman and CEO of General Motors, had an ambitious goal: bring General Motors back to the public markets within a year. It was also an audacious goal: just a few months before, GM had declared bankruptcy and been bailed out by the federal government in one of the most iconic business failures in American history. But Ed was a seasoned CEO, having risen from an entry-level role at AT&T to chairman and CEO over a long and successful career. He knew that the first action he had to take to pull off such a dramatic turnaround was to, in the words of business writer Jim Collins, "get the right people on the bus."[1]

Ed got to work deliberately constructing a team that blended seasoned industry and company experts, including current CEO Mary Barra and president Mark Ruess, with outsiders who brought new expertise, including me as CFO and vice chairman. Then he set the mission, goals, and roles for the team. I was initially skeptical about our ability to achieve a task of that scale as quickly as Ed thought it could be done, and I expressed that view to Ed. I will always recall his response, one delivered without any criticism in his dry Texas accent: "I didn't hire you for your opinion." Eleven months later, Ed's vision and savvy ability to put together the right leadership team allowed us to execute what was at the time the largest initial public offering (IPO) in history.

Presidential candidates facing a similarly herculean task and short time frame should also construct an outstanding executive team around them. The candidate's closest advisers shouldn't consist only of his or her top policy or political hands—the team also needs to incorporate people with management experience to deliver a White House ready to govern.

CHOOSE A COMBINED TEAM THAT CAN RUN THE CAMPAIGN AND ESTABLISH A SUCCESSFUL WHITE HOUSE

Even as recently as fifty years ago, campaigning to be elected president didn't start until around the beginning of the election year. In the 1972 race, most candidates on the Democratic side entered between November 1971 and March 1972—twelve to nine months ahead of the election. On the Republican side, incumbent President Nixon announced eleven months ahead of the election.

However, in recent decades, declarations of candidacy have come progressively earlier in the presidential cycle. In the 2020 presidential cycle, most contestants on the Democratic side entered the race between twenty and twenty-four months ahead of Election Day. The incumbent president, Donald Trump, announced his intention to seek reelection in June 2019, sixteen months ahead of the election.

Formal or informal campaigning now tends to start as early as immediately after the midterms (indeed, Donald Trump announced his intentions to run in the 2024 presidential election roughly two years ahead of Election Day), with declared or purported candidates making strategic visits to early primary states, launching fundraising efforts, releasing political autobiographies, and giving speeches to build momentum for their candidacy.

Once the campaign swings fully into action, it completely consumes the time and focus of the candidate and his or her senior team. Transition planning at this stage is nonexistent, as cash-strapped campaigns must focus on staying alive by generating adequate fundraising and competitive polling numbers. In the last few presidential cycles, most candidates had a very small transition operation that started around April/May of the election year and initially consisted of only a few people. Serious planning and increases in personnel didn't occur until around June or July of the election year, when it was clear that the candidate would likely become the nominee. The largest infusion of personnel onto a transition team then happens after the party conventions, when each party definitively nominates its candidate, and government funding and resources become available.

This approach accurately reflects the limited resources of a presidential campaign. But it also hamstrings what a candidate can achieve, especially in his or her first year in office. In a Five-Year Presidency, candidates would continue to start early on their campaign activities, but they would also construct the following leadership structure approximately a year from the election:

A Governance Team that will oversee both campaign and Year Zero activities.

A Campaign Leadership Team that will report to this Governance Team.

A Year Zero Leadership Team that would also report to the Governance Team.

The Campaign Leadership Team is self-explanatory—these are the leaders of the team trying to get the candidate elected. The Year Zero Leadership Team (Y0LT) consists of the individuals who would be appointed at least twelve months before Inauguration Day to manage all of the Year Zero tasks, which I will elaborate on in subsequent chapters.

The overall Governance Team would be comprised of the senior members of the Campaign Leadership Team and the Year Zero Leadership Team. This Governance Team exists to ensure tight coordination between the two parallel efforts, and so that there is a forum to resolve any issues that might arise between them. It would report directly to the candidate and consist of

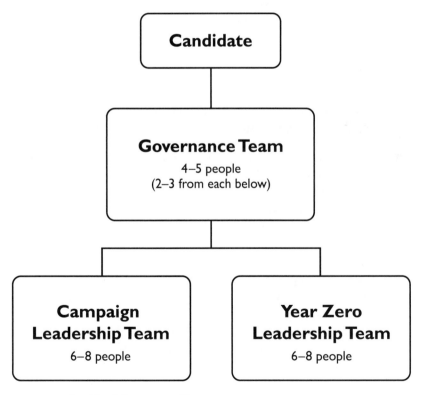

FIGURE 3. Combined Governance Team

his or her most trusted advisers. It should strive to resolve as many issues as possible without the candidate's involvement—resolving issues specific to their respective work streams as well as resolving issues between them (for example, how stated campaign policies should be prioritized, which decisions the candidate would articulate that could impact governance, or how to place campaign staff into political appointee roles after the election). Designing the structure and choosing the right people to populate the YOLT are clearly critical tasks in their own right, especially to ensure that the teams function well for the candidate's benefit. Traditionally, the transition planning team is seen as junior to the campaign team, and therefore the new approach requires the Campaign Leadership Team to buy into the concept and see the benefits of working closely with the YOLT.

The approach for a second-term "Year Zero" is somewhat different but parallels the above. Presidents should still appoint the equivalent of a YOLT in the fourth year of the first term, focused on planning and delivering a Year Five agenda. These people may or may not have existing roles in the White House (it is a good chance to bring in new blood and perspectives), and their efforts work in tandem with the running of the White House. For example, in 2020, as well as my duties as deputy chief of staff, I both carried out planning for a transition to a new president and ran a team planning for a possible second term.

THE YEAR ZERO LEADERSHIP TEAM SHOULD HAVE POLICY, PEOPLE, AND MANAGEMENT SKILLS

Given its focus on preparing policy items for presidential action well ahead of Inauguration Day, the YOLT should be composed of six to eight individuals who bring distinctive expertise in various subject matter areas, such as foreign affairs and economics. They should also have members with political background, knowledge of D.C., and congressional relationships.

One of its leaders should be someone with strong skills in discerning people suitable for presidential appointments, since preparing a presidential administration to more quickly deploy political appointees, and in greater quantities, is a major component of the Year Zero concept. One of the reasons that George W. Bush was able to stand up a White House so quickly in 2000–2001, despite the abbreviated transition period, was that he had enlisted a confidant, Clay Johnson, to run the transition a year ahead of the election. Johnson had been a Bush friend since their days at Phillips Academy and Yale, had been his chief of staff as governor in Texas, and was an outstanding people selector. He had a perfect combination of personnel skills and knowledge of what the candidate wanted. Johnson was instrumental in selecting the initial staff of the White House and subsequently ran the Office of Presidential Personnel as part of the administration.

An equally important skill set for the YOLT is general management. While the candidate and the Campaign Leadership Team focus on winning the election, the YOLT needs to manage and coordinate delivering on the Year Zero presidency tasks, including planning and designing the White House, building and managing a transition team of hundreds of people, and raising funding for their efforts. The team ought to be a blend of people who have been associated with the candidate for some time, specialists who are brought in for their policy expertise, and, where possible, people with experience in previous presidential transitions or White House and federal government service more generally. This diversity of experiences can serve a president well. As David Gergen, a former adviser to four presidents, has pointed out, "The success of the Reagan blend was he brought some people who knew him well and were extremely loyal to both his program and the man, all of whom were newcomers to Washington. . . . But he blended that with a team of experienced Washington insiders who didn't know the man as well but knew Washington well."[2]

The YOLT should determine a budget for the planning and transition activities. The main costs that will be incurred are for people and travel / accommodation. These can be kept low by the use of volunteers where possible (there are a large number of people willing to give their time for no payment and, in some cases, to pick up their own travel costs) and locating as much as possible of the activity either close to the candidate's home base or in Washington, D.C., where the government facilities and a number of the skilled staff will be located. The Presidential Transition Act provides government assistance for transitions, but it can only be accessed after a candidate has formally become his or her party's nominee at their respective conventions. The act does, however, allow for the creation of a separate 501(c)(4) nonprofit organization that can privately fund transition activities before the convention, or any activities after the convention where government-provided resources aren't deemed sufficient. Donations to that 501(c)(4) are limited to $5,000 per person or entity, but they do not count toward campaign donations so can be raised separately.

Total privately funded costs have varied considerably in recent campaigns, but all are very modest compared to the hundreds of millions spent on the campaign itself. The amount we estimated had candidate Romney won was approximately $10 million for the entire pre- and postelection transition activities. Donald Trump's campaign had some $5 million total transition costs (although that lesser amount reflected less preparation), while Joe Biden's were more than $20 million, which is a more representative number for Year Zero planning purposes. Initially, all that needs to be raised to fund the YOLT activities is an amount that is sufficient to get to the convention (after which public funds become available and private funding is much easier to raise), covering any salaries or incidental expenses. Depending on the mix of salaried employees versus volunteers, this amount should be tiny compared to campaign costs, potentially less than $1 million. Detailed funding for the postconvention period can be done closer to, and after, the convention.

The Advantages of Assembling the YOLT Early

Ideally, the YOLT should be assembled at least one year before the election. This time frame is earlier than virtually any campaign currently begins thinking about transition planning, but this earlier start has a number of benefits.

For one thing, if a candidate is serious about doing more during the first year in office, he or she needs to make critical decisions before being caught up in the full-time rigors of campaigning. Candidates need not be particularly interested or involved in the details of the YOLT activities, but they should be interested in setting the overall objectives. If the right people have been put in charge, the candidate need not have any more substantial involvement thereafter and can focus on winning the electoral race. They will inherit the results, and those results will help shape the success of their presidency. Either they set the shape and tone early, or their staff does (or, worst of all, no one does, and it evolves in an unconscious fashion). Clearly the best choice is for them to set the direction, and then focus on the campaign, only making the weightiest decisions that the YOLT are empowered to implement.

Starting early ensures that the people selected for the Governance Team are those committed to delivering results for the eventual president. The closer the date to the election, the more likely it is that potential members of the Governance Team are to be politically expedient allies or, worse, political opportunists seeking their own agenda. This is also certainly the case in the postelection period. It is possible to add people to the team as the year progresses, but ideally the core is in place very early.

Another advantage of starting early is that it allows a potential president and the YOLT to start to shape White House structure, processes, and culture before they face the storm of governance. Task conflict (the good faith contesting of policy ideas) needs to be promoted, but not personality conflict. Administrations can struggle in the early days of governance as newcomers adjust to each other. This was most obvious in the Trump

White House, where incompatible personalities drove much of the Trump White House turnover in its early months, as people moved in and out of senior-level jobs such as chief of staff, national security adviser, chief strategist, and communications director. The runway of Year Zero also gives the presidential candidate the ability to assess individuals' performance and the team's compatibility. Some turnover will happen during Year Zero, but it is a lot less disruptive to have a key team member depart before the election than during the early governing period.

If the Y0LT is successful individually and as a team during the period leading up to the election, then (assuming no firings or voluntary personnel departures) it will likely form the core of the White House senior staff. The Y0LT can then start to build a shadow White House immediately after the election, in parallel to the other transition activities. January 20 is too late to learn how to act as a fully functioning governing unit.

By the official Day One of a presidential administration (January 20), the main parts of the White House should have been operating as a cohesive unit for some weeks. Day One of the administration should, in effect, be Day Seventy-Six. All that changes is the location from which they are operating (from a transition workspace to the actual White House). At the core of that team will be the former Y0LT, the members of which will have been operating together for a year by that point, building muscle memory on both process and interpersonal work style.

CONTINUE TO EVOLVE THE CHIEF OF STAFF OFFICE: OPOTUS

The creation of the Y0LT has an even larger utility—it can plan for, and be itself the forerunner to a more powerful entity inside the White House: what I am describing as the Office of the President of the United States, or OPOTUS. To understand the OPOTUS concept it is useful to review the history of what it would replace—the Office of the Chief of Staff.

Historical Development of the Chief of Staff Role

The internal support structure around the president has gone through a series of evolutions. Initially the White House was simply the president and a very small number of personal aides. Most of the aides were generalists holding administrative responsibilities. The president relied almost entirely on the cabinet for policy and other more substantive advice. In Lincoln's day, for example, he had two personal assistants: John Nicolay and John Hay. But, as intimately depicted in Doris Kearns Goodwin's *Team of Rivals,* substantive advice came from figures such as Secretary of the Treasury Salmon P. Chase, Secretary of State William H. Seward, Secretary of War Simon Cameron (and later Edwin M. Stanton), Attorney General Edward Bates, and Secretary of the Navy Gideon Welles.

The initial evolution of this approach commenced when Congress appropriated money for presidential staff support for the first time in 1857. Staff numbers progressively grew in the following decades, but remained small, and there was little formal structure, with everyone reporting to the president.

The creation of the Executive Office of the President in 1939 was the second major evolution of White House staff, creating a formal structure of assistants around the president. Initially, the Executive Office of the President was still small enough that the president could manage it himself. However, as it grew in the number of staff and complexity, the president needed a layer of management between him and the resulting organization.

The resulting third evolution was the creation and development of a "chief of staff," a person who had a general managerial duty of overseeing the staff who carried out presidential orders.

Today the chief of staff role has evolved to entail a responsibility for executing on multiple lines of effort, including

advising the president on policy and political issues,
managing the flow of work (meetings, briefings, papers) to and from the president,
representing the president with key external constituencies such as Congress,
managing internal constituencies such as the cabinet,
communicating with the press both on and off the record,
managing the White House staff,
creating a positive culture,
choosing (and firing) staff, and
being the president's friend and confidant, often spending hours at a time in the Oval Office or on the road traveling to key events.

The chief of staff's duties have become so vast and complex that it is almost impossible for one person, no matter how hardworking, to carry them out effectively. Moreover, the scope of the role is so large, the pressure is so immense, and the need to deal with crises and conflict is so constant that those who try to do it all burn out quickly. Few can last a whole term with a president, let alone two terms. President Obama, for example, went through five chiefs of staff over eight years, and Ron Klain, one of the most effective recent chiefs, stepped down after two years of President Biden's term. This is not an optimal result, as changes in chiefs of staff result in disruption, lost time, and a new learning curve for the incoming chief. Over time the chiefs of staff have built their own offices, with support staff to assist with the function. For example, the chief of staff has deputy chiefs of staff to take the lead on specific functions, and this distribution of labor has lessened the burden. But deputy chiefs are generally more junior officials and cannot fully substitute their authority for the chief's.

Furthermore, a major limitation of the chief of staff role is that it concentrates in a single person powers that ought to be *institutional* in nature. Presidents' ability to be effective shouldn't depend on the management habits or personality of their principal assistant. Some chiefs of staff are inevitably strong in one area and weaker in others, meaning some of their responsibilities are performed well, but others aren't carried out optimally. Overall performance can go well or poorly, depending on who happens to inhabit the office. Weak chiefs of staff are ineffective, forcing presidents to do too much of the management themselves, which makes the White House significantly less impactful. Chiefs who are too strong or domineering are equally a problem, shutting down important debate, hijacking the president's agenda, and causing cultural issues by overpowering rather than empowering staff. Inevitably, since they are confrontational in nature, the strong chiefs are very hard to get rid of and are seldom capable of admitting they are the problem, not the solution.

It is also not unreasonable to ask the obvious question, "if the president with the hardest job in the world can be expected to serve four (or eight) years, why can't the person with the second-hardest job"? There have been thirty-six chiefs of staff under fourteen presidents. The first eight chiefs served on average roughly four years, but now two years is considered a lengthy service. If the president wants a change, then fine. But burnout implies that something is wrong with the job description, not the person.

OPOTUS

My recommendation is to use the Five-Year Presidency to launch a fourth major evolution of the chief of staff function: the creation of an "Office of the President of the United States" (OPOTUS). This office would be made up of the president's three to five most senior advisers, and, while headed by the chief of staff, would collectively manage the White House as a team. These advisers would not assume newly created positions—most of these advisers' individual roles are likely to already exist in the form of the national security adviser, White House counsel, etc. The key modification would be the conscious reworking of the chief of staff office to make it more of an institution, not the domain of one person, for supporting the president and directing the White House.

The creation of the OPOTUS will be a significant step forward in effective management of the White House and will help rectify issues that arise from chiefs of staff who are too weak or too strong. Management becomes easier to do with a team that between it has a blend of skills capable of covering the weaknesses of any one chief of staff. It will also assist in giving more longevity to chiefs, spreading the load among a larger and diverse group.

At a minimum, the current Office of the Chief of Staff should be strengthened. However, a more fundamental change is worth considering, as is the name change, which signifies that the office is there to serve the president's needs, not the chief of staff's.

Certain White Houses have had teams that in some ways had characteristics of an OPOTUS. President Reagan had the "troika" of James Baker, Ed Meese, and Michael Deaver. John Podesta, President Clinton's second chief, built up his office to include two counselors to the president and a senior adviser. President Obama had David Axelrod, Valerie Jarrett, and Pete Rouse, who were influential additions to the chief of staff. President Biden has a "quint" of Mike Donilon, Steve Ricchetti, Anita Dunn, Bruce Reed, and Jen O'Malley Dillon. So, the concepts discussed here aren't entirely novel. These were useful prefigurations of what I am proposing, but going forward with a model that would be more formalized than them and with clear and specific shared responsibilities.

The main responsibilities of the OPOTUS would be as follows:

"Protect" the president: The historian Richard Neustadt wrote that the president needed to be "his own best protector." By this he meant that presidents must fiercely defend their interests. While that is still true, it is impossible for presidents to do this by themselves—the job is too complex, information streams are too many, and the White House staffs are too large and divided on matters of policy and personality. The Brownlow Committee's mantra—"The President needs help"—remains as relevant as ever, but presidents need help of a different kind. They need a team of people whose only interest is the president's political and reputational "protection." This team needs to be the eyes, ears, and conscience of the president. They need to look at every decision through the lens of what is best for the president. And they need to be strong enough collectively to stand up to the president to stop him or her from making mistakes, a task that is all but impossible for one person whose job depends on the president's favor.

Run the system: The OPOTUS needs to manage the White House—a task in itself a significant challenge for a single chief of staff. They must have a collective system capable of capturing all the formal and informal information they and the president need to make decisions. They need a decision-making approach that leads to the best possible decisions. They need an implementation system that ensures that decisions result in action, and that action is effectively carried out and "sold" to the public.

Manage people: The OPOTUS needs to build the culture of the White House to suit the president. In doing so, they need to be instrumental in selecting and managing people (and their egos), and firing people. Very few presidents like firing people, so they need a person or people to be the enforcers. And the OPOTUS needs to be able to collectively tell presidents when it is time for one of the staff to leave, and not have that staff member go around them to get a second hearing from the president.

Focus and conserve the president's energy: Presidents are strong individuals, but they don't have infinite energy. If an activity requires positive energy, such as building relationships with congressional or foreign leaders, it should be reserved for the president. If it requires negative energy, such as dealing with clashing personalities, the OPOTUS should handle it.

Focus the president's time: The OPOTUS should also protect the president's time. There are an infinite number of topics presidents can be "briefed on," but unless there is an essential decision associated with the topic, it simply dissipates the president's focus. Steve Jobs famously minimized the number of decisions he made in a day and focused entirely on the most important ones. The OPOTUS can be the guardian of which activities rise to that level and shield the president from well-wishers and nonessential tasks.

The only way to do all of the above with any effectiveness is to do it as a team. Each member of the OPOTUS leadership team can have responsibility for a certain policy or functional portfolio, but each must act as part of a team in the performance of his or her presidential support responsibilities. Whom presidents select to be part of their OPOTUS is one of their most important decisions, so they need to choose each member in view of how he or she will work as part of a team. Thereafter the team needs to be self-governing in accordance with explicit rules, guidelines, and agreed team culture. Their rules should be codified in a charter created during Year Zero. As mechanistic as this sounds, the process of creating those rules, being explicit about their existence, and setting expectations for their obedience is critical to the OPOTUS's success.

Above all, an effective OPOTUS demands the president's complete support. It must be seen to be their advocate and representative to all outside of it. In Henry Kissinger's words, "In the final analysis the influence of a Presidential Assistant derives almost exclusively from the confidence of the

President, not from administrative arrangements."[3] This maxim still holds true. The best way to ensure the OPOTUS can execute on its intent is to have its authority backstopped by the confidence and trust of the president of the United States. That is why they must choose the members of it and have it operating seamlessly well ahead of their administration's start date.

Operating the OPOTUS

The members of the OPOTUS should think of themselves as a partnership—a team, not a group of individuals. That being said, no administrative unit can function well without a clear leader. The OPOTUS will not obviate the chief of staff role; he or she will still be the president's top aide but will otherwise be simply first among equals in the context of the OPOTUS. Other members should be chosen for their ability to perform the team roles, not seniority. Candidates to be other members could include the vice president, the national security adviser, the White House counsel, the communications director, the head of the Presidential Personnel Office, and any special advisers. Consideration should also be given to adding the First Lady as part of the team, potentially on a part-time but regular basis. Active first ladies such as Nancy Reagan and Michelle Obama have played important and powerful roles outside of their ceremonial duties and are the one person who reliably represents the president's best interests.

All of the members of the OPOTUS must be "honest brokers" in the tradition of the best White Houses. They are there to represent the president's interests, not their own. They can and should be involved in decision-making but only on the basis of what decision is best for the presidency.

The OPOTUS must be leak-proof, both individually and collectively. Its members should also have the "passion for anonymity" that characterized senior staff in the White House in bygone eras. That doesn't mean that they don't interact with the press—it just means that they would do it as part of a precoordinated plan. When a member of the press hears from one of them, he or she should know it is effectively the president speaking. As James Baker pointed out, "You have to be willing to background the press. Background, not leak. There's a big difference. But one of the things Cheney told me before I took the job: 'Be sure you spend a lot of time with the press giving them your spin, why you're doing these things. Talk to them. But always do it invisibly.'" When members of the OPOTUS do go on the record, it should clearly be on behalf of the president, not themselves. Former White House chief of staff Ron Klain, for instance, promoted President Biden's agenda through his official Twitter account in a way that didn't seem self-serving.

Consistent with their duty to be honest brokers, part of the OPOTUS culture will be to know how to dismiss one of their own. Senior staff, including the chief of staff, are difficult to dismiss, even if in concept they serve "at the pleasure of the president." One of a president's most difficult decisions is to dismiss their own chief of staff, and history shows a few cases where he left one in place too long. The OPOTUS must be able to self-govern in a way that makes replacement possible. It is difficult to prescribe a mechanism by which a chief of staff is removed once they are in role, so the time to do it is before that person is in place.

The creation of the OPOTUS would clearly need the support of the chief of staff himself or herself. This requires picking someone who is strong enough for the role but personally secure enough to be willing to share responsibility, a unique blend, but one worthy of one of the most important roles in D.C. To quote James Baker talking about chiefs, "the people who succeed in Washington are the people who are not afraid to surround themselves with really good, strong people."[4]

CONCLUSION

Year Zero is the time to start the trial of individuals who may form the core of the White House leadership group.

The creation of a Year Zero Leadership Team sets the platform for all Year Zero activity, and allows the candidate to focus on the key activity of winning the election, while still having a management structure ready to govern on Day One.

The team will, with any luck, morph into a new, more powerful White House component: the Office of the President of the United States. An OPOTUS will help facilitate more and faster outcomes in the first year of a presidency, relieve the chief of staff of the total burdens of management that are currently too heavy for any one individual to carry, and better ensure that the president's interests are well-served.

I recognize that this model depends substantially upon relationships— not just the candidate's relationship with the members of the OPOTUS, but that which exists among the members of the OPOTUS themselves. The OPOTUS bond must be based on teamwork, trust, and a total commitment to the candidate. These are characteristics that are not always found in surpassing quantities among those who work in the political sphere, which is why it is critical for a candidate to "get the right people on the bus."

5

TASK TWO
Develop a Strategy and Operating Model

Start ten months before the inauguration.

As I walked around the White House on the morning of January 20, 2021, I was struck by its vacancy. The offices had some furniture but were devoid of papers, books, and documents. The filing cabinets were empty. As the incoming Biden administration officials started to arrive, they looked more like new renters come to occupy a barren office building than the inheritors of a hive of power that had been buzzing with activity just days before.

The desertedness of the center of American government power illustrates the reality any incoming president will face: he or she, and his or her staff, must start from scratch. The Year Zero framework therefore offers a special opportunity to build the institutional knowledge that incoming staff need before they enter an office containing nothing but a desk, a phone, and a computer, avoiding the need to spend the first six months learning how to run the White House.

Indeed, at least one White House team wishes they had taken such an approach. As the *Los Angeles Times Sunday Magazine* wrote in 1993 of President Clinton's team, "though it had studied the operations of every other major government agency . . . [it] assigned no one to study the workings of the White House." One Clinton aide put it this way, "We knew more about FEMA and the Tuna Commission than we did about the White House. We arrived not knowing what was there."[1]

The Five-Year Presidency model will help mitigate this kind of void. Year Zero is the time when a candidate's overall governing strategy should be determined. This strategy—which history can be a useful guide in developing—should primarily focus on determining the legacy a candidate wants to leave and how to turn that into real actions in Year One. But it should also include determining a coherent operating model that takes into account the structure, process, and people that will best serve the future president's agenda. Though the best-laid plans will always be disrupted by unforeseen events, setting objectives and a governing strategy to achieve them will ensure the best possible outcomes regardless of circumstance.

LEARN FROM HISTORY

"In history," wrote the Roman historian Livy, "you have a record of the infinite variety of human experience plainly set out for all to see, and in that record you can find for yourself and your country both examples and warnings: fine things to take as models, base things, rotten through and through, to avoid."[2] Future presidents and their teams would do well to look to history as one guide for understanding how they might govern. John F. Kennedy famously employed the historian Arthur Schlesinger on staff. Several months into his first year in office, President Obama met with major historians like Robert Caro, Doris Kearns Goodwin, and Paul Kennedy, and Joe Biden did the same with other scholars of the past in 2021. Among other topics, reported one outlet, President Biden and the historians "talked a lot about the elasticity of presidential power, and the limits of going bigger and faster than the public might anticipate or stomach."[3] The Obama and Biden confabs were excellent ideas, but they took place in those presidents' first year of governing. They would have been even more useful had they happened during Year Zero, when the insights and lessons generated by these conversations could have been baked into the early days of an administration.

The Year Zero Leadership Team (YOLT) should designate an advisory board of not just historians but also private sector and political strategists, scientists, operational experts, and former officials who can help build the knowledge base for a successful design of the White House. Interviews with White House veterans are useful tools for understanding what to expect inside the nerve center of American power. Even today, these fact-finding missions can occur across partisan divisions. Most people who have served in the White House are willing to share their knowledge for the betterment of the country. Think tanks, too, can be tremendous sources of information on the basics of governing, especially when their products are based on the experiences of White House personnel.

Finally, there is a wealth of written material for would-be officeholders to read on the best practices of previous administrations. These include memoirs of presidents and White House staff and publications on the mechanics of transitions. In 1960, Lauren Henry published the first book specifically on transitions, *Presidential Transitions,* covering transitions to that point in the twentieth century. Carl Brauer updated Henry's work to include the decades of the 1950s through the 1970s with *Presidential Transitions: Eisenhower through Reagan*. John Burke then added additional studies of George H. W. Bush and Clinton with *Presidential Transitions: From Politics to Practice*. Martha Kumar and Terry Sullivan collected an excellent set of essays that helped the George W. Bush transition team, which were subsequently published as *The White House World: Transitions, Organization, and Office Operations*. Martha Kumar also wrote an excellent book on one of the most successful transitions ever in *Before the Oath: How George W. Bush and Barack Obama Managed a Transfer of Power*. I've already mentioned the manual I co-wrote with Daniel Kroese and Clark Campbell, *The Romney Readiness Project 2012: Retrospective and Lessons Learned*, published in 2013 after the unsuccessful campaign, with the intent of providing a playbook on how to run a transition organization. Stephen Hess and James Pfiffner published the fourth edition of *Organizing the Presidency* in 2021, updating it to include laydowns of management structure of all modern White Houses from Franklin Delano Roosevelt to Donald Trump. And in 2022, David Marchick published *The Peaceful Transition of Power*, a series of written transcripts of podcasts that he recorded with notable figures discussing aspects of transitions. Chris Whipple wrote about the most recent tumultuous Biden transition in the book *The Fight of His Life: Inside Joe Biden's White House*. And other extremely useful general White House books include George Edwards, Kenneth Mayer, and Stephen Wayne's *Presidential Leadership; The Managerial Presidency*, edited by James Pfiffner; and *The Presidency and the Political System*, edited by Michael Nelson.

For second-term planning it is equally important to bring in outsiders for fresh perspectives. Living in "the bubble" can isolate members of the White House and cause bad habits to set in. It is never too late to build on the positives of the first term but with new approaches. Also, transitions to the second term have special characteristics of their own that are worth studying. There have been just five in the last fifty years, but each is instructive.

Although I don't discuss in detail every president's White House transition or governance approach, it is worth reviewing some notable aspects of more recent presidents' transitions into office and/or operating styles, and some of the resulting lessons learned.

Harry Truman

Arriving in the Oval Office, Harry S. Truman had little concept of the policy-making or managerial demands of the presidency, despite having been vice president. His was perhaps the most sudden transition in modern times, with the incoming president learning of Roosevelt's death while playing a card game at the Senate. Roosevelt's team had prepared no plans for how a formal handoff of the presidency might happen if the president should become incapacitated or die. On his twelfth day in office, President Truman received a briefing on the Manhattan Project, the first time that he had learned of this world-changing nuclear weapons development program. The only benefit of his experience of being thrown into the deep end is that it encouraged him to plan the transition *out* of office, starting a tradition of presidents taking the handoff of the White House more seriously. Also the White House operations became slightly more regimented under Truman, with the first equivalent of a chief of staff in John Steelman, and the establishment of the National Security Council in 1947 as a body for coordinating policy.

Dwight Eisenhower

The information deficit Truman suffered as vice president motivated him to ease the Eisenhower administration's transition into power, marking the first time a departing administration prepared information for an incoming one. Said Truman, "Now, whoever's elected this fall, whether he be a Republican or Democrat, I don't want him to face the kind of thing I faced when I came into office in 1945, completely unbriefed and unprepared. . . . I want this to be a smooth transition."[4] Truman was as good as his word, bringing both Eisenhower and Democratic candidate Adlai Stevenson to the White House for classified briefings.

Eisenhower also had the advantage (and challenge) of entering office sooner after the election than other presidents had. As a result of the Twentieth Amendment, Eisenhower's inauguration was the first to take place on January 20, significantly earlier than the March time frame that had been in place up until then. Additionally, and perhaps unsurprisingly given his military background, Eisenhower built out the machinery of government, with a hierarchy to match: the earliest formal incarnations of the Offices of White House Chief of Staff, Staff Secretary, and Director of Legislative Affairs emerged at this time, and though the National Security Council (NSC) had been created in 1947 with an executive secretary, it was in 1953 that the first national security adviser was appointed as an assistant to the president.

Perhaps reflecting both his disdain for political fights and his goals of minimizing debt and sustaining peace, Ike's cabinet was composed mostly of successful businessmen ("eight millionaires and one plumber," as the *New Republic* wrote at the time).[5] Eisenhower's approach to governance factored in the prevailing popularity of the New Deal model that Roosevelt had instituted: He continued all the major New Deal programs still in operation, especially Social Security. He expanded its programs and rolled them into the new cabinet-level agency of the Department of Health, Education, and Welfare, while extending benefits to an additional 10 million workers. Thus the quiet growth of the federal government continued.

John F. Kennedy

The youthful John F. Kennedy wanted his administration to be seen as the opposite of the perceived stodgy Eisenhower bureaucracy, continuing a pattern of each president trying to distinguish himself from his predecessor in style. Kennedy consequently eliminated the chief of staff role on the advice of the historian Richard Neustadt (before eventually installing longtime aide Kenneth O'Donnell in a quasi–chief of staff role), held few cabinet meetings, and dismantled the Operations Coordinating Board of the NSC. Kennedy relied on a culture of informality, one undergirded by his long-standing relationships with political loyalists stemming back to his days in Boston, including O'Donnell, David Powers, and the president's brother, Attorney General Robert F. Kennedy. Kennedy was more enthusiastic about foreign affairs than domestic ones, and a "little State Department" of NSC staffers emerged inside the White House, largely in response to the bureaucracy inside the State Department and the failure of the Bay of Pigs invasion. In time, Kennedy and his team came to see professional civil servants as, in the words of Arthur Schlesinger, "a force against innovation with an inexhaustible capacity to dilute, delay, and obstruct presidential purpose."[6]

Lyndon Johnson

Coming to power as a result of Kennedy's assassination rather than his own election, Lyndon Johnson kept on most of Kennedy's people, even if they were not his hand-picked advisers. No changes in the cabinet were made for thirteen months. As time went on, Johnson populated his administration with many Texans, and young ones at that. "I'll get my action from the younger men and my advice from the older men," he remarked.[7] Largely because of his own superhuman energy, Johnson set in motion a White House work ethic that persists today: owing to the enormous time commitments and constraints on family life, White House jobs below the senior staff level are most often populated by men and women in their twenties and thirties. Like Kennedy, Johnson also held sway over a culture of informality, and different advisers wore many different hats.

As a manager, Johnson inserted the White House (and himself) into as many functions of the federal government as possible. A small group known as the Tuesday Cabinet, which effectively substituted for formal National Security Council meetings, became Johnson's main sounding board for his policy on the Vietnam War. On a number of Tuesdays, Johnson would have lunch with this group, which included, over time, Secretary of State Dean Rusk; Secretary of Defense Robert McNamara (and later Clark Clifford); National Security Adviser McGeorge Bundy (and then Walt Rostow); CIA Director Richard Helms; the chairman of the Joint Chiefs of Staff, Earle Wheeler; and Press Secretary Bill Moyers. Having such a small cadre of advisers informing the president on the course of the war has led to suggestions that Johnson's Vietnam policy suffered from groupthink.

Richard Nixon

President Nixon was the first president whose transition into office occurred under the Presidential Transition Act (which had been introduced under President Kennedy and subsequently passed under Johnson). The impact of the act wasn't significant, as the resources provided through it were modest ($1 million), and Nixon was already a seasoned Washington insider from his many years of service as a senator and vice president. However, the act did at least set a precedent for transition planning that subsequent transitions and legislative amendments built upon. Anecdotally, one event during the transition turned out to be significant. President Johnson supposedly showed Nixon the taping system he had recently installed.

Nixon initially promised that domestic policy would be driven with the full involvement of the cabinet, with the White House taking the lead on foreign policy. However, as early as the first year, his personally suspicious nature led him to start to distrust the advice of the agencies and their leaders, and the White House began to lead every area of policy. The establishment of formal management structures also continued apace: Nixon created the Office of Policy Development, the forerunner to the Domestic Policy Council, and turned the Bureau of the Budget into the Office of Management and Budget, indicating a broader scope for their activities.

Gerald Ford

President Ford sought advice on how to best transition, even though Richard Nixon's resignation in the wake of the Watergate scandal led to Ford's nontraditional accession to the presidency. He appointed a formal transition advisory group, headed by Donald Rumsfeld, who at the time was ambassador to NATO. Ford wanted to differentiate his style from that of Nixon, at least initially. He may have been wise enough to set up the group, but he didn't accept all their recommendations. He eliminated the chief of staff role (H. R. Haldeman's strong chief of staff role having been seen as contributing to Watergate), although he eventually brought it back after the White House proved unmanageable without it.

Ford empowered cabinet officers to take a strong role in policy formulation, and cabinet meetings commenced once a week. These large meetings proved unproductive relative to the time they took, and they moved to once a month. Policy generation continued its trend to the White House through the creation of entities such as the Economic Policy Board, which can be thought of as an early forerunner to the National Economic Council. As Lyndon Johnson did when he assumed the presidency from the deceased John F. Kennedy, Ford tried to create continuity with the previous administration by keeping on Nixon's cabinet members and a number of aides, but this caused as many problems as it solved, due to personality clashes between the loyal staff he also bought with him. Significantly, he kept Henry Kissinger on as national security adviser (and secretary of state, relinquishing the NSA post to Brent Scowcroft only in November 1975), reflecting Ford's greater background and confidence in domestic policy.

Jimmy Carter

President Carter was characteristically thorough in his transition planning. He started it in April of the election year, very early by the standards of the day. It was headed by his trusted colleague Jack Watson but was hindered by internal feuds with the campaign staff, headed by Hamilton Jordan. Carter campaigned as an outsider and tried to govern as one. He brought in only Georgians to his top staff, recruiting few D.C. people. Consistent with the themes of Carter's campaign, they were dismissive of the political establishment, and Carter's ability to get things done suffered as a result. Carter tried to introduce multiple pieces of legislation, but a lack of clear priorities and often conflicting objectives led to legislative overload, and little was achieved in the early months. Like other presidents before him, he made a commitment to cabinet government but then steeped himself in the details of every decision. Said Joseph Califano, Carter's secretary of health, education, and welfare, "Carter read hundreds of pages of material on welfare programs and did almost everything but draft the legislation." He was "the highest paid assistant secretary for planning that ever put a reform proposal together."[8] Carter's obsession with detail also extended into his management approach: he tried to run the White House himself, using his prodigious energy to delve into the nuances of everything. He would be the last president to try managing without a chief of staff.

Ronald Reagan

In contrast to Carter, President Reagan chose a mixture of loyalists and D.C. experts, most famously appointing a "troika" of aides as his inner circle. Ed Meese and Michael Deaver were longtime Reagan loyalists and were balanced by the appointment of the experienced James Baker as chief of staff, even though Baker had managed Gerald Ford's and George H. W. Bush's campaigns for president in 1976 and 1980, respectively. He is regarded by many as the finest chief of staff to serve in that role and went on to serve in other roles such as secretary of the treasury under Reagan and secretary of state under George H. W. Bush. The troika took time to be effective, given that Baker's appointment happened during the transition, and he had never worked with the others before, but it came to be extremely effective in managing the White House. Other positions similarly were given to a mix of Californians who had served Reagan, and others who had been in previous federal administrations. Reagan became yet another president to make a commitment to cabinet government, and he achieved some success with cabinet councils (seven subgroupings of the cabinet members clustered around common themes such as economic affairs and natural resources). These smaller groups met significantly more often than the cabinet. Decision-making was largely concentrated in the White House through the Legislative Strategy Group, a small group designed and run by Baker.

George H. W. Bush

President Bush was the first sitting vice president to be elected since Martin Van Buren in 1836 and came to the job with a wealth of government experience. Bush had served not only for eight years as Reagan's vice president but also, prior to that, as director of the CIA, ambassador to the UN, and a member of Congress. However, Bush faced a difficult situational context: a Democratic House and Senate, as well as the task of distinguishing himself from his predecessor. Bush built a team that was partly inherited from the Reagan era but then was slow to nominate new people. A notable setback came when the Senate rejected the nomination of John Tower to be the secretary of defense, a defeat that was exacerbated by Bush sticking with the nomination for too long. Bush's presidency was also hamstrung by the fact that, despite his long service to the nation, he came into the role without a strong and clear policy framework, in particular with respect to a domestic agenda (he was much more comfortable with foreign policy). He did appoint a strong cabinet, although they operated more as individuals than a collective entity. His White House staff were less domineering over the cabinet than in previous White Houses, with the strong exception of his initial chief of staff, the hard-line John Sununu. The national security adviser, Brent Scowcroft, was seen as the archetypal "honest broker" and devised a decision-making process within the federal government that is still used today.

Bill Clinton

Martha Kumar, the noted presidential historian, reported that on the day after his defeat in the 1992 election, Bush told his team to "be helpful and leave no ticking time bombs for the incoming Clinton administration."[9] Clinton spent little time worrying about how to run the White House. He also focused too much on cabinet nominations, to the exclusion of placing the proper people in White House staff roles. Additionally, Clinton's nominee for attorney general, Zoe Baird, had to withdraw her name from consideration because of ethics issues, as did his second nominee to lead the Justice Department, Kimba Wood. The "bottom line" for the first year of the Clinton presidency, write Hess and Pfiffner, was that "President Clinton was not willing to delegate enough power to anyone else to manage the policy process, and the administration consequently suffered from poor organization."[10] His initial chief of staff, Mack McLarty, was only appointed almost six weeks into the transition and had to work hard to impose order on a White House featuring a high number of inexperienced staffers and Clinton's freewheeling style. Despite a slow start, Clinton managed to achieve some successful first-year legislative initiatives.

George W. Bush

President George W. Bush had the disadvantage of an abbreviated transition period, owing to the ballot-counting litigation surrounding the 2000 presidential election. At the head of the Bush team was Vice President Dick Cheney, a longtime D.C. fixture with government experience inside and outside the White House, including as chief of staff and secretary of defense. He worked alongside the talented Clay Johnson, who was Bush's chief of staff while he was governor of Texas. Andrew Card, a Bush loyalist since 1980, was selected as Bush's White House chief of staff, following Bush's declaration that, in the words of Clay Johnson, he "did not want someone to be chief of staff who was over-territorial or was a control freak."[11] The experienced team and an early start (Bush had asked Johnson to commence planning almost a year in advance) got the Bush White House off to a relatively smooth start despite the shorter transition period. However, it did mean that the Bush team had less time to vet and prepare to nominate potential Senate-confirmable appointees, and the Brookings Institution could write that by March 2002, the Bush administration was "the slowest in modern history to fill its top appointee positions."[12] Rising political polarization by the turn of the century also played a role in that lag.

Where the management of the Bush White House was concerned, Vice President Cheney played a stronger role than any vice president in history in steering policy and influencing presidential decisions. As the Afghanistan and Iraq Wars consumed the administration's attention in the post-9/11 years, Bush, in an echo of President Johnson's Tuesday Cabinet, stood up a war cabinet of his own in Cheney, Card, Secretary of Defense Donald Rumsfeld, Secretary of State Colin Powell, National Security Adviser Condoleezza Rice, and CIA Director George Tenet. Powell departed after the 2004 election because of disagreements over the Iraq War, marking one of the few voluntary defections from the Bush team.

Barack Obama

Out of a desire to preserve continuity of government as America waged two wars in Afghanistan and Iraq, Bush wanted to ensure, in the words of Bush's final White House chief of staff, Josh Bolten, "the smoothest, most effective, most coordinated transition out ever."[13] Today the Bush-Obama transition is considered the gold standard for transitions, given the cooperation between outgoing and incoming administrations, the quality of preparation from the both sides, and joint activities such as tabletop exercises during the transition period. On the Obama side, two wars and a raging economic crisis escalated the need for thorough planning. The team eventually scaled up to more than 500 people covering 62 agencies, and the Senate was able to hold twenty-five preinaugural hearings for Obama's nominees, a record.[14] The Obama White House generally had a high degree of stability and loyalty to the president. But it featured a succession of five chiefs of staff over eight years, who variously mirrored or contrasted with the president's personality, the most dominant of them being the future Chicago mayor Rahm Emanuel.

Donald Trump

Donald Trump's transition planning was a departure from the increasingly comprehensive efforts of the two presidents before him. As a candidate, he had tapped former New Jersey governor Chris Christie to lead transition planning. Christie, largely replicating the 2012 Romney team's thorough approach, did months of work identifying personnel, hammering out policy plans, reviewing agencies, and designing a support system for the president-elect. But Christie did not have one of the essential qualities of a transition leader: a strong bond with the president-elect and his key staff. After Trump's victory, the president-elect's team literally threw the Christie team's work into a dumpster and installed Vice President Mike Pence as the head of the transition, thus negating months of planning work. The Trump team's rushed transition effort was later evident in some abandoned nominations and legal defeats of early presidential executive orders.

Multiple senior staff, including Chief of Staff Reince Priebus, turned over in the first year. Trump ran through four secretaries of defense, four national security advisers, two secretaries of state, two UN representatives, and three directors of national intelligence in a single term. Trump's initial national security adviser, Michael Flynn, was forced to resign after less than a month.

Joe Biden

Joe Biden's transition into office was complicated by Donald Trump's claims that he had been cheated out of victory in the 2020 election. Consequently, a delayed ascertainment of Biden's victory slowed up the team's access to government office space and resources. Some federal agencies also minimized their cooperation with the Biden team. Nonetheless, the Biden team had planned for such a contingency and were not fatally hampered by it. With former senator Ted Kaufman, a Biden confidant since 1972, at the helm, the transition had a leader with an airtight relationship with the candidate. Kaufman and his team built up a transition staff of more than 600 people, covering more than 100 agencies. They also prioritized the identification and vetting of non-Senate-confirmable appointees, allowing the Biden administration to get more of its people into place, faster. Inside the White House, the president has been served by a cadre of loyal and discreet aides, many of whom have worked for Biden for years and served in the Obama administration. Thus, to the outside observer, the Biden White House has been characterized by a relatively smooth operational climate.

Lessons Learned: Balance

There are a number of common themes that come through in a study of past presidents' transitions and early attempts at governance. The first is balance. The concept of balance permeates the U.S. political system, going back to the fundamental constitutional principles of balance of institutions, balance of electoral methods, and balance of the time frame of terms.

There are multiple instances in which a balanced approach, or lack thereof, has dramatically shaped a presidency. One of the most important areas requiring a balanced approach is the background of the president's staff. The strongest incoming administrations have generally been constructed of a senior team with balance across different axes: for example, between D.C. insiders versus outsiders; knowledgeable and experienced staff who may have served in previous administrations versus newcomers who bring a fresh perspective; and ideologues versus technocrats.

Jimmy Carter's administration offers an example of one that focused too heavily in one direction. Carter's stacking the White House with staff from Georgia gave him the benefit of a staff characterized by loyalty and familiarity but also impeded his ability to achieve his goals as his team struggled with navigating the workings of Washington, D.C. As scholar Paul Quirk has commented, "If there was a single root cause of the Carter Administration's failure (underlying even its management of decision making), it was the president's refusal to recruit people with successful experience in Washington politics for top advisory and political jobs in the White House."[15] A contrasting example of balance translating into effectiveness was the Reagan presidency. Quirk went on to observe, "In short, the political strategy for policy promotion by which the 'Reagan Revolution' was pushed through Congress in 1981 was devised and executed by hired hands who were latecomers, at most, to Reaganism."[16]

Another area in which balance is needed is in the personality of the chief of staff. He or she must have an appreciable amount of fearlessness in doing "dirty work": enforcing discipline of process, reining in rogue actors, killing bad ideas, and protecting the president from mistakes of his own and others' doing. Failing to perform these duties will cause the White House to unravel. Reince Priebus, for example, was not a strong manager of the White House and was unable to prevent end runs around established protocols for briefing the president. But a chief of staff who approaches his job in an authoritarian—not authoritative—fashion will cause issues as well. Domineering chiefs of staff such as Donald Regan and John Sununu caused problems for the president by blocking debate and imposing their own agendas.

Presidential involvement in the details of governing also benefits from a balanced approach. A "hands-off" approach such as President Reagan's was effective when it was spearheaded by an outstanding chief of staff, James Baker. When Baker became treasury secretary, however, the lack of presidential involvement in governing the White House led to destructive and unauthorized behavior, with the Iran-Contra affair almost sinking Reagan's presidency. At the other end of the spectrum, President Carter's attention to every detail of governing (famously represented by him supposedly authorizing requests for use of the White House tennis court) led to a logjam of activity and few tangible results, despite his prodigious energy. A balanced approach to most issues of management is likely to prevent both breakdowns of order and wasteful diversions of presidential energy.

Lessons Learned: Cabinet Government

Most presidents start with the explicit or implicit intention to have "cabinet government." What they specifically mean by that can differ, but in essence the term expresses a president's desire for heavy involvement of the cabinet in decision-making. Before the advent of the Executive Office of the President (EOP) in 1939, the cabinet was the primary source of advice for the president, and a number have wanted to reinstate the importance of the body, especially given the high-profile nature of some of the members.

However, there are few modern examples where the cabinet as a whole becomes the main decision-making body once the president starts governing. There are a number of reasons behind this trend. For one thing, presidents have found the body, numbering more than 20 people, too large for effective decision-making. The members know a lot about their policy area but often not much outside of that. Second, even though cabinet members are handpicked by presidents, they are often new faces to the presidents. Over time they can lose confidence or trust in some of the individuals, out of concern that the cabinet members have been "captured" by their agency.

Presidents need to be realistic about the degree to which the cabinet will be an effective decision-making body. As John F. Kennedy grumbled, "Why should the Postmaster General sit there and listen to a discussion of the problems of Laos?"[17] They should consider full cabinet meetings as useful for communication purposes and instead rely on smaller groupings for decisions. These can be formal standing entities, such as the NSC, or temporary, such as task forces or the subcabinet groups such as those under President Reagan.

Lessons Learned: If It Isn't Broke, Don't Fix It

Most presidents have effectively sought to differentiate themselves from their immediate predecessors in both policy and personal style. John F. Kennedy's youthful verve and grand visions for American power abroad was a self-conscious contrast to Eisenhower's avuncular bearing and agenda focused on domestic tranquility. George W. Bush cut a figure of moral rectitude after Bill Clinton's personal transgressions inside the White House. And Joe Biden cast himself as an empathetic restorer of democratic norms after the turbulent Donald Trump. This tendency can be multiplied by the hubris that comes from a recent victory in the most challenging political race of any candidate's life.

Often the best of intentions founder in the face of the reality of governing. As Nixon himself said, "I would operate differently from President Johnson. Instead of taking all power to myself, I'd select cabinet members who could do their jobs, and each of them would have the stature and power to function effectively. Publicity would not center at the White House alone. . . . [W]hen a President takes all the real power to himself, those around him become puppets."[18] But as early as the end of Nixon's first year, these ideals had been largely discarded, and the White House was the center of all policy.

The desire to differentiate can discourage copying best practices from previous administrations, but this is a misguided approach. The way a White House operates will vary enough from administration to administration through personality changes alone—a team does not need to exacerbate the inefficiencies that come with changes in administrations by recasting roles or processes out of public relations considerations. The NSC is perhaps the best example of a degree of continuity, with some sharing of best practices across administrations. Dismissing the fear of what might not play well politically, learning from the past, and retaining the best parts of previous administrations should be imperatives for any White House.

Lessons Learned: Legislation versus Executive Actions

Presidents can prefer to create policy through executive action rather than working with Congress to pass legislation. This is a function of the increasing difficulty in passing legislation, a multilateral undertaking, compared to the relative ease of signing executive orders, a unilateral one. But presidents would do well to heed the words of President Obama from 2016: "My suggestion to the President Elect is . . . going through the legislative process is always better, in part because it is harder to undo."[19] Obama hit on a key reality: the ease of issuing executive actions is equally offset by their lack of longevity and the ease with which they can be extinguished by a future president. In recent presidencies, one of the first Day One actions has been for the incoming president to sign a series of executive actions countermanding those issued by the previous president. Developing politically symbolic but largely ineffective executive orders is something of a waste of precious time in Year Zero. Thus, to the extent presidents are resolved to use executive actions, they should focus their administration on developing those that put down policy roots deeply and quickly, and thus become difficult to reverse.

Lessons Learned: Mistakes

Every president makes mistakes, and the early days of an administration are particularly fraught with the potential for misjudgments. Looking at history should help presidents avoid them but also instruct them on how to recover. How presidents deal with mistakes—and learn from them—leads to them either limiting damage or having them metastasize into larger problems. John F. Kennedy learned from the Bay of Pigs fiasco—the overconfidence and hubris of predetermined victory was replaced with much more deliberate thoughtfulness and testing of options in the Cuban Missile Crisis. Early and unproductive culture clashes in the Reagan administration such as that between Secretary of State Alexander Haig, a strong cabinet member, and the relatively weak national security adviser, Richard Allen, were only rectified when both were replaced. Bill Clinton picked a fight he didn't need with "Don't Ask, Don't Tell" because he didn't have a good system for priorities. His nomination of Zoe Baird also highlighted his need for a good system for identifying ethics issues. In her case, the president held on too long and ended up with a nomination fight he didn't need. Clinton's intervention in Somalia led to the death of eighteen U.S. soldiers, but he recovered by the time of the Bosnian peacekeeping mission. Year Zero is an opportunity to build a good system to minimize the chance of mistakes, and also a system for dealing with them when they do happen to stop them from becoming larger.

DECIDE WHAT YOU WANT YOUR LEGACY TO BE

An aphorism commonly paraphrased from the Lewis Carroll tale *Alice in Wonderland* holds, "If you don't know where you are going, any road will take you there." This idea is certainly applicable to any organization, and especially for the presidency. Without identifying a desired end, presidents are liable to move through four years in an unconcentrated way, thereby generating a lot of activity, but not necessarily a legacy.

Most presidents have set ambitious goals on the campaign trail or during their first year. Few have managed to succeed as memorably as, say, John F. Kennedy did when he famously said in May 1961 that the United States "should commit itself to achieving the goal, before the decade is out, of landing a man on the moon, and returning him safely to the Earth," a legacy for which he is still remembered.

The logical approach to determining a president's governing strategy is to start with the end in mind, and then work backward to craft a Year One agenda. The candidate should have at the start of the campaign a vision of the legacy that he or she wants to leave. That vision must then be turned into a set of campaign promises—a dynamic process that will unfold over the campaign itself, driven by the candidate and the campaign leadership team. Simultaneously, it will be the job of the YOLT to take those promises and determine a set of four-year goals. Those four-year goals should then drive the annual priorities, the Year One agenda, and the operating model necessary to deliver all the above. All this fits into a logical framework as set out in figure 4. Rarely is it as easy to implement it in real life, but the framework is a useful guide. If followed, it allows the building of a legacy one tangible step at a time.

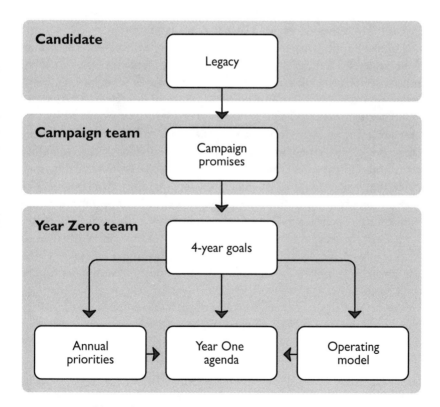

FIGURE 4. Building a legacy, one year at a time

Determining specific goals is a challenging process, especially since they can compete with one another. In the private sector, a public company has a primary goal: delivering shareholder value. The rise of ESG (Environmental, Social, and Governance) measures, and frameworks such as the Balanced Scorecard, have expanded the perceived goals, but generally shareholder value remains the single or primary measure for most private sector organizations.

By contrast, most political organizations have multiple, ambiguous, and sometimes conflicting goals. What Abraham Lincoln once said is still true: "There are few things wholly evil or wholly good. Almost everything, especially government policy, is an inseparable compound of the two, so that our best judgment of the preponderance between them is continually demanded."[20]

Also, ironically, shareholders in the private sector can be more tolerant of a slow build than citizens in the public sector. Rather than expecting to see results in the first one hundred days, research suggests the time it takes for a new CEO to develop a vision is eight months, to build a new team, fourteen months, and to reinvent how the company does business, twenty-two months.[21] New presidents don't have that luxury of time.

From the 1990s onward, there was a series of reforms internationally done under the banner of "New Public Management" that tried to apply private sector principles of defining goals, measures for achieving them, and accountability for those responsible to the public sector. Results were, and still are, mixed.

The Government Performance and Results Act (GPRA) of 1993 mandated that agencies prepare strategic plans. Those plans needed to define goals and performance measures. However, the GPRA notably didn't include the White House in its mandate. Also, there is a fundamental difference between the White House and agencies. In concept, the White House makes policy, and the agencies implement it. Agencies can therefore be measured against a delegated target. In contrast, the White House mandate is open-ended and can be defined by incoming presidents, who are constrained only by law, level of ambition, and context in determining their agenda.

Detractors will suggest that worrying about legacy before a candidate has spent a single day as president signals a hubristic attitude, one consonant with the pejorative connotation of "measuring the drapes." Moreover, the law of unintended consequences, and the general presence of Murphy's Law in politics, would seem to militate against the idea that one's legacy should be predefined. I don't suggest that a president's legacy won't be influenced by unforeseen events or that presidents won't have to concentrate on unanticipated priorities (think of George W. Bush's presidency and the impact of 9/11). I do mean that every president must have a North Star to come back to. Lyndon Johnson had his Great Society program. When Ronald Reagan was asked what his vision of the Cold War was, he replied, "We win and they lose"—and his approach to the Soviet Union issued from there.[22] George W. Bush executed a domestic policy agenda rooted in "compassionate conservatism." Donald Trump insisted it was time to put "America First"—and from that ideology came tariffs and withdrawals from multilateral endeavors he perceived as worthless. The spirit of a president's legacy must trickle down throughout the administration to guide behaviors and policy and to endure despite crises.

Furthermore, although defining goals, annual priorities, a Year One agenda, and an operating model are hard work, the very act of doing this work during Year Zero brings benefits. Problems are easier to identify and resolve before facing the daily pressures of governance. Conflicts can be identified and either minimized or accepted and managed. And teams that brainstorm together operate better together (or at least identify the issues that divide them).

For second-term planning, Year Four is a perfect time to reflect on the progress toward the legacy, and reset the goals. Most substantial change takes two presidential terms to achieve and lock in. Based on the performance of the first term (which should be significantly enhanced by a Five-Year Presidency approach), aspirations can be raised even higher for a second term, and a lasting legacy will be constructed.

Effectiveness versus Efficiency

Delivery of a positive legacy will only truly be possible with a White House that remains committed to driving the president's ideas agenda and is organized to achieve it. One factor in the question of legacy is whether to design the White House for effectiveness or efficiency. Effectiveness would be to regard the White House budget and head count as relatively set and look for the ways to use those resources in the most productive fashion. Efficiency would be to look for ways of simplifying the White House through means such as decreasing the budget and/or eliminating head count.

In my private sector experience, I have been involved in multiple successful (and at times unsuccessful) efficiency programs. These occurred not only because of the organization's financial imperatives; sometimes they were also seen as healthy "regular checkups" for the organization, eliminating bad habits and wasteful spending that have built up. However, I do not favor it for the White House for the following reasons. First, the organization has a regular "cleansing" every four to eight years that provides plenty of opportunity for resetting. Second, its budget as a proportion of overall federal spending is tiny, and a major cut would make virtually no difference to the federal deficit but almost certainly damage the White House's effectiveness. Various presidents have tried to shrink the size of the White House, but all have eventually returned it to something like the size with which it began.

I do favor, however, seeking to significantly improve the effectiveness of the White House—getting more done with the same resources. Once the overall legacy has been determined, it needs to be converted into actual, measurable goals—for example, the number of pieces of significant legislation that are passed to support highest-priority goals and the number of executive orders issued toward the same ends. The YOLT should work to determine what can be done in Year One to facilitate the achievement of legacy goals. They should also take a clean-sheet approach to the structure of the White House and shift resources between departments to the extent they deem it wise to do so, with a view to increasing overall effectiveness.

THE OPERATING MODEL IS A SYNCHRONIZED COMBINATION OF STRUCTURE, CORE PROCESSES, AND PEOPLE

After the YOLT and the candidate have studied history, determined a desired legacy, and set goals, the next step is to build an operating model for achieving it. We can think of any organization's operating model as being the sum of three parts: core processes, structure, and people. Each of these components is important in its own right, but to be effective they also need to work together in a synchronized fashion. For example, no structure or process can survive the wrong sort of people or culture. Similarly, a structure that doesn't align with the core processes will be extremely ineffective.

The ability of the operating model to endure is paramount. The White House is an institution, but it is also a collection of people. It therefore needs a solid design but should also adapt from administration to administration. Woodrow Wilson wrote that the "government is not a machine, but a living thing. It falls, not under the theory of the universe, but under the theory of organic life. It is accountable to Darwin, not to Newton. It is modified by its environment, necessitated by its tasks, shaped to its function by the sheer pressure of life."[23] His point is well-taken. A White House will naturally shift its characteristics according to the external pressures placed upon it. Hence comes the importance in Year Zero of determining the operating model of the White House—one that needs to be both resilient against external pressures and adaptable to circumstances and personalities. Its design needs to be more systematic than "it depends on the president" and less simplistically reflexive than "do what came before."

Looking to history for guidance in designing the White House certainly can be useful, but one of the challenges in designing an ideal model is the very small sample size of White House designs in the modern era. There have been only fourteen presidents since the creation of the EOP under President Franklin Roosevelt. The lack of firm conclusions that may result from a small sample size can be overcome by looking to general principles of organization design and drawing on private sector ideas, where appropriate. Conversely, the Y0LT has the benefit of starting with essentially a clean sheet, so they do not have to be concerned with institutional inertia, patch protection of existing structures, or trying to accommodate existing personalities.

Operating models will look different across administrations, but the approach to developing one should be the same. A detailed approach to developing both core processes and structure is set out in chapters 6 and 7, respectively, and they should be developed in tandem with each other. The first design concept should be process (chapter 6) because the key outcome that a president needs is action, and that is achieved through process. The structure (chapter 7) is there to facilitate the process, not the other way around. People selection should be considered the last of the three components of the operating model for a similar reason. Everyone in an incoming White House is new and can be selected to suit the structural and process design. This approach is different from how some White Houses have historically evolved, with organizational building blocks molded around the people chosen as part of a bargaining process, and to suit their personalities, not the president's agenda. A more deeply articulated approach to people selection is set out in chapter 10.

SHAPING THE ANNUAL PRIORITIES

Not all periods of a four-year term should reflect the same priorities and be concentrated on the same activities. An approach that does not align what happens and when to the rhythms of a four-year term diminishes a White House's outcomes. Part of an optimal governing strategy is to tailor the timing of specific activities in a way that maximizes effectiveness. As the presidency unfolds, it will need to adapt to trends and changes in circumstance, but an overall plan can be determined in Year Zero along the lines set out below.

Years One and Three Should Focus on Achieving Results

The best window for locking in legislative achievements and accomplishing other significant policy actions is the first year of the administration. Presidents' political capital is generally at its highest point during the first year, nor do they have to immediately worry about the electoral impact of their actions. Similarly, Year Five, the first year of the second term, holds the best chance for passing signature legislation. The closer to the end of the second term, the more the specter of "lame duck" hangs over the presidency.

Year One should also be a good year for issuing executive orders, although doing so requires prioritization. There can be a flurry of activity in the first few weeks as the president signs the executive orders that have been prepared in Year Zero. In recent presidencies, many of the executive orders issued first are more symbolic than substantive and are limited in their policy impact. Also, to the extent that they simply stop a previous policy that would otherwise happen, citizens don't see positive impact. Good planning should focus on ensuring that meaningful executive orders are at the front of the line.

A focus on results in Year One also means deprioritizing everything else—a course of action that requires political willpower. While there are certain activities and events that presidents are expected to do, there are few that they *must* do as a matter of holding office under the Constitution. Consequently, any activities that are not essential and contributing to delivery of results should be minimized. Traveling domestically and internationally should be kept to a minimum, and their time and energy should be focused on passing signature legislation. Year One is also the time to build the foundations for later results, in particular nonlegislative ones. Agencies should be tasked with improving citizen services, programs that can often take years to effect.

The second-best window for legislation is the year after the midterm elections, Year Three. Clear successful outcomes in Year One, followed by a year of implementation and selling those outcomes, should help position the president's party for the best possible outcome in the midterm elections, thereby strengthening the ability to deliver on Year Three actions. But even assuming a relatively unfavorable midterm result for a president, the period immediately after the midterm election is the next-best possible time for achieving the passage of significant legislation. A favorable window for political dealmaking reopens; expectations for what can be accomplished need to be recalibrated to the political context in which the president must operate. If they must deal with one or both houses of Congress controlled by the opposition party, for instance, their legislative strategy needs to become more moderate and bipartisan. Elections have consequences, but close or split elections have moderate consequences.

Consequently, any activities that do not contribute to delivery of results should be minimized in Year One. As regards attending to their presidential duties of conducting diplomacy overseas and demonstrating leadership at home, there will be plenty of time for travel in Year Two (and Year Four), and, indeed, this is when it should be done. There will be some events to which the president is obligated to travel, such as the G7 and NATO summits, but the great bulk of foreign travel can be saved for Years Two and Four. Additionally, virtually every foreign leader is happy to travel to Washington, D.C., and be seen in the Oval Office. The White House should invite them to visit and let them, not the president, suffer the time zone and travel fatigue.

Nor is Year One the time to focus on "selling" accomplishments. The president has just won an election and doesn't need to win it again, so he or she should be highly selective in doing media events, speeches, and other such activities. They consume time and energy that is better spent on generating results.

The president's bully pulpit has been shown to be of limited use in building support for legislation that wouldn't otherwise pass. "Going public"—that is, direct appeals to citizens to try to build support—should be minimal as it is ineffective. As Paul J. Quirk has written, "In short, presidents cannot generally accomplish anything that requires moving public opinion."[24] Despite all of his magnificent oratory skills, President Obama couldn't rally public support sufficient to overcome Republican intransigence on an issue such as gun control. Nor could Donald Trump achieve the immigration and border security reforms he sought, despite his public elevation of the issue as a top priority. It is unlikely that rhetoric will change the public's minds in a polarized world; only results will do that.

Appeals to the public to try to influence legislative action can actually be counterproductive as that undercuts the more important process of negotiating with Congress. As Samuel Kernell notes, "Going public violates bargaining in several ways. First, it rarely includes the kinds of exchanges necessary, in pluralist theory, for the American political system to function properly. At times, going public will be merely superfluous—fluff compared with the substance of traditional political exchange. Practiced in a dedicated way, however, it may displace bargaining. . . . Second . . . going public is more akin to force than bargaining. . . . Third, going public entails public posturing. To the extent that it fixes the president's bargaining position, posturing makes subsequent compromise with other politicians more difficult."[25] The net result is that it is just as likely to entrench divergent positions as to bring them closer together.

The president should use some media outreach in a targeted way in Year One, but this is overwhelmingly the time for Neustadt-like "bargaining" with Congress. The president is often the only one who can broker opposing views on the most contentious pieces of legislation and get warring parties to come to a compromise. Neustadt observed that, "when the chips are down, there is no substitute for the president's own footwork, his personal negotiation, his direct appeal, his voice and no others on the telephone." Outside of a skillful handling of a major crisis, that ability to bargain will be the single-biggest determinant of the success of his or her presidency.

Years Two and Four Should Focus on Implementation and Selling

If the focus of Years One and Three is on achieving results, the focus of Years Two and Four should be on the implementation and selling of those results. Implementation drives the action that will lift the president's standing with the voting public. Selling the results will focus attention on those actions, which may not help directly drive policy but will indirectly help by enhancing reelection prospects.

The importance of implementation cannot be overstated. Policy decisions and announcements mean nothing unless they result in action that citizens can see and experience. Unfortunately, the White House has a mixed record on the implementation of major initiatives. There have been some high-profile successes, such as Operation Warp Speed. However, high-profile failures such as the launch of the Obamacare website, the 2021 withdrawal from Afghanistan, and the violence that engulfed post-Saddam Iraq show the need for not only good planning but also the subsequent careful, thorough implementation of those plans. The history of the presidency also abounds with politically salient initiatives that are announced but never accompanied by actual results. For example, there are numerous executive orders issued that mandate a report on a given topic, often in 180 days or so. The reports are then delivered with recommendations, but those recommendations die on the vine without a formal mechanism for turning them into action.

The reality of Years Two and Four being election years means that significant legislation is unlikely to occur. The White House thus can and should focus more of its attention on implementation. Assuming there have been meaningful policy accomplishments in Years One and Three, there will likely be a pipeline of statutory and regulatory actions that must be implemented through the federal agencies (which, for a variety of reasons, are often sluggish in implementing them).

The president needs to be the champion of implementation. Years Two and Four are the time to be engaged, for example, by holding results reviews with cabinet secretaries, visiting agencies and meeting with their senior staff, and holding press conferences where senior officials explain the benefits of actions. All are visible signals that the president is a competent chief executive and that the White House is a high-functioning unit.

The core senior staff must also be intimately involved in implementation work: reviewing implementation plans, holding people both inside the White House and at senior levels of agencies to account, and designing the president's schedule to deliver on the activities above. In Years Two and Four, the main policy councils and staff also need to change their focus to building a policy pipeline for Years Three and Five (assuming the president intends a second term).

This division of activity is hard work. It requires perseverance and the willingness to shun some of the more high-profile activities. But it is critical to the success of the presidency. Clearly not all policy work will stop. There will still be legislation to work on, and if the context allows for victories, they should be taken. Significant executive orders can still be produced and rolled out. Crises don't happen on a convenient schedule, so they can interrupt the best-laid plans. But other than major crises, these activities are secondary in importance to ensuring that the accomplishments of Years One and Three are locked in.

Presidents and their teams will also accordingly need to adjust their focus in Years Two and Four to "sell" what they've done in Years One and Three. Selling accomplishments will aid presidents in their quest to get things done by producing (they hope) electoral results favorable to their mission. Recent midterms have not been favorable to the incumbent president. Clinton lost both the House and Senate; and Obama, Trump, and Biden each lost the House. Only George W. Bush retained control of both chambers, mainly a patriotic vote of confidence after the 9/11 attacks. The negative swings against the president were influenced by a lack of perceived results. They hobbled the legislative agenda and significantly decreased the presidents' expectations and hence their legacy. For example, by initially focusing on healthcare, which consumed most of his early time and political capital, President Obama was unable to address immigration legislatively in his first two years. After the "shellacking" he took in his first midterm election, he was forced to try to achieve something through executive action in the form of DACA (Deferred Action for Childhood Arrivals), a much less permanent solution than his DREAM Act.

In keeping with a focus on selling, Years Two and Four are the times for the president to travel domestically. Years Two and Four are also a good time to make up for the foreign visits that were relatively underinvested in the previous years. Time that is freed up from legislative bargaining can be used for showcasing relationships with foreign leaders, which also strengthens the president's profile as a global leader going into an election.

The president should highlight results as they start to be implemented, constantly reinforcing the benefits of resulting actions. The core of the communication strategy should be to highlight the full timeline of a policy's history: from promises during the campaign, to Year One action, to tangible results. These benefits may take time to achieve, but timing the communications strategy for selling them once they are evident is public relations at its most effective. Celebrating with a Rose Garden signing of a bill is good theater, but highlighting human-interest stories of people receiving something of real value from the president's initiative is more powerful. In other words, telling people they will be happy through promises is not as good as making them happy through results.

Countering negative narratives is also part of "selling" accomplishments. As some scholars have pointed out, "risk aversion and distrust of government make people wary of policy initiatives, especially when they are complex and their consequences are uncertain."[26] A fulfilled campaign promise and Year One results will still need to be explained to a skeptical public and reinforced multiple times, in particular in Years Two and Four. For example, President Trump's tax cuts were still often perceived as "tax cuts for the rich" months and even years afterward—a narrative he never satisfactorily countered as he moved on to other issues. This approach of engaging the public to build support after the event has been successful throughout the history of the presidency. Rather than try to sell Washington's controversial Neutrality Proclamation before its issuance, Hamilton organized a series of meetings to generate support for it afterward.

Clearly these prescribed divisions of activity should not occur to the exclusion of everything else—it is a matter of emphasis. The resulting strategy of emphasizing producing results and selling them in alternating years will therefore look something like figure 5.

CONCLUSION

Thinking about a legacy isn't a presumptuous action for a candidate not yet elected to office. Rather, it should guide all the subsequent activities and enable a focus on the biggest goals he or she is trying to achieve in office,

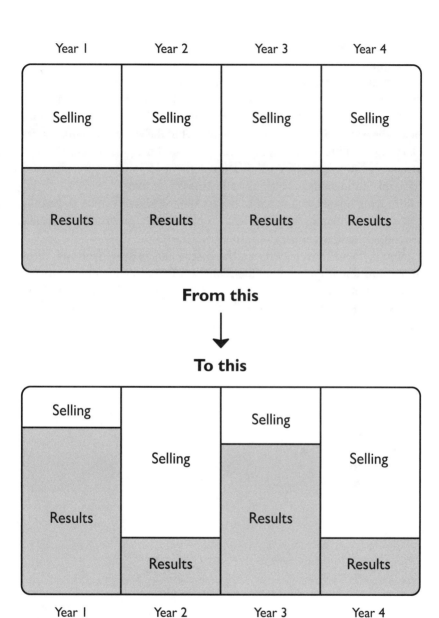

FIGURE 5. Annual priorities

etching into stone the core ideological beliefs that will characterize his or her administration.

Setting a legacy is also the basis for a governing strategy, serving as the end point of where a president wants to take the country. Defining a legacy is then the basis for designing a White House that is conducive to the goals he or she wants to achieve. Clearly events get in the way and circumstances change over four or eight years. But with the linchpins of legacy and a strong operating model for action defined in Year Zero, a new president will have the foundations to be significantly more effective.

Studying history, and specifically past White Houses, can be powerfully instructive in helping to shape ideas for successful governing strategies, personnel configurations, and responses to crises.

And by following a pattern of achieving results in Years One and Three and selling and implementing them in Years Two and Four, presidents can deliver on their promises to the voters who have asked them to lead the country. A very similar pattern applies to Years Five and Eight. The first and third years of the second term are the best opportunities to achieve results and build an even stronger legacy.

6
TASK THREE
Design Core Processes to Achieve Action

Start nine months before the inauguration.

In the spring of 2006, reporters were hounding George W. Bush for standing by his embattled secretary of defense, Donald Rumsfeld. Bush famously said, "I hear the voices, and I read the front page, and I know the speculation. But I'm the decider, and I decide what is best."[1] Bush said out loud what presidents face—they sit atop a decision-making pyramid and are (or should be) the ultimate judge of competing policy ideas that work their way up to them.

Making those decisions, however, relies on the institution and system around the president. The early days of an administration are particularly fraught with the potential for poor decisions if that institution isn't functioning properly. During the planning of the Bay of Pigs operation, carried out in the months after inauguration, several of President Kennedy's top aides, such as Secretary of State Dean Rusk, had doubts about the mission but failed to voice objections. It was Kennedy's decision to go ahead, but it was a poorly conceived one. The failure to advise the president properly led to a debacle in April 1961, with the U.S.-trained rebels getting slaughtered moments after hitting the beach. It embarrassed Kennedy as well as the nation and emboldened Castro. Thankfully, by the time of the Cuban Missile Crisis eighteen months later, Kennedy's team had learned their lessons and had a much more robust decision-making process.

Presidents shouldn't require a catastrophe—or a near-catastrophe—to get them to focus on the importance of their decision-making process. Similarly, presidents should expect to see action when they make a decision. This, however, requires more than just the institutional power that comes with the office. It requires a system to make it happen.

Every president needs a comprehensive and systematic approach to making decisions and turning those decisions into lasting results. Year Zero is a time when decision-making style and processes can be developed, road-tested directly with the presidential candidate, and supported by a clear structural design.

THE WHITE HOUSE NEEDS CORE PROCESS DESIGN THAT ACHIEVES IMPACT

Having a well-conceived process for making decisions is particularly important in the White House, for multiple reasons. First, few presidential decisions can be made in isolation. Most impact other policies and have interrelationships to other decisions. Second, it is not only the initial decision that matters, but all the chain of subsequent follow-on decisions, actions, and scenarios that need to be considered. Third, there are usually multiple people—with multiple responsibilities—inputting (or hoping to input) their views into the decision-making process. Fourth, very few decisions fit neatly into "silos." For example, domestic issues almost always have economic consequences, so the Domestic Policy Council and the National Economic Council, and the agencies they represent, need to share input into decisions. Alternatively, foreign policy decisions need to consider diplomatic, military, and economic issues either in tandem or sequentially.

The style of presidential decision-making is also important. Some presidents, such as Carter and Obama, preferred briefing books and written material; others, such as Trump, preferred dialogue and debate in front of them. Carter's approach was to dive into detail ("My ability to govern well would depend upon my mastery of the extremely important issues I faced"),[2] whereas Reagan's was hands-off ("Surround yourself with good people, delegate and get out of the way").[3]

There is a natural interest and focus on "the decision"—that is, what momentous policy decision does the president have to make—as the terminus of a policy development process. However, the decision is actually in the *middle* of the process. To make the best decision, the process leading up to it is critical. And even more important is the implementation of the decision to create impact after it has been made. Although eventual "street-level" implementation primarily resides with departments and agencies, accountability for policy delivery needs to be controlled through the White House.

A simple framework for the core process of making and implementing decisions is set out in figure 6 and covered in depth in this chapter. It consists of deciding priorities, building options, making a decision, implementing that decision, and then locking in the impact.

The key agents in a White House decision-making process differ at each

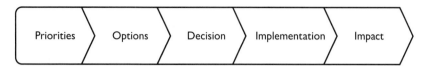

FIGURE 6. Making and implementing decisions

step. Although the presidents are clearly the decision-makers, they should not be the most active participant during other steps. They therefore need a system that they can rely on to bring them the best decision options and to carry them out effectively.

The Decision-Making Process: Structured or Fluid?

All presidential decisions should follow essentially the same path; the main variables subject to change in the process are speed and comprehensiveness. That is—how quickly will a decision get made, and how much information will be input into the process along the way? A rigorously structured decision-making process will by necessity have a low degree of speed and a high degree of informational inputs, whereas a more fluid process may go faster but may allow less time for information-gathering and deliberation. Generally, the best overall system requires a combination of these structured and fluid processes. A structured process is like the train tracks of public policy—it keeps the flow of policy generation regular and on time. It aids in determining the selection of priorities, who gets input on those choices as they are debated and collated, and how options arrive on the president's desk for the final decision. The structured process also should have a clear communication and implementation plan with responsibilities assigned.

At the same time, a decision-making framework also should allow for a level of less structured process, because uncontrollable external events and changing presidential directives drive so much activity. In this way it would be more like the banks of a river that provide the overall pathway but allow for more rapidity in the flow. These fluid processes involve putting out fires quickly, swarming resources to a crisis, and redesigning priorities at a moment's notice. The basic flow of generating options, making a decision, and ensuring implementation still apply, and in the same order, but the process is more dynamic.

Although the specifics of a crisis can't be anticipated, the methods for confronting them can be designed in advance. In my role as deputy chief of staff, I would typically have time each day to discuss policy with the president. Yet my first task every morning was to reassess and replan everything based on what had happened in the previous twenty-four hours, and thus shift processes and priorities accordingly. Sometimes that meant minor adjustments, at other times a complete overhaul. Sometimes we were dealing with decisions that had followed a carefully managed process for weeks or months, other times only days. The tightrope to walk was to have enough structure for every plane to land on time but also have the flexibility to respond to unforeseen changes. By having the bulk of decisions follow a structured path, time can be freed up to overlay more fluid processes on top when needed.

Other Processes Are Important but Exist Only to Support the Core Process

Besides decision-making, a number of other processes run in the White House that generally come under the umbrella of what is colloquially called "care and feeding of the president." That is, these functions are important but essentially exist to support the core process of decision-making and turning those decisions into action. They include managing the president's calendar, arranging trips, arranging events such as state dinners, and running the operations of the White House itself. These activities to a large extent are managed centrally by the deputy chief of staff for operations. They are critically important but to a large extent invisible and in the background.

Presidents are also considered to be the "chief executive" of the executive branch, so they are responsible, at least in concept, for all the activities of all agencies of the federal government. In practice, their role overseeing the government is limited to determining key policy, setting some goals for the agencies, and choosing the political appointees to the agencies. Other processes that would be typically found in the private sector, such as performance reviews, regular budget and spending reviews, or people development for senior management, are seldom or never carried out by the president. Realistically, given the scale of the government, the massive activity of "running it" will continue to require significant delegation to agencies, with occasional interjection from the president.

LIMIT CHOICES: BE RUTHLESS IN IDENTIFYING PRIORITIES

One of the most pressing issues that any White House faces is the almost infinite number of policy areas it could focus on. This is clearly both an opportunity (the ability to impact every aspect of life) and a challenge (lack of focus can lead to lack of impact in any one aspect). Therefore, the design of the system requires a means of determining priorities, and being ruthless in shedding those that may be attractive but are not essential. This filtering is not just about giving up bad policies or low-value ones; it is also about giving up ones that the president really cares about but are simply impractical to achieve. Being ruthless in choosing priorities must also allow for the president and the White House to have bandwidth to execute decisions arising from circumstances that are outside the White House control, such as international or economic crises. They crowd out the priorities that would otherwise be chosen.

Ideally, given the work done under the task of defining a legacy as set out in chapter 5, an administration's overall goals will already be clear. The Year Zero Leadership Team (YOLT) will have been active in the pregoverning period in understanding and starting to prioritize those goals. Once in office, the president—with strong involvement from the OPOTUS—must lead the process of deciding priorities. The OPOTUS needs to discourage and, where necessary, eliminate ideas on priorities that come bottom-up from White House staffers. When White House staff are chosen (see chapter 10), it should be made clear that their personal agendas are not important, and if the priority doesn't arise from the president, it won't be resourced.

Once a priority has been agreed on, and hence will be run through the core process, the OPOTUS needs to identify other related aspects. The members of the OPOTUS must define the objective the decision is trying to achieve; decide who should make the decision (the president should make virtually all the most important policy decisions, but sometimes lesser decisions can be delegated); and agree on who should be involved. On this point, initially there should be broad participation by many agencies and components of the White House, but the field should narrow as the process unfolds.

Establishing these important parameters may appear overly bureaucratic, but agreeing to them, and specifying them to participants, will spare all parties from confusion, improve the quality of decisions, and free up time to make the system significantly more effective.

IN ORDER TO MAKE GOOD DECISIONS, THE PRESIDENT NEEDS GOOD OPTIONS

Multiple Advocates: The PC Process

Having decided the priorities, the president's team's next step is to generate good options for each of those priorities. The Tower Commission of 1987, organized in the wake of the Iran-Contra scandal, summarized a framework for how options should be generated. The wisdom in this framework still holds true today. The following recommendations were made with reference to the National Security Council but can equally apply to all councils in the White House:

That matters submitted for consideration by the Council cover the full range of issues on which review is required.
That those issues are fully analyzed.
That a full range of options is considered.
That the prospects and risks of each are examined.
That all relevant and other information is available to the principals.
That legal considerations are addressed.
That difficulties in implementation are confronted.

These principles still equally apply today. A process model exists inside the White House that is designed to give principals comprehensive information for a decision. This model, known as the Principals Committee (PC) Process, was developed by Brent Scowcroft, the national security adviser to President George H. W. Bush, who also served on the Tower Commission.

Though there may be variations on the process, in essence, the PC Process entails multiple rounds of meetings in which the seniority of the participants increases over time, terminating in a decision by the president. The need for many meetings with many hands is due to the fact that the amount of information to be considered and the variety of implications in a policy-related decision are too great for even the more foresighted staffer to properly understand and assess alone. At the start of the process, a Policy Coordinating Committee (PCC) is convened by a White House policy council. The PCC is made up of staff tasked with carrying out background work to generate options. This PCC usually has broad representation from agencies and components of the White House. The seniority of the participants is mixed but is generally at the level of special assistant to the president or equivalent. They typically meet several times until multiple options are generated, and quality data and analysis are produced to support the options. In Year Zero, all of this approach would be designed, including a governing body to guide it. Under my model, the governing body would be the OPOTUS.

The PCC results are then reviewed by a Deputies Committee (DC), which generally consists of deputy secretary–level staff from the agencies and deputy assistants to the president from the White House. The DC is chaired by the deputy of the relevant White House council—so, for instance, the deputy national security adviser. This is a key group, because the deputies generally have the necessary time that their principals often lack to ensure quality control and the seniority to work through disputes to the extent possible. If necessary, the DC can send the options back to the PCC for further work or refinement. It can reach alignment on some options, and disputes on others, and in the latter case note the extent of the dispute to the next level of review.

That next level above the DC is the Principals Committee (PC), which consists of agency leads (secretaries) and White House assistants to the president. It is generally chaired by the head of the relevant White House council. It is at this level that the true final options are developed for presidential decisions.

Honest Brokers and Advocates

Ronald Reagan's chief of personnel, Scott Faulkner, once remarked, "Personnel is policy."[4] This familiar comment may be descriptive of what typically happens, but it shouldn't be. Policy is the president, or at least policy decisions ought to reflect his or her ideological bent and priorities. The people who work in the White House should not be deciders of executive branch policy but, to the extent possible, dispassionate option generators and implementers. In particular, the chairs of each of the committees at all three levels (PC, DC, and PCC) need to follow the classic "honest broker" role to be effective. Part of that role is to ensure that all options are generated and equally considered. The role requires reaching out to all impacted or interested parties to seek ideas, collate, and synthesize them.

Expecting people to put their personal agendas aside and not "be policy" may seem to work against human nature, but it is fundamental to the working of an effective presidency. It does not mean that staff cannot be advocates. Indeed, they should be. Advocates are those staffers who throw their weight behind specific policies when providing options to the president. It just means that, as advocates, they have a specific role in the process, which is to generate options, but not to decide them.

Honest brokers, in contrast, have a governing role. They do not put their thumb on the scale when suggesting courses of action. More technically, the presidential scholar John P. Burke defines the key attributes of an honest broker role as "(1) a concern for the fair and balanced representation of views amongst principals and others at various points in the deliberative process; and (2) attention to the quality of the organization and processes in which deliberation occurs at various stages."[5] The role of honest broker doesn't usually exist in the private sector (although the role of the chief financial officer in some ways comes closest), as various division heads compete for attention and resources.

The meanings of the words "honest" and "broker" capture the large investment of trust in these individuals that the system requires to function. Honest brokers are to arrange different options, and do so out of a genuine desire to seek the best result, in a way that builds trust in the person and the system. This is significantly more than a passive coordination role. It requires active management of the process and the people in it—being an honest broker means encouraging and synthesizing views, accepting or rejecting ideas. It requires enough domain expertise to filter the arguments at an intellectual level and adjudicate between the parties making them. It requires the strength of personality to deal with conflicting advocates, who often aggressively push their agendas. Honest brokers must often force participants in the decision chain to make decisions that allow the process to move forward. In Roger B. Porter's words, honest brokers "do more than simply insure due process. They promote the genuine competition of ideas, identifying viewpoints not adequately represented or that require qualification, and augmenting the resources of one side or the other so that a balanced presentation results."[6]

Poor honest brokers fail to subordinate their personal desires to their professional duty to generate the best result. This has occasionally been an issue with the national security adviser: "Since the Kennedy administration, the assistant to the president for national security affairs (a.k.a. the 'national security adviser') has played two roles: manager ('honest broker') of the day-to-day policy process and substantive policy adviser. . . . [P]residents clearly want both, but the roles are in tension. . . . Some national security advisers have balanced these roles adroitly. Others have not, generating discord within the president's senior advisory team."[7] Brent Scowcroft, who designed the template of policymaking still used within the federal government today, was considered a model for the honest broker. He said of the role, "If you are not an honest broker the system doesn't work well. The first thing you have to do is to establish in the minds of the members of the NSC that their views will be presented honestly and straightforwardly to the President."[8]

My role in the White House as deputy chief of staff for policy coordination was a classic honest broker one and required significant discipline to remain independent of the decision. Being in the Oval Office most days during decision time posed a great temptation to steer decisions toward what I perceived as the "right" direction. I used physical layout as a means of limiting that temptation, setting up the room with the main advocates sitting around the Resolute Desk directly in front of the president and consigning myself and others to the background. My main role was then to try to ensure the conversation culminated in a clear decision from the president.

After they have put all options on the table in a balanced manner, it is sometimes appropriate for honest brokers to put on their "advocate" hat at the end stage of a decision-making process. When and whether it is appropriate to do this is a matter of discretion—certainly presidents might ask their chief of staff or national security adviser for his or her opinion. To truly be both a useful honest broker and advocate, the person needs to keep an open mind until the decision time. They must remember that they are helping to make a decision on behalf of the president, not themselves. It is possibly the most challenging and important personal discipline required of a senior White House adviser. Because it is so difficult, the OPOTUS needs to be the "collective honest broker" over the policy process and not just leave that function to one individual.

Whether staff are acting as an advocate or an honest broker, in neither case should they be the decision-maker. Personnel are policy *options*.

OVERCOMING ISSUES ASSOCIATED WITH DECISION-MAKING

While the decision-making process set out above makes logical sense and, if done correctly, can be very powerful, it will need to overcome several aspects of human nature.

Groupthink

One of them is groupthink. The purpose of the PC Process is to generate multiple options, but groupthink—when members of a team concentrating on a problem all come to consider it in the same ways—can limit principals' ability to give all options their proper consideration. The concept of groupthink was introduced by Yale University social psychologist Irving Janis in his 1972 work *Victims of Groupthink,* which featured a case study on President Kennedy's Bay of Pigs invasion decision. The book found that Kennedy's advisers, despite massive misgivings about the operation's ability to succeed, nonetheless kept silent for fear of looking stupid by positing alternative views outside the group's consensus position. Later works applied Janis's ideas to other case studies such as the Iran hostage rescue mission and Iran-Contra. In both cases, groupthink influenced the decision-making process. More recently, Condoleezza Rice stated that the trajectory of the Iraq War happened because "we had not . . . done a good enough job of thinking the unthinkable."[9]

It is here that the "multiple advocates" play a useful role in shaping decisions and avoiding groupthink. At the core of the problem is a lack of diversity of thought, so a decision-making group needs to ensure that it has a diversity of backgrounds, perspectives, and approaches. Choosing not only the right agencies and components of the White House but also the best representatives from those entities is important. Of course, as John F. Kennedy's speechwriter Ted Sorenson observed, "The most formidable debater is not necessarily the most informed, and the most reticent may sometimes be the wisest."[10] Therefore, it is important that the honest broker facilitate all views being equally represented and does not let any single view or person dominate the others. The honest broker must also encourage participants in the decision-making process to not be intimidated by the presidency and the president. Said President Gerald Ford, "There's a majesty to the office that inhibits even your closest friends from saying what is really on their minds."[11] Barack Obama insisted, "What I know concerns me. What I don't know concerns me even more. What people aren't telling me worries me the most."[12]

Cross-Cutting Issues/Linkages to Other Decisions

Decisions must also carefully be made in consideration of overlapping currents. Since World War II, both domestic and foreign issues have become progressively more multifaceted and intertwined. Most domestic policy issues have an economic perspective, as well as implications for international affairs. Foreign policy issues have also become more complex, with many decisions having some mixture of diplomatic, military, and economic consequences. Generally speaking, they also have a domestic implication. Sanctions on Russia, for instance, cause energy and food prices to rise, and tariffs on China can lead to manufacturers pushing higher prices on to consumers.

Virtually no one White House staffer is knowledgeable enough, let alone an expert, in every area to properly consider the multiple dimensions of every policy decision. Thus, numerous stakeholders must contribute to the information input and option generation. The policy committees need to synthesize these diverse views and ensure that an option is not oversimplified. At the same time, the benefits of more input need to be balanced by the diseconomies of scale involving too many people. This is a balance that needs to be determined at the start of the process.

Quality of Information Flows

The White House needs a comprehensive information system to supplement the option generation process. Ideally, this system will be a combination of formal and informal inputs. Information flowing through formal channels—federal agency intelligence reports, collected firsthand experiences, and knowledge of existing government programs, for example—ought to come through the PC Process. The information flows should be supported by a first-class technology platform for disseminating them. If the process is carried out well, all the agencies and components of the White House that have relevant information will provide it, and it will be distributed at the relevant levels of the decision-making process.

Informal channels of information should supplement the formal information. The OPOTUS and the honest broker in charge of the process should reach out to sources such as trusted external experts, selected members of Congress, think tanks, and some informed media to gain diverse perspectives and "contrary opinions."

Somewhat controversially, despite staff's desire to control access, presidents should be free to reach out to trusted sources outside of the formal PC Process as they desire. Neustadt's 1960 maxim is still true: "[The president] must become his own director of central intelligence."[13] He or she should have unconstrained access to opinions outside of the formal channels. FDR was the master of using informal channels to gain important perspectives and contrary opinions. Arthur Schlesinger commented on FDR, "The first ask of an executive, as he evidently saw it, was to guarantee himself an effective flow of information and ideas. . . . Roosevelt's persistent effort therefore was to check and balance information acquired through official channels by information acquired through a myriad of private, informal, and unorthodox channels and espionage networks."[14]

Since Roosevelt's time there has been a tendency to formalize the process so that only official channels of information are acceptable, in the belief that the president should be "shielded" from unofficial sources. This in concept seems intuitively to make sense but is wrongminded. The best system is a combination of both.

Presidential Influence in Decision-Making

The president can unintentionally limit the generation of options by being involved too early in the process. The natural tendency of staff to wish to please the president can tip the balance of options, with people wanting to have an option that aligns with what they believe his or her preference to be. Additionally, the president's presumption of the correct solution might be misguided. To return to the Bay of Pigs example, as Paul J. Quirk has written, "The president unwittingly inhibited debate by his tone and manner of asking questions, which made it obvious he believed, or wanted to believe, the invasion would work."[15] The best way to solve the problem of presidential bias or interference in the option general process is to limit the president's involvement in it. He or she should only become involved at the decision-making stage. Presidents can always ask for more or refined options that require a second or third round of consideration. But the initial round should be free of their influence to the greatest extent possible.

Implementation Preplanning

A viable implementation plan needs to be considered and created as part of the option generation process, as well. Experiences such as the aborted Carter administration rescue mission of the Iranian hostages, the crashing of the Obamacare website, or the scenes in 2022 from Kabul airport as the United States withdrew from Afghanistan are not only failures in their own right, but they also reinforce the impression of an incompetent and impotent government. There is a natural human tendency to remember the failures and overlook the successes (who remembers a website that worked properly?), so there is an even greater imperative to make sure decisions always work in practice.

No option should be put forward to the president without a fully agreed-upon plan of execution that includes timelines and resources needed for successful implementation. The implementation components should also include strong legal clearances, especially in the case of executive orders, which virtually always face legal challenges. In the case of proposed regulations, the president must also have an opportunity to see information such as economic cost/benefit analyses produced by the Office of Information and Regulatory Affairs (OIRA).

MAKE THE DECISION WITH THE RIGHT PEOPLE AT THE RIGHT TIME

The deluge of decisions a president must make prompts us to consider three important aspects of the decision-making process: Which decisions should the president make? When should the president make them? How should the president make them? Determining the approach to these questions is something that should be done in Year Zero with the input of the presidential candidate. Thereafter, identifying which decision falls into which category is a decision in its own right and should be an eventual responsibility of the OPOTUS. This is not something that the president should have to be concerned with once governing begins. While they certainly have the prerogative to resist pressure to make a decision if they feel uncomfortable with the options presented, they should trust the system to bring them the right decisions, at the right time, in the right way.

Which Decisions Should the President Make?

In concept, the president must make every decision in the White House. Everyone else is there to assist the president with the decision-making process in some form, not to make the decisions. In reality, there are simply too many decisions to be made, and some should be delegated to save the president's time and mental energy for those that matter the most.

Any decision that relates to policy should be a presidential one. Decisions that have reputational implications should also be the prerogative of the president because they influence the ability of the administration to drive change. As Matthew J. Dickinson, paraphrasing Neustadt, observed, "Presidents must continually ask how their choices today influence their sources of power down the road."[16]

All other decisions should be considered "for delegation." The president should start by delegating the act of categorization (which is itself a decision) to the OPOTUS. They need to use their collective judgment as to the level of presidential involvement. This will help minimize the president's involvement in some decisions, especially in the administrative, or "care and feeding," category. If necessary, the chief of staff can then summarize lower-level decisions for a final sign-off from the president before dissemination to the White House.

When Should the President Make the Decision?

Decisions come in two categories. Some should be made as soon as possible. Either external events require an immediate response, or more time and information will not significantly improve the quality of the decision, or their significance is small, and making a decision will free up time for other more important decisions.

Other decisions benefit from time and multiple iterations, for the opposite of these three reasons. They have no deadline, either external or self-imposed, so they can be deferred in preference to more urgent ones. More relevant and important information could be coming, and that information could lead to a better decision. Sometimes a "preliminary" or partial decision could be made and floated to gather feedback from key stakeholders, and that feedback is itself important information in the final decision.

Timing a decision cannot be reduced to an exact science, and it may rely on the president's intuitions. Arthur Schlesinger observed Franklin Roosevelt's sense of when to make a decision:

> His complex administrative sensibility, infinitely subtle and sensitive, was forever weighing questions of personal force, of political timing, of congressional concern, of partisan benefit, of public interest. Situations had to be permitted to develop, to crystallize, to clarify; the competing forces had to vindicate themselves in the actual pull and tug of conflict; public opinion had to face the question, consider it, pronounce upon it—only then, at the long frazzled end, would the President's intuitions consolidate and precipitate a result.[17]

Delaying a decision by asking for more options is a decision in its own right. It should be done if the president is uncomfortable with the options and/or the strength of the implementation plan, and if timing allows.

How Should the President Make the Decision?

There are several dimensions to the answer to this question. The first is to decide how many consensus versus still undecided options are appropriate to present to the president. This choice is more about the individual president's style than the decision itself. President Reagan, for example, wanted a lot of consensus, and for his advisers to try and iron out differences as much as possible before decisions were brought to him. He disliked open conflict, even if it was issue-based. In contrast, other presidents wanted to see all the options that had been considered and see them debated, even if a consensus had been reached at a lower level.

In the Trump White House, I learned that the most productive meetings in the Oval Office were small, with up to five advocates of different viewpoints gathered before the Resolute Desk and with few bystanders. One of my roles was to organize these sessions. The most memorable example was the trade group, whose members represented the full spectrum of ideologies, from strong protectionist Peter Navarro to free trader Larry Kudlow, with Ambassador Robert Lighthizer, and Secretaries Steve Mnuchin and Wilbur Ross falling in between. Debates both before and during the meetings were both vigorous and designed for what the president was seeking, full contestability.

This anecdote also illustrates a larger point: meeting dynamics matter for quality decisions. The decision itself should seldom be made in a large meeting. As discussed in chapter 5, cabinet decision-making has been tried and failed numerous times. A large meeting can be arranged if it is critical that several principals be heard, but generally smaller is better, even if that upsets potential participants. If the honest brokers have done their job well, the process should have given all the relevant stakeholders the chance to air their views. In the meeting with the president, designated lead principals can represent the main views.

The decision should then be made in two stages: debate and decide. The debate phase should be a presidential discussion with the principals—the advocates—on the options, followed by a smaller "decide" meeting with just the OPOTUS for the president to make the decision itself. This two-stage approach has the following benefits. The first stage gives all the relevant parties a chance to express their views. It is important that an effective advocate for each position is there and that the options are presented fairly. The honest broker needs to ensure that the right people are there and that their positions are presented equally to the president. This may require a lot of meeting management, as some personalities are naturally more dominant than others and need to be compensated for.

The second stage allows the president and his or her inner circle to freely debate options without relitigating them in front of advocates. A smaller decision group can also consider not only the decision itself but the secondary and tertiary implications, in particular the effects on the president's reputation and power. It is also easier for the president to make a decision without the pressure of offending or disappointing a key advocate in person, or "splitting the baby" with a decision that, in attempting to satisfy multiple advocates, fails to adequately address the problem. And there is significantly less chance of that decision leaking out until it is ready to be communicated.

No decision should ever be made with just the president, or just him or her and one other adviser. At least two members of the OPOTUS should always be present to ensure decision clarity and communication.

The chief of staff (or other designated OPOTUS member) is then responsible for communicating the decision to the relevant parties, and at the relevant time (to minimize leaks). He or she can shield the president and take the "heat" of an unpopular decision from those whose options weren't chosen. They should eliminate the opportunity to relitigate thereafter.

Clearly this system relies on a high amount of goodwill from all parties and is particularly susceptible to "end runs" from staff who are excluded from the debate discussion meeting or the subsequent decision meeting. The OPOTUS needs to be ruthless in their discipline and solidarity—end

runs are not acceptable and should be a dismissal-worthy event. It is difficult for presidents to enforce this level of discipline, but he or she must
support the OPOTUS in doing so. The more they make it a matter of principle, not a reflection of the person, the easier it will be to hold the line. In
the long term they will welcome that discipline.

LASTING IMPACT IS ACHIEVED ONLY THROUGH EXCELLENT IMPLEMENTATION

While final action primarily resides with departments and agencies, accountability for policy delivery needs to be controlled through the White
House. The White House is full of policy offices and experts, but it often
fails to focus on implementation. As President Truman observed about his
successor, President Eisenhower, "He'll sit here, and he'll say 'Do this! Do
that!' *And nothing will happen.* Poor Ike—it won't be a bit like the Army.
He'll find it very frustrating."[18]

Impact is only achieved when citizens experience "street-level" change—
whether it be lower prescription drug prices, more medical services for veterans, new infrastructure completed, or new stimulus funds in bank accounts. Proper impact can require months or even years to achieve because
of headwinds of various kinds. Fragmented views between federal agencies
of how to proceed is one issue. Unclear or conflicting orders is another. New
programs must be properly resourced, given that federal agencies are reluctant to eliminate any existing programs to make way for new orders. Implementation plans need to deal with issues such as the new skills needed for
starting up programs and the degree of discretion granted to those implementing a decision at street level.

The first step of turning a decision into action is to ensure that all the
parts of the executive branch, and the White House in particular, can implement the decision in a coordinated way. For example, implementing a
decision may require the White House to persuade Congress to pass or
modify legislation. Impact in this instance would be the application of that
new legislation in a way that tangibly affects citizens' lives.

Richard Neustadt has suggested the characteristics of a presidential decision that will lead to effective execution. It must have the president's full
backing, be unambiguous in intent, be widely publicized to the people who
need to know it, provide the people who received the order the ability to
carry it out, and be backed by the presidential authority to issue the decision. Ensuring that these features are reflected in any decision is a job
for the OPOTUS. They can communicate the decision through the staff

secretary or other channels, but they are responsible for ensuring that these factors are present.

Implementing a Decision through Congressional Legislation

Assuming the decision conforms to something resembling Neustadt's standards, presidents have a key role in bargaining with any party outside of their direct authority that will be instrumental in executing the decision—and specifically Congress. When it comes to legislation, the decision is just the beginning of the bargaining process. To quote President Johnson, "There is only one way for a president to deal with Congress, and that is continuously, incessantly and without interruption."[19] The OPOTUS also has a key role in engaging with a significant number of the 535 members of Congress. The president cannot cover the whole list and should spend his or her time focusing on conference leaders and key swing votes. Members of the OPOTUS can cover the rest, as long as legislators know that they speak for the president.

Turning Passed Legislation into Action

Very often when Congress passes legislation, it leaves statutes open to interpretation by the executive branch, which is expected to create regulations in line with congressional intent. Creating regulations that act as the functional follow-through to presidentially endorsed legislation should be a primary goal of the policy councils inside the White House, and be one of the key goals for any relevant agency. Given the deluge of regulations that the White House's OIRA is expected to review, reallocating personnel from lower-value roles to OIRA would be a smart step for increasing its speed and capacity. Additionally, bottom-up proposed regulation from the agencies should be discouraged and deprioritized relative to regulation scheduled to be implemented via legislation. The secretary and deputy secretary of each agency should use their power to give priority to the regulatory actions of highest priority to the president.

The necessary oversight doesn't end once the regulations in question are issued. Their promulgation is necessary but not sufficient for achieving impact. An implementation team needs to monitor regulatory rollout and subsequent supporting agency programs—usually a multiyear process. Political appointees inside the agency should be selected and given responsibility for ensuring implementation. An Agency Implementation Unit (see chapter 7) would work with those appointees, providing central support and guidance. And the OPOTUS would support the multiyear approach by taking ownership of the results. It should have as part of its mandate that implementation does not fall off the radar screen, overtaken by the fresh new policy challenges.

There is also a role for the president to play in ensuring agency follow-through on implementation. In the private sector, corporate CEOs often do a deep dive into a business unit to see if it is actually doing what it is supposed to. Likewise, presidents should deep-dive into an agency from time to time to see if action that they care about is happening. This could take the form of briefings from working-level staffers, reviewing proposed implementation plans, and asking for progress against milestones. These would not cover all agency actions, only the ones that build toward the president's main agenda. Symbolism is as important as the activity. Not only is this a powerful tool for ensuring that work gets accomplished, but it puts other agency units on notice that they are liable to the same examination. Additionally, it accrues to the president's political benefit, as voters see him or her ensuring that otherwise invisible organs of government are doing what taxpayers pay them to do.

Implementing a Decision through Executive Orders and Executive Actions

While executive orders are relatively easy to issue, they still may require implementation through, for example, the issuance of a report, or for a federal agency to create a plan that is subsequently turned into street-level action.

Executive orders need to be issued with time frames and deadlines for implementation, along with a specific plan for ensuring these deadlines are met. Hitting the mark requires active management, not assumption of completion or compliance. Members of the OPOTUS must perform regular check-ins with all the impacted parties (generally representatives of federal agencies) on a defined timetable. There need to be interim deadlines that monitor progress, actions, and resources available to course-correct and to ensure the final delivery on time in full.

Some executive orders call for an agency or multiple agencies to create a report within a time frame—180 days is a common one. The report is not the end product but simply an interim step to a final action. Reports need to lead to recommended actions, and those actions need to result in tangible action within a defined period. An Implementation Unit needs to coordinate the various parties that create that report but, more importantly, have a subsequent follow-up plan to deal with the report's conclusions. Recommended actions may need to go back to the president for a decision and subsequent executive order, which in turn triggers another set of processes, all of which require management and monitoring.

Similarly, executive agreements between the United States and other countries also need an explicit action plan. Take, for example, the Paris Agreement, which was signed in 2015 and committed the United States to reduce its carbon emissions by 25 percent by 2025. The commitment is ineffective unless it is then converted into specific actions that create a pathway that leads to change. In the case of something as significant as the Paris Agreement, this should mean legislation and numerous regulations. There is no hope that these can be passed without a plan driven by the White House, led by an individual who has specific responsibility to coordinate and make agreed actions happen.

Of course, executive agreements become even more complicated than executive orders because they require working with other governments. Therefore, a joint implementation plan—decided *before* the executive agreement is signed—needs to be agreed upon between all parties. The team that is negotiating the executive agreement needs to contain implementation experts who create a plan that should be approved prior to signing. Depending on the level of significance of the executive agreement, that plan should be signed off on by the White House, either the OPOTUS or a delegated senior staff member.

I recognize this articulation of vital processes may sound dull and procedural, but an effective White House does not measure its success in terms of the number of decisions it makes or executive orders it issues; it measures its success in terms of what they achieve. There is nothing more futile than an order that is only partially complied with or a report that leads nowhere.

Selling for Impact

Presidents have a key role to play in promoting the policy they are trying to implement. The aforementioned occasional presidential deep dive into agency units should also be accompanied by efforts to promote this work. The president can do interviews, speeches, or other public engagement events to encourage the fast implementation of a decision, especially where implementation requires citizen engagement (think of the Obama administration's advertising blitz to ask Americans to enroll in coverage newly provided by the Affordable Care Act). The emphasis in Years 2 and 4 on selling citizen services pays off only if there are tangible benefits to showcase.

CLARIFY ROLES IN EACH STEP

Having "too many cooks in the kitchen" is fatal to any organization's speed and productivity. Even worse is to have confusion about who is the head cook for each course. Different people in the White House will lead different steps of the decision-making process at different times, for different reasons. Clarifying the nature of the roles, especially the president's, is important to ensure a decision-making process that produces maximum impact. The nature and scope of participation is consistent with the emphasis above—the president's time should be used strategically, such that their participation adds value that only they can add. Equally important is to clarify who is *not* the lead, active in the process, or involved at all. Enforcing this clarity falls, once again, to the OPOTUS.

Three types of roles in the decision-making process are shown below. Obviously, these are indicative only, and will need to be customized to the context:

> *Lead:* the person or people who are in charge of the process step.
> *Active:* the person or people who are in the key meetings and actively shape work performed in the step.
> *Input:* the person or people who provide input as determined by the Lead.

For each of the steps:

> *Priorities:* The president should be the Lead in determining the administration's priorities, with Active impact from the OPOTUS. Input can be requested from others—such as cabinet secretaries—but the default setting is for no one else to be involved, with unsolicited suggestions of priorities discouraged.
> *Options:* Once presidents have determined their priorities, they should step back from the option generation process and take virtually no role until they must decide to adopt one of them or request further refinement. Their active input will more than likely limit the number and quality of options generated. A member of the OPOTUS should take the Lead in overseeing the process. Given the importance of this step, that member should enlist Active participation from as many components of the White House and agencies as necessary (following the outline of the PC Process).
> *Decision:* This is clearly where the president should Lead, with Active involvement from OPOTUS, and a very select number of other EOP staff and cabinet members giving Input as necessary.

	Priorities	Options	Decision	Implementation	Impact
POTUS	LEAD	—	LEAD	Active	Input
OPOTUS	Active	LEAD	Active	LEAD	Input
EOP	—	Active	Input	Active	Active
Agencies	—	Active	—	—	LEAD

FIGURE 7. Roles in the decision process

Implementation: The OPOTUS needs to Lead and ensure a proper and successful implementation of the decision. The president should be Active as necessary to enforce implementation. Other components of the EOP would also be active, for example, a newly created Implementation Unit inside OMB (see chapter 7 for more details).

Action: This is the step where agencies take the Lead and turn the implementation into long-term and sustainable action. The president should have a small but important role, such as selling the implementation. Components of the EOP should remain Active in overseeing progress, to ensure that federal agencies tasked with implementation meet White House expectations.

In figure 7 the main participants' roles in each step are delineated.

CONCLUSION

A carefully designed and managed White House decision-making process may seem like anathema to the political world, a place where informality, instincts, and in-group dynamics make decision-making much more art than science. However, better-structured EOP decision-making and follow-through mechanisms will clarify responsibilities, minimize crowded decision rooms, and maximize the throughput of the most important decisions. Moreover, having a foundation of well-structured processes will free up the time for the fluidity needed for dealing with crises and unforeseen events.

If a White House follows the steps set out in this section, it should lead to a change in emphasis in the decision-making process. In many White Houses, too much effort is spent on just the decision phase. Activities such as arguing over who is in the room with the president, and when, consume too many man-hours, as does relitigating unclear or partial decisions resulting from poor meetings. This energy ought to be rebalanced into meaningful work on what happens prior to presidents' decisions (generation of multiple sound options) and afterward (thorough plans for implementation of their decisions).

Transforming the machinery of the White House to concentrate on well-structured option generation and implementation of decisions will massively increase the number and quality of decisions, and the lasting impact of those decisions, while still allowing all the flexibility needed for fluid decision-making. Year Zero is the time to design these processes and start to road-test them.

By the second term, all these processes should be well established and running effectively. However, a reset is always a good chance to review and correct course. Carrying out a detailed comprehensive historical analysis of the quality of decision-making and implementation will show the way to an even more effective system. This should be done in Year Four of the first term.

7

TASK FOUR

Design a Coherent White House Structure

Start nine months before the inauguration.

As Dick Cheney was finishing his tenure as President Ford's chief of staff in 1977, his colleagues gave him a curious going-away present: a bicycle wheel mounted on a piece of plywood. Every spoke connecting the center of the wheel to the rim was broken, except one. It was a metaphor as well as a joke: a symbol of the administration's poorly conceived management style, in which Ford initially had rejected hiring a chief of staff. Ford's motive in trying to be his own chief was to send a signal that his presidency would be different from that of Richard Nixon, whose chief of staff's zealous sequestering of the president from certain staff and information was seen as one of the contributing factors to the Watergate scandal. Yet Ford's creation of a system in which too many people (the spokes) reported to him directly, rather than through a chief of staff, was a huge mistake. Predictably, disorder reigned, and an old comment of President Eisenhower's was vindicated: "Organization cannot make a genius out of an incompetent. . . . On the other hand, disorganization can scarcely fail to result in inefficiency."[1]

Eventually, Ford reversed his stance and appointed Cheney as chief of staff. When Cheney left the White House in 1977, following the election of Jimmy Carter, he gave the wheel to his successor, Hamilton Jordan, and attached a note: "Dear Hamilton. Beware the spokes of the wheel."[2] Cheney intended to convey that having every spoke (presidential staffer) tie directly to the president (the inner part of the wheel) was bound to fail. Sadly, Carter repeated Ford's mistake and attempted to function without a chief of staff. This was a mistake, said Carter aide Jack Watson. "It pulls the president into too much; he's involved in too many things."[3]

My early weeks in the White House in 2017 were similarly full of confused lines of communication and reporting. It felt like an Odyssean voyage, as the new staff explored overlapping power centers and the perplexing mechanics of getting things done in the modern White House. For instance, we spent a lot of time and energy on patch disputes such as who had "walk-in privileges" to the Oval Office, who would be entitled to membership on the National Security Council, whether or not the Homeland Security Council would be part of the NSC, and whether the newly created Office of Trade and Manufacturing Policy would stand on its own or become a part of the National Economic Council.

These problems are best solved before an inauguration and not after it, when all efforts should be directed at governing. The Year Zero team can design a new architecture well ahead of time that reflects a closer alignment of structure with achievement of the president's goals.

This chapter proposes an approach to organizing the White House that ties structure to the core decision-making processes. This model is intended to overcome a fundamental shortcoming of White House design—it must be able to be replicated in an "evergreen" fashion, no matter who is president.

START WITH AN (ALMOST) CLEAN SHEET, AND A SET OF PRINCIPLES

Given the many components that must be brought together to carry out effective processes within the White House (as described in chapter 6), a systematic approach to an organizing set of principles for a productive structure is essential. While no human entity operates strictly according to organization charts, they do bring some clarity to the guardrails of activity.

Most studies of organization design have focused on private sector organizations. There are some similarities between private sector entities and the White House—for example, both involve a large number of tasks to be performed, limited resources, and organizational hierarchy.

Most organizations, whether private or public, need to assign specialized tasks and then coordinate multiple activities, often with insufficient resources. Hence arises the need to set priorities and make trade-offs. There is also generally a hierarchy of roles. Assuming the organizations are larger than one person's effective span of control of approximately 10 to 15 people, the roles need to be organized in a logical fashion. A hierarchy with span-breakers is the normal model in the private sector once a company gets to a certain size.

However, successful private sector models, while potentially useful to some extent, cannot be applied in their entirety to the White House. There are considerable differences between public and private sector entities in general, and the White House in particular.

In the public sector:

Objectives are often less clear.

Very few decisions are binary yes/no choices.

Decisions require much more consensus building.

There are more shared and overlapping responsibilities between organizational actors.

There is a mix of elected officials, political appointees, and civil servants executing on policy.

A political body has a finite life span defined by elections.

Differences for the White House in particular include:

The whole team is formed very quickly (they come together on "Day One").

Presidents are central to everything (in theory everyone reports to them, and they are the only ones who can make policy decisions).

Its staff may consist of only a few hundred people, but it is at the center of an organization that employs several million people.

It has no "competition" existing at the same time—the White House has a constitutional monopoly on the federal executive branch. This means that innovations in design must be self-generated.

To add to the complexity, there are dozens of units in the Executive Office of the President with differing organizing principles. As an analogy to the private sector, some can be thought of as being designed around "functional" areas, such as the lawyers in the Office of Legal Counsel. Others can be seen as "product" areas, such as the National Economic Council, which organizes itself around economic themes such as taxes. Still more can be thought of as the equivalent of "customer" areas, such as the Office of Legislative Affairs, which organizes itself around its customers—Congress. Others have geographic subunits. And some can be a combination of the above or a matrix. For example, the current National Security Council has a mixture of all the above—geographic (Middle East, Russia and Central Asia, Western Hemisphere, etc.), product (cybersecurity, international economics and competitiveness, technology and national security, etc.), function (strategic communications, strategic planning), and customer (partnerships and global engagement).

Some functions can be distributed across multiple domains. Responsibility for technology policy, for instance, can sit with any or all of the National Economic Council, the National Security Council, the Domestic Policy Council, and the Office of Science and Technology Policy. The result of such multiple owners and overlapping jurisdictions can be patch disputes, poor coordination on policy delivery, and a lack of accountability.

The problem is compounded by the dozens of people who technically report directly to the president, from more than 20 cabinet members to about 25 assistants to the president. This is a theoretical span of control that is totally impractical, which no organization would consciously choose.

A good chief of staff can handle some of the resulting turmoil and be, in the words of President Clinton's chief of staff, Mack McLarty, "the javelin catcher."[4] However, effective management is extremely difficult. Many businesspeople who come into staff roles at the White House often struggle to adapt and succeed (e.g., chiefs of staff such as William Daley and Donald Regan). They are used to a clean hierarchy of reporting that doesn't exist in a defined way in the White House. Sometimes they have tried to control the whole White House in a hierarchical fashion, acting more like a "chief" than "staff."

The Year Zero team should take a "clean-sheet" approach that involves a broader reimagination of White House structure and management but is based on the same core principles. One of the benefits of the 100 percent turnover of top White House staff from one administration to another is that the Year Zero team can take a first principles approach, and there is no need for "change management." The White House can be designed for maximum impact, with people hired into that structure as it is designed. A conscious choosing of priorities can and should also inform the level of resources allocated to each office.

Creating an Evergreen Approach

A commonly accepted, reflexive approach to designing the White House holds that its design must be customized to reflect a unique president's background, management style, and method of decision-making. Although this approach makes intuitive sense, it is not an organizing principle, and it comes with no "evergreen" guidelines for implementation in the White House. Ironically, in practice in recent White Houses, most of the actual structure looks very similar to previous ones, mainly because a lack of a conscious design causes the president and White House staff to simply copy what has come before.

In trying to design an evergreen approach, it is important to differentiate structural factors that are common to all White Houses and personal factors that are particular to the president, and then balance them in the right way. More fundamentally, letting the president's style alone dictate the structure of the White House is a mistake. If presidents are chaotic in their decision-making approach, that doesn't mean the White House should be chaotic. Alternatively, just because the president is very structured and prefers detail doesn't mean the White House should become overly bureaucratic. Just because the president has a preference for preagreed solutions doesn't mean that the White House should try to seek consensus on every issue. The trick is to customize those elements of the White House where it is important to reflect the president's style and standardize the rest.

Structural Factors

There are several structural factors that undergird the design of the White House. First, the White House is an environment characterized by high levels of complexity and change. Second, it must engage with a number of external entities, for example, the two other branches of the federal government, state governments, and other nations. Third, it has a small central unit (a few hundred people) that sits over a massive federal government, comprised of several million direct employees and contractors combined.

A fundamental principle of organization design holds that a complex environment should lead to high levels of unit differentiation, attendant integrating mechanisms, and a decentralization in decision-making. However, White House decision-making is centralized in one person, the president. Resolving this tension requires a unique design that accommodates the actual decision-making process and the personality of the decision-maker.

The President's Personal Characteristic Factors

Presidents come in many different flavors, and the structural design of the White House needs to accommodate the chief executive's particular manner of operating. For example, one categorization is that there are two models of presidential leadership style, "one in which a strong president dominates his environment as a director of change, and one in which the president has a more limited role as a facilitator of change." In the "director-of-change" model, "presidents lead the nation by creating opportunities to move in new directions, and leading others where they would otherwise not go." On the other hand, in the "facilitator" model, "presidents work, bargaining and pleading, at coalition building to further the attainment of their goals and the goals of their constituencies."[5] Presidents will reflect both of these models to some extent but can generally be placed into either bucket.

Presidents often differ according to decision-making style. Some presidents, such as Obama, have been very analytical in their decision-making style. Others, like President Clinton, adopt a more personal method of relying on the strength of the argument presented by individuals in person. Still others, such as Trump, have made their own intuition the ballast for their judgments, after observing competing arguments being voiced.

DESIGN THE STRUCTURE AROUND THE CORE DECISION-MAKING PROCESS

In order to have an evergreen approach capable of accommodating the conflicting structural and personal factors, the fundamental and enduring principle that should govern design is that the White House should be built around the core decision-making process. Figure 8 summarizes what such a model could look like.

In essence there are three levels to the structural design, with each level having a unique design based on its primary role in the core decision-making process.

The top level is customized, consisting of the president and the OPOTUS. These individuals collectively lead in four of the decision process steps. The top layer needs to be designed entirely around the personal characteristics of the president. It also provides a "translation layer" between the POTUS/OPOTUS offices and the rest of the Executive Office of the President (EOP). This customized layer interfaces with and manages the (standardized) structure below it.

The second level consists of the rest of the EOP. It should be heavily standardized in every White House in terms of the processes and the nature

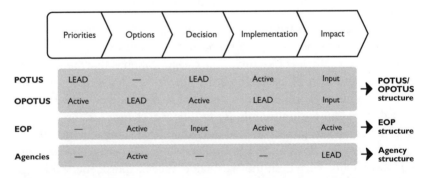

	Priorities	Options	Decision	Implementation	Impact	
POTUS	LEAD	—	LEAD	Active	Input	→ POTUS/OPOTUS structure
OPOTUS	Active	LEAD	Active	LEAD	Input	
EOP	—	Active	Input	Active	Active	→ EOP structure
Agencies	—	Active	—	—	LEAD	→ Agency structure

FIGURE 8. Decision process drives structure

of the roles in the offices. The EOP has two primary areas of responsibility according to my prioritization of activity in the White House: generating policy options and implementing decisions. These areas should have separate but coordinated structural designs. The second level should also have a structure for managing the noncore administrative and operational "care and feeding processes." That structure should be designed separately but is consistent in terms of design principles—a high degree of standardization.

The third level is also standardized, consisting of the agencies and, in particular, members of the cabinet and other senior, Senate-confirmed, politically appointed leaders of federal agencies. They have an active role in option generation and a lead role in implementation, and their structure relative to the White House reflects that. Agencies are generally statutory bodies, so they are already reasonably standardized in their personnel composition and responsibility allocation. The interface between the EOP and the agencies needs a standardized architecture—one that will be durable between administrations—that allows the EOP to appropriately drive agency implementation of presidential decisions.

CUSTOMIZE THE INNER CIRCLE TO SUIT THE PRESIDENT

A president brings a certain set of characteristics, and White House design should not expect him or her to change to suit the office. An evergreen approach needs to anticipate and be flexible enough to cater to all types, styles, and personalities in the president, building on his or her strengths and covering his or her weaknesses. However, only a small part of the White House (that part that the president interacts with on a daily basis) needs to be customized, not its entirety.

Chapter 4 introduced the concept of the "Office of the President of the United States" (OPOTUS). The main idea behind it is that the OPOTUS collectively assumes the responsibilities of the White House chief of staff, which have become too numerous for any one person to perform optimally. The OPOTUS should operate as a team, protecting the president and representing his or her interests unfailingly in every context.

Given each member's proximity to the president, the principle of design for the OPOTUS would be to make it completely customized to the president's needs and style. The members of it need to organize everything about his or her professional life, in particular the decision-making processes, with an objective of making it optimal for him or her. They should individually and collectively spend considerable time with the president to properly understand his or her likes and dislikes, and patterns of thought and expression. Depending on the skills of the OPOTUS team members,

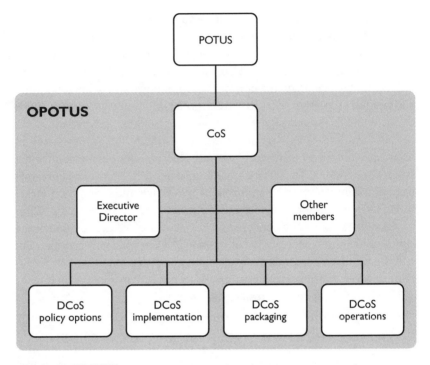

FIGURE 9. OPOTUS structure

they would split the responsibilities of the office between them and ensure that the usual cadence of the president's day met his or her requirements and that meeting structures (in particular those involving decisions) were designed to suit his or her style.

The OPOTUS would then act as a "translation layer" between the president and the rest of the White House. This concept is an important one. One of the roles of the OPOTUS is to shield presidents from the workings of the second and third levels. Presidents should neither see nor care how they function. Whether they are inclined toward highly organized processes or not, they should only care about what they must know, not the "sausage making" behind it. That is for the OPOTUS to manage.

The guardians and operators of this translation layer would be the deputy chiefs of staff. The OPOTUS should have up to four deputy chiefs of staff (DCoS), who as individuals report to the chief of staff but who have responsibility to the whole OPOTUS. The first DCoS should coordinate all the policy processes up to the level of presidential decision-making. The second should then oversee all the steps associated with implementation.

The third DCoS should oversee "packaging and selling"—activities such as communications and press. The fourth should be in charge of all logistical operations in support of the president—the "care and feeding" of the president. The OPOTUS should be run by an executive director—someone who is senior enough to monitor and coordinate all its activities and be an arbitrator as necessary—potentially an "honest broker to the honest brokers."

STANDARDIZE THE REST OF THE EOP

The second (middle) level consists of the rest of the EOP. The EOP's structure should be reconceived such that offices are categorized according to functions: offices with responsibility for generating policy options, offices responsible for overseeing implementation efforts (including packaging and selling), and offices responsible for White House and presidential operation.

In order to keep decision-making highly centralized (i.e., within the domain of the president) and still control the volume of decisions, there are two fundamental principles that need to be observed in the design of the EOP: standardization and coordination.

The offices of the EOP should be standardized to the maximum extent possible. Roles should be explicitly defined, and processes made standard and predictable. Institutional knowledge should be codified and carried over from one administration to another.

Henry Mintzberg characterized standardization as occurring on a continuum, from direct supervision at one end of the spectrum, through standardization of work processes, standardization of outputs, standardization of skills, to mutual adjustment at the other end.[6] In a highly decentralized decision-making system, simple systems, such as standardization of skills, are sufficient. As decisions become more centralized, then more standardization is necessary all the way to direct supervision—essentially a bureaucracy. In the White House, a middle ground needs to be sought. It should be standard enough to be predictable but flexible enough to reflect the realities of the complex issues that have to be dealt with, the highly skilled people inside the offices, and the fluid nature of daily life. The optimal resulting blend should be standardization through the work processes (in particular the decision-making processes) and coordination through the policy councils.

Councils therefore play a critical role in allowing the White House to standardize but not become overly bureaucratic. Hal G. Rainey, commenting on the findings of Paul R. Laurence and Jay W. Lorsh, has written,

"Firms that were successfully operating in uncertain, complex, changing environments had more differentiated internal structures. By differentiated structures, they meant that the subunits differed a great deal among themselves in their goals, time frames, and internal work climates. Yet these highly differentiated firms also had elaborate structures and procedures for integrating the diverse units in the organization."[7] The policy councils are the integrating force in the White House.

The area of presidential appointments is another good example of the need to standardize processes such that they are invisible to the president. Some presidents like to be very hands-on with people selection, others less so. But regardless of their approach, the same discipline is needed to screen and short-list the right candidates. Having a good process that is invisible to presidents can also shield them somewhat from the pressure to do favors—they can pass the handling of that difficult issue to the Presidential Personnel Office.

Below the OPOTUS, other than the heads of various policymaking councils, the great bulk of people only see the president on a very occasional basis (in some cases, virtually never outside of ceremonial occasions), and their lives do not need to be "customized" to a particular presidential style. They need to be extremely good at what they do, in a manner that is reasonably consistent across administrations.

The members of the rest of the EOP will be a mixture of honest brokers and advocates. The heads and deputies of the policy councils should be honest brokers, because their roles are to coordinate components of the White House and agencies to come up with policy options. That requires some subject matter expertise (they need to have enough intimate knowledge to be able to synthesize competing policy choices), but more importantly, they must have skill around managing people, processes, and meetings. As the size of the White House has grown, assistants have moved from being generalists to specialists, so it is necessary to have some staffers skilled in management techniques.

Lower-level staff (special assistants to the president and below) can be policy specialists, and advocates as needed, although to the extent they wish to be advocates, they limit their potential for promotion. Given that they are likely to have strongly held policy preferences as a result of spending years working on the issues within their domains, staffers should be explicit about them where they exist. As Reagan's political adviser Michael Deaver observed, "Everyone who runs a department within the White House has a constituency."[8] Staffers with policy biases will exist as a matter of human nature; they just need to be explicit and transparent about their beliefs.

Reporting Relationships between the President, the Chief of Staff, and Assistants to the President

Reporting relationships should also be standardized. All staff in the EOP should report to the president through either the chief of staff or some member of the OPOTUS.

This will require a major adjustment in current thinking about the reporting relationships between the president and assistants to the president. In concept, all assistants to the president (and, through them, all other more junior political appointees) report to the president. But the resulting span of control is impractical. The chief of staff role was introduced to manage the staff, but often it is unclear what the chief's actual responsibility is.

This informal structural design should be recast as a formal one characterized by a dual reporting relationship. Any assistant to the president should have a "solid-line" reporting relationship to the chief of staff and a "dotted-line" reporting relationship to the president. The solid line would cover what in the private sector would be called performance management—performing daily and weekly responsibilities and delivering results against tasks set by the chief of staff or the OPOTUS. The dotted line would essentially cover only the decision to be hired and to be fired.

The president is clearly free to reach out directly to any assistant to the president at any time, but not the other way around. This is critical for presidential time management. Staff may carry the rank of assistant to the president, but this should not give them direct, unobstructed access to him or her. All access must be through a member of the OPOTUS, which will schedule time to discuss policy and other issues. It is critical, therefore, that the OPOTUS does its collective job as honest brokers to minimize staffers making end runs around them to get to the president.

This reporting configuration should also apply to the national security adviser, a role that has often been occupied by advocates or individuals accustomed to direct access to the president outside the chief of staff line of reporting. The president must decide whether the national security adviser should be an honest broker, in which case he or she is a candidate for the OPOTUS, or if he or she wishes to be an advocate, in which case he or she needs to report through a member of the OPOTUS (probably the chief of staff). To become a member of the OPOTUS, he or she needs to be an unambiguous team player willing to subject himself or herself to the self-governance of the team, not, as can be the case, a lone ranger.

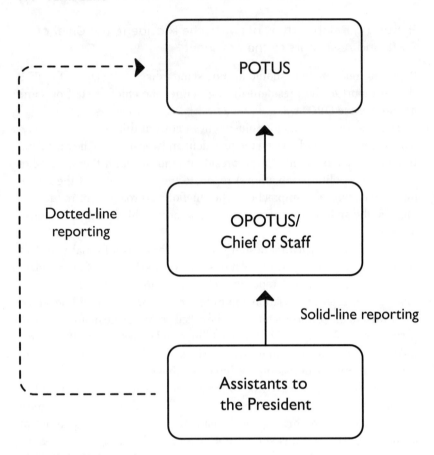

FIGURE 10. EOP reporting

Building Charters and Allocating Resources

Designing all of the above should occur in Year Zero. The Year Zero Leadership Team (YOLT) should draft a series of charters documenting roles and responsibilities for not only the OPOTUS but every office in the White House. These charters should define goals, roles, and resources. These should not be cumbersome or lengthy bureaucratic documents; they should be simple, clear descriptions of the general purpose and specific duties of various White House offices and councils. The idea behind them is to help streamline and clarify roles depending on the distinctive priorities of a potential White House administration.

A "clean-sheet" approach should include a reallocation of head count and resources between offices (to the extent federal statutes or funding permit it) to reflect the administration's policy goals. Commissioned officers (approximately 25 assistants to the president, 25 deputy assistants to the president, and 50 special assistants to the president) are the most senior people in the White House. At a minimum, these commissions should be allocated by office in Year Zero, each with a short job description and, more importantly, the key goal the occupant of the role should pursue. This allocation and definition should not be left until after the election—no priorities are likely to arise that aren't known before—and it is much easier to recruit senior people if they know what is expected of them and what resources they will have. Also, preallocation and definition will minimize the time and energy wasted during the transition and early weeks of the administration as senior hires otherwise contest and negotiate for limited precious resources.

Staff numbers in other offices should be allocated according to the president's priorities. During Year Zero, the team should do a bottom-up exercise on the minimum number of staff needed to carry out the core functions of each of the offices. This number should be the only guaranteed staff level, and the team should resist the temptation to democratically allocate the rest. Additional billets should only be allocated according to priority, not historical precedent. Staff numbers can always be reassigned in subsequent years, but the initial allocation should match the priorities for Year One as determined in the legacy planning step.

In the White House, staff in policy offices such as the National Economic Council, the Domestic Policy Council, and the Office of Science and Technology Policy should be concentrated in high-priority policy initiatives, not across all subject areas. The Office of Legislative Affairs should get a disproportionately high number of staff, given the Year One focus on legislation. In the wider EOP, the number of staff and resources in offices such as the Office of the U.S. Trade Representative, the Council on Environmental Quality, and the Office of National Drug Control Policy should reflect the priority the president assigns to trade, environment, and illegal drug issues, respectively.

There will be additional customization in the EOP to suit nontraditional objectives of a particular administration. Some offices will be added that reflect a particular presidential priority (for example, the White House Office of Faith-Based and Community Initiatives in the Bush administration). But these are the exception, not the rule, and they should follow the same basic template as other offices. They should have a clear charter that encompasses their mandate and goals. And they should have a predefined expiry date. In the Trump White House, we established an American Technology Council, which I led. It was focused on modernizing government technology platforms, a particular focus of the administration. But rather than create yet another office that an incoming administration may or may not want based on their priorities, it had an automatic expiration date of the end of our administration.

Shadow Staffers

One feature of the White House is the duplication of roles across different offices. For example, the National Security Council and the Office of the Vice President each have their own communications, legal, and legislative relations staffs. This can create the undesirable tendency for these staffers to have a primary loyalty to the principal or office they routinely serve, not necessarily the president.

These "shadow staffers" can exist, but in keeping with optimizing all offices to serve the president's agenda, they should all report primarily to the central White House offices overseeing their areas of responsibility. In other words, the "solid lines" are drawn to White House offices, and the "dotted lines" to the unit in which they work (e.g., the vice president's office, etc.).

THE EOP NEEDS A UNIT RESPONSIBLE FOR IMPLEMENTATION

Good implementation is critical to good governance, as only successful implementation achieves the results for citizens necessary to increase faith in democratic government. And yet implementation is generally the least developed area of focus for any White House. Assistants to the president are generally chosen as policy experts, not implementation experts, and therefore implementation doesn't get the attention it needs.

To rectify this, the YOLT must define effective implementation as a key objective, design structures and systems inside the White House to achieve it, and recruit people with an effective track record of operational excellence. Policy people can seldom be reskilled, so they should not be expected to play a dual role; other experts should be selected as part of the recruitment process to be the implementation leaders.

An effective implementation mechanism could be set up in one of two ways. Either the YOLT can create a series of units inside the policy councils led by implementation experts, or it can create one centralized unit inside the Office of Management and Budget (OMB) responsible for leading all implementation efforts. My recommendation is to do the latter. The concept of implementation is consistent with the core function of OMB. OMB also has head count numbers (approximately 500 staff) that can be allocated to a dedicated unit that should have a large staff. Present OMB staff are a good mix of political appointees (about 20 percent) and civil servants (about 80 percent). The civil servants are generally highly skilled, professional, and evince a high degree of bipartisan commitment. OMB should therefore play an even more critical role in the White House of the future.

The following concepts would underpin the Implementation Unit. It would be staffed by people expert in project management and led by someone also expert in management, and with the rank of assistant to the president. It would work with other parts of the White House that have responsibilities for aspects of implementation (e.g., the Office of Legislative Affairs, Press, Communications, etc.). It would have a dual reporting relationship to the head of OMB and the deputy chief of staff for implementation. In addition, individual implementation units would be created inside each agency that would be coordinated by the central unit.

Changing OMB to have more focus on implementation would also reverse the trend of it being increasingly politicized. In Terry Moe's words, "Politicization is deplored for its destructive effects on institutional memory, expertise, professionalism, objectivity, communication, continuity and other bases of organizational competence."[9]

For OMB to perform a strong implementation role, the "M" part of its mandate needs to be emphasized and redefined. Reconsidering the qualities that inform the selection of OMB leadership is one possibility for sending a strong signal about the new direction. Traditionally, the head of OMB has had more of a budget background, but as part of the move to an implementation focus, he or she could be hired from an operational background. There could still be a strong budget hand at the deputy director level, but having a director with a managerial orientation would signal a strong commitment to lasting change through effective implementation. Reallocating resources that currently are used to create the president's budget could also catalyze a switch in emphasis. The president's budget is not quite "dead on arrival," but is close to it, and has become more of a messaging exercise than a true financial commitment.

There are also very good existing vehicles within OMB that can help achieve implementation goals, and they need to be utilized with that objective in mind. The program associate directors (PADs) are political appointees who can be very effective for reaching into agencies and effecting change through budgetary control. They direct Resource Management Offices (RMOs) separated into six functional units: National Security, Health, Natural Resources and Energy, Transportation and Homeland Security, and Treasury, Commerce, and Housing. The RMOs are powerful entities that control apportionment, the process of signing off on funds progressively released to agencies throughout the year. The RMOs therefore have good insight into, and significant knowledge of, agency programs.

The Office of Information and Regulatory Affairs (OIRA) is one of the least known yet most influential parts of the White House, being the central authority for the review of executive branch regulations. Consideration should be given to upgrading and increasing the head count in OIRA. This is a major opportunity to increase the amount of regulatory throughput, a key part of the president's ability to achieve impact. OIRA should be mandated to coordinate with the RMOs on implementation.

In addition, the President's Management Council, CFO Council, and CIO Council are all directed out of OMB. They can be vehicles for change, given more status and tools, and be a forum for sharing best practices. The President's Management Agenda—a vehicle for modernizing the federal government—is a process that already exists and is also OMB-generated. But it needs to be revitalized and focused on implementing a small number of priorities.

Policy Promotion

Consistent with the need to prioritize "selling" activities in Years Two and Four, presidents should tout their accomplishments as part of a sound implementation plan. Their public reinforcement of the importance of what they have done signals to the federal workforce to take action to achieve implementation and raises awareness among the public of the benefits they will receive through them. Presidents should be the champion of the programs, taking every opportunity during Years Two and Four to highlight citizens who are benefitting. Public events outside of Washington, D.C., in which presidents meet with beneficiaries of their policies are particularly attractive to the press and effective in getting the word out. Writes Neustadt, "One should never underestimate the public's power to ignore, to acquiesce, and to forget, especially when the proceedings seem incalculable or remote from private life."[10] Having presidents publicly selling their accomplishments will keep them front of mind.

Selling associated with implementation efforts should also connect to a wider messaging approach highlighting how government is working. Some may question the need for as sizeable a communications team as a White House typically has (around 35 people), especially since messaging seldom shifts opinion in favor of policies ahead of their legislative passage. But having well-stocked communications and press offices is essential—not just for informing the citizenry of what their government is doing but for selling the accomplishments that give them confidence it is doing it well.

AN AGENCY'S STRUCTURE SHOULD FACILITATE POLICY OPTIONS AND IMPLEMENTATION

There are more than one hundred agencies within the federal government. They all have a dual reporting structure—to both Congress and to the president. The president appoints the most senior staff in those agencies, but the great bulk of the people who work in them are civil servants (i.e., employed by the government, but not appointed by the president). The structure inside the agencies is therefore reasonably standardized, other than for the political appointees, and even with them there is a high degree of regularity. Each agency typically has an appointed secretary, deputy secretary, chief financial officer, general counsel, and so on.

The most important agencies, from the president's perspective, are the fifteen executive departments where the secretary forms part of the cabinet (although some noncabinet independent agencies such as the Federal Reserve or the CIA are also very important due to their policymaking or national security functions). The Constitution does not explicitly establish a cabinet, and, as a unit, it has no statutory executive powers of its own. There are typically 20 to 25 members, with the secretaries of fifteen agencies always represented, and others who are occasionally added at the president's direction (e.g., ambassador to the United Nations).

In terms of how to structure the agencies, the main decisions that the YOLT should recommend to the president-elect are the number of political appointees per agency, which additional agency heads should get cabinet rank, and how, when, and who to involve from the agency in a decision-making process. Of these decisions, the last should be the main organizing principle.

Agency Input into Decision Options

As shown in the core decision-making process, agencies have an active role in the option generation stage. Their participation should primarily come through the PC Process, where staff (political and career) are involved at multiple stages. As the option generation process evolves, political staff take a greater role with deputy secretaries and then secretaries debating options before the decision is taken to the president.

Involving all cabinet members in any one decision is a poor use of time for any of those whose direct contribution is not necessary. But where multiple cabinet members' input is necessary, one concept that has been tried with some success is cabinet subgroupings organized around themes. These subgroupings can range in formality, size, and longevity depending on the White House. Some are as follows:

TABLE 1. Cabinet members listed in order of presidential succession

Agency	Rank
Secretary of State	1
Secretary of the Treasury	2
Secretary of Defense	3
Attorney General	4
Secretary of the Interior	5
Secretary of Agriculture	6
Secretary of Commerce	7
Secretary of Labor	8
Secretary of Health and Human Services	9
Secretary of Housing and Urban Development	10
Secretary of Transportation	11
Secretary of Energy	12
Secretary of Education	13
Secretary of Veterans Affairs	14
Secretary of Homeland Security	15

Formal and long-standing: These exist throughout the administration and may be governed by statute. An example would be the NSC, with members including the vice president, secretary of state, treasury secretary, and secretary of defense.

Informal and long-standing: These have less structure but exist for long periods, perhaps the whole term. An example is President Johnson's Tuesday Cabinet, which consisted of lunch every Tuesday with Secretary of State Dean Rusk, Secretary of Defense Robert McNamara, NSA McGeorge Bundy, Chairman of Joint Chiefs General Earle Gilmore Wheeler, and CIA Director Richard Helms.

Formal and short-lived: These address specific issues, such as the Coronavirus Task Force.

Informal and short-lived: These also address specific issues, but with less governance formality. An example could be cabinet subgroups organized for a policy issue such as reducing student debt. Generally, these should be avoided in favor of a PC Process.

The design of how cabinet members and other agency heads should interface with a policy process can vary according to the circumstances, but they should be determined by the following principles:

1. Agency leaders are there to generate, advocate for, and debate options for the president to consider. They have no decision-making responsibility besides the authorities legally delegated to them.

2. Their gatherings should be coordinated by an honest broker. In the case of the NSC, it is the national security adviser. It may vary in the other cases, say, for a task force, a member of the OPOTUS, the vice president, or another White House appointee would be fit for the task.

3. Agency heads should act as advocates, not honest brokers. Consequently, cabinet secretaries should not lead the group, as they should act as advocates for their agencies. Eisenhower told his cabinet, "You are not supposed to represent your department, your home state, or anything else. You are my advisers."[11] This view may have been correct in the past, but it should not be applied to the modern White House—cabinet secretaries must represent their agencies' interests and diverse constituencies. This is the opposite of commonly accepted wisdom. Additionally, because agencies are often the prime implementers of laws and regulations, agency heads should outline for the president the implications of various options.

4. Cabinet subgroups should not be led by the president. For the reasons explained in chapter 6, the president's involvement will tend to limit debate around options and should generally be avoided. An occasional exception to presidents' noninvolvement is the NSC, which they have a statutory role in chairing. However, even then they can delegate that responsibility so that the NSC can meet without them, with the NSA as the acting chair.

5. The structures above can be replicated at lower levels of the agency, for example as part of the PC Process.

Agency Implementation through Action

Federal agencies assume the bulk of the responsibility for turning decisions into action. Doing it well requires deft coordination and management to ensure the agencies uptake those responsibilities in the way a president expects.

To achieve good outcomes, there should exist within every agency a senior political appointee whose specific responsibility it is to lead implementation efforts as part of an Agency Implementation Unit. That person needs to have operational skills and be hired specifically with these duties in mind. He or she needs to be responsible for crafting agency plans reflecting all aspects of the delivery of citizen services—whether that be the production of regulations, and/or specific citizen programs that deliver tangible benefits. This individual will have a dotted-line relationship with the OMB's newly created central Implementation Unit, which would oversee the network of parallel Implementation Units inside each agency.

Permanent change will require a project management system capable of monitoring and assisting multiyear commitment. Ideally this system would be a combination of some "light touch" central monitoring from the White House, and progressively more decentralized management inside the agency. The responsibility for implementing a sustainable plan should be handed off to the Implementation Unit inside the agency. The White House's role is to ensure the agency has a plan, enough resources to achieve it, a system to ensure it happens, and agreed reporting mechanisms. It can also resolve any interagency disputes, for example, those that arise around which agency will lead the management of shared programs.

The corresponding White House oversight system needs to be characterized by a high degree of involvement in the initial phase of the implementation of management of short-term projects, and lighter involvement on longer-term projects. This system itself requires a well-organized structure and organization. Ideally it is driven by career staff inside the Implementation Unit, who will likely still remain in their roles—and be around to shepherd implementation efforts—beyond the tenure of the administration that started them.

Creating totally new programs is challenging and requires perseverance to embed deep into an agency, all the way down to street-level delivery of services. However, the degree of permanence and impact is often highly correlated with the degree of difficulty in implementation. Programs are difficult to create but once in existence are hard to reverse, and large programs are even harder. So the effort of creating and implementing a new program is difficult but has long-lasting impact—well past the life of the administration.

Agency Reporting Relationships

The role of the chief of staff and the rest of the OPOTUS relative to the relationship between presidents and their cabinet also needs to be clarified. Unlike White House staff, cabinet members should expect to have a direct "solid line" to the president for important issues. The role of the chief of staff is still important, but ultimately it is secondary to the personal and formal relationship the president should have with his or her cabinet members. They are Senate-confirmed, have very broad responsibilities, and hence should have a higher status than White House aides. The chief (and

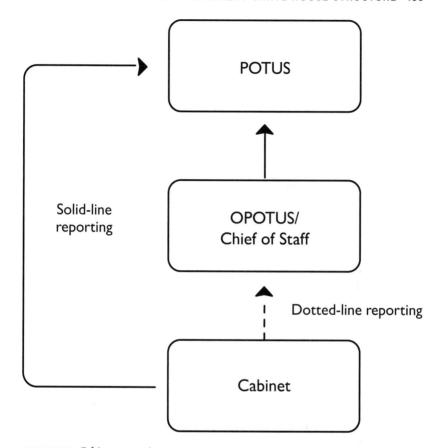

FIGURE 11. Cabinet reporting

where appropriate, the OPOTUS) should stand between the president and the cabinet only for more logistical issues such as scheduling and meeting attendance.

SPOKES OF THE WHEEL REIMAGINED

Early White Houses were managed with something that looked akin to a spokes-of-the-wheel approach, with every one of the small number of staff and all the cabinet reporting to the president. One of the most successful presidents of all, FDR managed this way. However, the concept became unwieldly and eventually made no sense by the 1970s, given how large the entity had grown.

However, ironically, what replaced it, a chief of staff, has some of the same characteristics and the same challenges. In theory, everyone at the White

House (and, to some extent, cabinet members) reports to the chief (although, confusingly, also to the president at the same time). Given the increasing responsibilities of the chief, this burden now also needs to be shared and a different management layer created between presidents and their staff.

With the approach set out in this chapter it is worth reconsidering the spokes-of-the-wheel concept, underpinned by the development of the chief of staff's role into a broader leadership office. This office allows for a significantly greater managerial span of control. For example, assuming all 25 assistants to the president (and to some extent the cabinet) report through the OPOTUS, which consists of, say, 5 to 6 people, each of the resulting number of direct reports becomes very manageable. And the overall system would be run at an operational level by a series of deputy chiefs of staff with clear lines of responsibility.

The resulting structure would allow presidents to reach into the EOP as they like, either directly or through the OPOTUS. Unburdened by the logistics of management and the complication of people issues, they can manage their time and interactions in a way that suits their style and in a very effective manner. They can also be shielded from the incoming distractions that previous incarnations of the spokes-of-the-wheel approach allowed—in particular unchallenged access to their time.

Under this approach, each member of the OPOTUS would have a responsibility for clusters of offices. Those offices in turn would represent the principal White House interface with the outside world. Some are shown in figure 12. The diagram is indicative only; clearly there is some overlap in the relationships that would need to be adjusted in conjunction with the relevant agencies, as they are today. The National Security Council (NSC) would remain the primary White House interface with other countries and multilateral organizations such as NATO. The National Economic Council (NEC) would take that role for most private sector companies and organizations. The Domestic Policy Council (DPC) would cover some relevant private and other sector entities, for example in the health and education sectors. OMB would retain its primary responsibility for interacting with agencies on budget and adding implementation as set out in this chapter. The Office of the General Counsel (GC) would connect as necessary to the external legal system. The Office of Cabinet Affairs (OCA) would manage the day-to-day issues associated with the cabinet. The Office of Intergovernmental Affairs would interface with state and local governments, and in particular governors. The Office of Public Liaison would deal with a number of civil society entities. The press and communications offices would handle media of all forms. The Office of Legislative Affairs, and where appropriate

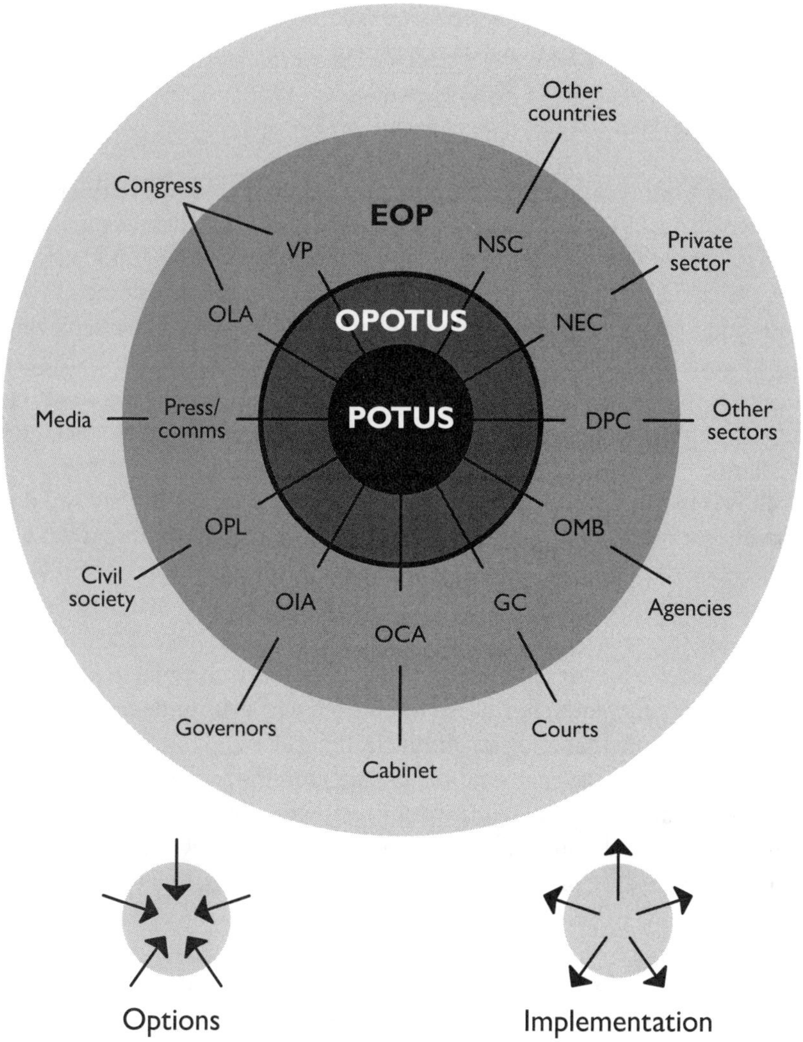

FIGURE 12. Spokes of the wheel—reimagined

the vice president, would have primary responsibility for nonpresidential outreach to Congress. And so on.

The overall management of the spokes of the wheel would follow the core process of presidential decision-making. Policy options would flow inward, and implementation outward. The formal structure would facilitate this flow, supplemented by informal lines of communication from the president or the OPOTUS. As Neustadt suggested, the president can and should remain their own director of central intelligence. They can now be assisted by an institutional structure that makes it possible.

CONCLUSION

Bringing a tighter and more coherent structure to the White House, which is often shaped by presidential idiosyncrasies, precedent, and personal relationships more than anything else, is a challenging proposal. And it's never easy to convince human beings to change how they are accustomed to doing things. But getting the structural element right is crucial for achieving significant impact. Perhaps counterintuitively, a strong focus in Year Zero on what may seem like bureaucratic detail in clarifying and regimenting reporting relationships will significantly free up time for governance, not consume it.

It is important not to confuse clarity with bureaucracy; they are two different concepts. It is possible to bring clarity to an organization so it can operate effectively without making it bureaucratic. The structure set out here seeks the former, not the latter. There is some degree of standardization where appropriate, but the core inner group is totally bespoke. The objective is to be clear to all the members of the White House on which parts of the organization should be flexible to the president's style, and which should look broadly consistent across administrations.

A customizable layer around the president in the form of the OPOTUS will help honor the president's work preferences. Having an EOP that is standardized in its ranks below the most senior level will prevent (or at least minimize) the need for every incoming administration to waste time reinventing the wheel. Focusing greater resources on option generation and implementation will allow the team to do what the public expects them to do—get stuff done. The success of this process depends much on the presence of honest brokers both within the OPOTUS and at the top of the policy councils, who will follow the norms established and conform to the expectations of their offices as laid out in a set of charters. At the top of all of this architecture will sit a president less distracted by process and management issues, and more freed up to achieve legacy impact.

Finally, the president's agenda will benefit from skilled managers making sure ideas and decisions are executed as envisioned. This can be delivered through the concept of dedicated Implementation Units at the White House and the federal agencies. The value-add of having people with management expertise devoted fully to agenda implementation is that policy will become tangible at the "street level" more quickly and comprehensively.

8

TASK FIVE

Plan for the First Two Hundred Days

Start eight months before the inauguration.

Presidential transitions are usually peaceful affairs. Both winning and losing participants are guided by a sense of patriotic duty and a belief in the fairness of the electoral process to concede the results, even in the aftermath of a bitter and hard-fought race. Yet this has not always been the case. The worst example came following the election of Abraham Lincoln in 1860, when a confederacy of states attempted to secede from the Union. In 2000, the electoral result between George W. Bush and Al Gore was so close and controversial that the Supreme Court had to intervene. Democratic politicians such as Hillary Clinton in 2016 and Stacey Abrams in 2018 complained that they had been cheated out of victory.

But the turmoil that surrounded the outcome of the 2020 presidential election, when President Trump refused to concede defeat to Joe Biden, was unprecedented in living memory. Nothing I had done over three decades in the private sector and four years in the White House could have prepared me for the presidential transition of 2020–21. As the White House officer in charge of the transition, I had to develop a plan of action to ensure continuity in government. The same was true of my counterpart in the Biden transition team.

The ascertainment of the election (a technical step that is normally automatic but that was hindered by the president's refusal to concede) was delayed, causing frustration and annoyance in the Biden camp. Our respective transition teams tried to maintain a good working relationship over that period, but it strained what was already a tense situation. After the ascertainment had been obtained, the great majority of staff did their best in what was still a difficult environment, but some people inside the government still refused to cooperate or did the minimum possible. And the events of January 6 raised the tension to a dramatic level. Fortunately, we were able to overcome these obstacles, and as I said on a subsequent podcast, "The institutions of this government have held."[1] But it was an exceptionally challenging time for all.

Although that tumultuous aftermath of the 2020 election is unlikely to repeat itself, it illustrated that a traditionally nonpartisan presidential transition process cannot be taken for granted in the future. The depth of today's political polarization may be a harbinger of future acrimony surrounding an election result. Consequently, many Year Zero tasks, such as designing people and policy pipelines, should be done assuming little to no assistance from an outgoing administration. Ultimately, the period between election and inauguration should be conceived as one of confirmation of priorities and processes, not exploration.

A contested election is just one type of contingency that demands that the Year Zero Leadership Team (YOLT) begin robust planning for the first two hundred days. Foresighted planning for this period will turn ideas into action on the fastest possible timeline.

PLAN FOR A TRANSFORMATIONAL FIRST TWO HUNDRED DAYS

Having determined the overall strategy, core processes, and structure that an administration will deploy, the next task is to combine them into an actual plan. This plan needs to cover three periods, determined in reverse order:

> What can be achieved in the *first two hundred days*?
> How will the *transition* (the time between election and inauguration) be used to produce successes in those two hundred days?
> How will the *preelection* time be planned to ensure an effective transition?

The two-hundred-day time frame is not an arbitrary one. The "First One Hundred Days" is often considered a meaningful window for action in the first year of a presidency, and the media love to assess a president's performance at that point in time. It was President Franklin Roosevelt who helped drive the popularity of this benchmark, passing fifteen major bills through Congress in the first 105 days of his first term in 1933. But two hundred days is a much more sensible period within which a president should be judged in the modern presidency. As my colleagues and I summarized in the *Romney Readiness Project*:

Plan backward:

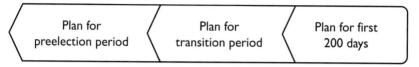

FIGURE 13. Planning for the first two hundred days

Two hundred days was chosen as the appropriate timeframe because it was short enough to force a tight set of actions, but long enough to provide ample runway for execution. A shorter period (100 days) was initially considered and is a time frame often cited in popular culture. However, it was agreed that the inherent difficulty surrounding policy implementation in Washington made 200 days a more realistic target to achieve a narrow but critical set of actions. It also roughly coincides with the August recess of Congress.[2]

The first two hundred days are critical because they set the scene for the following four years. The White House faces an almost infinite set of policy choices. It has the machinery and resources, if well applied, to carry out any of them. But it can't do them all, and if it chooses the wrong ones, or adopts the wrong approach, it risks using up its most valuable resource—time—and weakening the most important tool, the president's power. Presidential power either grows with success or weakens with inability to achieve action. The federal government has a natural inertia, and nothing will happen unless the president makes it happen.

A two-hundred-day plan will catalyze action early and set the tone for his or her entire term of office. It should be a visible part of campaigning. An example of this is President Eisenhower's 1952 campaign speech in which he famously declared, "The first task of a new Administration will be to review and re-examine every course of action open to us with one goal in view: To bring the Korean war to an early and honorable end. . . . That job requires a personal trip to Korea. I shall make that trip. . . . I shall go to Korea."[3] Eisenhower actually made the trip during the transition period, in November 1952, signaling an early commitment to that cause, which he eventually delivered on with the withdrawal of American troops from the Korean Peninsula in 1953.

Having a two-hundred-day plan for the second term is just as important if not more so. In the first term, new presidents have the benefit of fresh legs and high energy around them. They need to resist any tendency to be more measured with the start of the second term, driven by four hard years of governing and a bruising reelection campaign. Bringing in new staff, refreshing core processes, and charging the second-term equivalent of the YOLT with setting ambitious new two-hundred-day plans should be a priority.

Two-Hundred-Day Priorities: Choose Early Battles That Are Meaningful and Winnable

The president's two-hundred-day priorities should be decided in Year Zero, well in advance of the inauguration. Some candidates will feel this is too early to make such an important decision, believing that it will hinder their ability to maneuver politically and even, superstitiously, that it could threaten their chances of succeeding in the election. But if they want to set themselves up for an impactful administration, they need to generate early and sustainable momentum from Day One.

The key person who should determine the initial two-hundred-day priorities is the candidate. He or she needs to choose what they really care about and what they will shape their legacy around. Here they have an opportunity to turn perceived negatives (a public perception of "measuring the drapes") into positives (focused effort on governing). By showing managerial and planning capability, they can showcase exactly the skills needed in the actual job. Just as it has become commonplace for a candidate to say on the campaign trail something along the lines of, "On Day One I will sign an executive order on gun control," they should also say, "On Day One I will introduce to Congress legislation on issue X." The details of the legislation don't need to be disclosed, just the intent and high-level concept, and a demonstration of the ability thereafter to do it.

The YOLT should have an active role in making the decisions around two-hundred-day priorities. They need to gather the information around the choices and be part of the active debate with the candidate about which should be the priority focus. Just as important in deciding what to do is deciding what *not* to do. The list of achievable priorities in the first two hundred days should be realistic, and some campaign promises need to be tabled for Year Two and beyond. The team needs to build capacity for the inevitable unforeseen difficulties and activities that will consume time and resources. The team should avoid and eliminate bottom-up ideas that the president isn't either passionate about or committed to, or that don't have any meaningful long-term impact. They should mandate that no policy priorities can be generated other than those that the presidential candidate initiates. Priorities can change based on circumstance, but that is a decision that only the president and YOLT should make.

Understanding the reality that when everything is a priority, nothing is a priority, a mix of two-hundred-day priorities should ideally fall along the following lines:

one piece of transformational legislation;
executive orders that are lasting and create nonsymbolic policy impact;
one major goal communicated to each agency;
the beginning of a program to produce better citizen services across all agencies; and
more than 3,000 presidential appointments made.

The exact mix of top priorities can vary and reflects the fact that some have more significance than others, and also the president's varying degrees of unilateral control in executing them.

The first two hundred days are a time for bargaining and results, not travel and media, which should be kept to a minimum. The president has just won the election and doesn't need to win it again. Instead, the first two hundred days should prioritize achieving results by dealing with Congress, making decisions on policy issues, managing potential crises, and adjudicating a continuing flow of personnel decisions in order to hit the high target number of presidential personnel appointed in the first two hundred days (discussed in more detail in chapter 10). The filter for deciding which priorities sit inside these categories is, "Fight the battles we can win and avoid the battles we will lose." The first two hundred days are too important to waste time on efforts likely to prove fruitless.

Consider Congressional Makeup

Dealing with Congress should especially occupy the president's time, as the most durable policy achievements are secured through federal legislation. Samuel Kernell has written, "The ideal president is one who seizes the center of the Washington bazaar and actively barters with fellow politicians to build winning coalitions."[4] Robert A. Dahl and Charles E. Lindblom have similarly written, "The politician is, above all, the man whose career depends upon the successful negotiation of bargains. To win office he must negotiate electoral alliances. To satisfy his electoral alliance he must negotiate alliances with outer legislators and with administrators, for his control depends upon negotiation. Most of his time is consumed in bargaining."[5] Given the likelihood of the persistence of divided government and its impact on the scale and ambition of early legislation, the two-hundred-day plan needs to accommodate differing political compositions of Congress. Even if presidents have the benefit of their party controlling both houses, recent electoral margins have been razor-thin. Navigating factions inside a party with a small majority can be as difficult as between parties.

REIMAGINE DAY ONE

A president's inaugural speech on January 20 (Day One) is typically mostly visionary in content, proposing broad themes for future governance with few specifics attached. Consideration should be given to using that address—as large a platform a president will ever enjoy—to launch the first two hundred days in a more tangible fashion. If the planning has been done effectively, Day One could be a signal moment for:

- launching legacy legislation that the president announces and delivers in outline the following day;
- outlining a budget that supports the president's plans, also to be delivered the following day;
- outlining the program and specifics of executive orders, the first of which will be signed that afternoon; and
- outlining the plans and goals for a number of federal agencies, in particular cabinet agencies.

Every element of this program would be the result of Year Zero planning. They would require a more aggressive action plan and considerably more prework in the Year Zero period. The political consequences of boldly launching such a detailed agenda on Day One would of course have to be carefully weighed. Nonetheless, the benefits of rolling out a comprehensive set of specific initiatives are that the president can take advantage of the momentum and goodwill from the election, save precious weeks and months, and signal an active presidency.

PLAN THE TRANSITION PERIOD TO ACHIEVE THE TWO-HUNDRED-DAY PLAN

The transition period (the roughly seventy-five days between election and inauguration) should be mapped out to deliver the two-hundred-day plan. It should consist of the following main components:

how the president-elect's time is to be used;
how the shadow White House is to be built; and
how transition activities should be organized.

The President-elect's Time

The president-elect's time becomes his or her most valuable and con-strained resource the instant he or she is elected president. Each one of the roughly seventy-five days needs to planned out for maximum effectiveness. The days should be separated into meaningful blocks of time sufficient for accomplishing key activities. Here are a few of them:

Choosing key appointees: This is the most important transition activity. Sufficient time needs to be set aside during the transition period for the president-elect to choose the first wave of senior appointees (see chapter 10). This requires not only working through lists of potential candidates but interviewing a number of them in person. It may take more than one inter-view for the president-elect to identify the right candidate for senior White House posts and cabinet secretary positions. Other key roles also require personal presidential attention.

Signing off on Day One through Day Two Hundred policy priorities: The president-elect must now finalize his or her strategy for translating cam-paign promises into action. Assuming the preparatory work for a policy pro-gram has been done well (refer to chapter 9), this is the other major activity, albeit one that should be less time-consuming than choosing appointees. The final plan should mainly be a continuation of work in progress, adapted ac-cording to the latest information, such as the political makeup of Congress.

Responding to a multitude of well-wishers, domestic and foreign lead-ers, etc.: This activity could overwhelm all the others if the president-elect and his or her team lets it, so these engagements must be limited to those of an essential nature. The whole world will want to talk to the president-elect, and the ones critical to the first two-hundred-day agenda are the most important. The others can wait.

Briefings: There is an almost infinite number of topics the president could be briefed on. However, knowledge for knowledge's sake is unnec-essary. Briefings should focus on only those topics that have an associated policy or personnel decision.

Some time off: The candidate has just won the most grueling contest of all and will need some time before the onslaught of actual governing. Every candidate is different in terms of the amount of recharging they need, but some committed down days are essential.

The staff ready to carry out transition activities number more than 500

President-elect

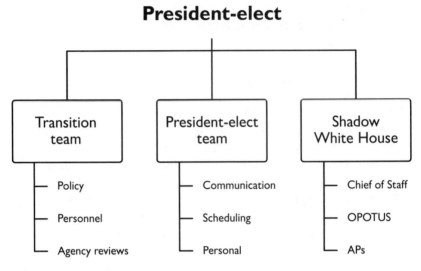

FIGURE 14. Transition organization

before the election and can swell from 500 to 1,000 immediately after it. Coordinating them to create an effective plan for the first two hundred days is a major management challenge. A simplified version of the way to organize is shown in figure 14.

Transition Team

The transition team will primarily oversee the core activities of personnel appointments, policy finalization, and agency reviews. Based on the targets I lay out in chapter 10, approximately 1,500 people need to be appointed by Day One. Assuming the prework has been carried out properly this is possible, but it is a large logistical exercise of finalizing short lists, interviewing, and selecting. The president will need to be involved in the most senior appointments with others delegated to achieve the target. The transition period is also when policy priorities are agreed upon and the prework gets turned into actual documents for Day One rollout. Last, the great bulk of transition staff will be dedicated to carrying out comprehensive agency reviews, again in preparation for effective exercise of control on Day One.

President-elect Support Team

A separate organization within the transition team, the Office of the President-elect, should be established. This organization would manage not only his or her calendar and the activities above but also other potential important though potentially distracting activities such as setting up the White House Residence and syncing with the vice president's schedule.

Building the Shadow White House

While the transition activities are being carried out, the White House itself starts to take shape. This begins with the announcement of the chief of staff, followed by other senior roles. These roles will start to be filled during the transition period as the president-elect or other individuals responsible for personnel sign off on candidates for political appointment. These people then come together in a "shadow White House." Assuming the Year Zero activities have been done, this shadow entity will be putting in place the work already done and getting ready for actual governing. It will start to operate in the same way as the eventual White House, building on the "muscle" created during Year Zero, so that by Day One its inhabitants will already have been tested as a team.

The shadow White House will operate in parallel to the transition team but will eventually supplant it. The transition team will continue activities as described above, but responsibility will progressively shift from the transition team to the shadow White House.

Detailed organization charts for the transition organizations including the president-elect's support are contained in the *Romney Readiness* book.

PLAN FOR CRISES

Former White House counsel and member of the 9/11 Commission Fred Fielding once told Congress that "the time of transition is a time of great vulnerability for our country."[6] Indeed it is: a terrorist attack or a cyberattack on the United States in the transition period, or shortly thereafter, would exploit the absence of Senate-confirmed authorities and the presence of leaders at the White House who are new to their jobs. Similarly, other "black swan" events such as economic crises or natural disasters can quickly overwhelm an administration in its early days unless it is ready to govern. The Year Zero team must develop plans to deal with such emergencies.

Crises can come in two forms: external and self-inflicted. In the latter case, they can be small mistakes that become a larger problem because of the way that they are mishandled. It is inevitable that all candidates and presidents make mistakes; the distinguishing factor in recovering from them is how they are dealt with. Instead of treating the wreckage of Hurricane Katrina as a visible priority, George W. Bush went to Senator McCain's birthday party and then to a commemoration of V-J Day in San Diego. He finally went to one of the affected areas five days after Katrina struck the Gulf Coast. His belated visit was better than nothing, but the delay signaled—unfairly or not—that helping the affected areas wasn't a priority.

Planning for crises during the transition and first two hundred days should be a primary task delegated by a presidential candidate to the Year Zero team and then taken up by the shadow White House. In this case they can borrow from the private sector. The classic example from the private sector of addressing a crisis well comes from 1982. When authorities discovered that multiple people in the Chicago area had been killed by cyanide slipped into Tylenol bottles, Johnson & Johnson pulled all its products off the shelves, urged people not to buy it, and offered refunds for medicine already purchased. This kind of speed and decisiveness continues to win acclaim to this day, and the case is taught in business schools as an example of effective crisis management.

A similar approach can be designed for the White House. This would involve techniques such as getting ahead of the crisis, being brutally honest about the state of play and ongoing effects to customers (citizens) and the company (country), taking responsibility for the narrative swiftly, and addressing and alleviating the issue in a comprehensive manner.

Task forces or similar special purpose entities can be extremely useful in dealing with crises, and their operating model should be designed in advance, even if the topic is unknown. The structure of a charter for a task force can be set out during Year Zero with governing processes embedded in the operating style. Task forces need to be composed of policy, political, and domain (e.g., scientific) experts but be run by operational people. Leaders should weigh expert opinion in their decisions, but experts should not drive decision-making. Broader perspectives are often needed.

Traditionally, during the transition period, the National Security Council (NSC) has held "tabletop" emergency exercises for the incoming administration, but these alone cannot be relied upon. The Year Zero team should use the wide-ranging expertise outside the sitting White House to develop its own plans that are tested well before Election Day.

Plan for a Contested Election

Many see the contested presidential election of 2020 as an aberration. One hopes that this is the case, but it is not a certainty in the polarized world we live in. And it is the second example in twenty years. An abbreviated transition also happened in 2000, albeit for very different reasons.

I commented in an interview with Martha Joynt Kumar on the significantly difficult, but eventually peaceful, 2020 transition: "At 12:01 we had a new president. And nothing happened on January 20th . . . other than what should happen. So, despite all the challenges, the institution held. It held to some extent because of the goodwill of a few people."[7] The presence of that goodwill should not be presumed in contested situations. A losing side may contest a future election even more vigorously, leading to an even more difficult transition. Thus, the guiding principle of the transition planning should be that, regardless of what the law suggests, the incoming administration should assume that they will get little cooperation from the outgoing one. The stakes are too high to assume otherwise, and good scenario planning can overcome a number of the disadvantages of poor cooperation. In other words, *plan for confirmation, not exploration.*

The Biden campaign team did good work in this regard. As David Marchick recounts in his book *The Peaceful Transition of Power:*

> Anticipating the many problems Biden would face, [Ted] Kaufman broke up his team's workflow into two streams: one for conventional problems—appointments, policy, agency reviews, and president-elect support—and another for "unconventional challenges," foreseeing President Trump's future posture as well as pandemic-related logistics issues. What if Trump delayed ascertainment? What if the Biden team could not assess agencies? What if the FBI, the Office of Government Ethics, or the Office of Personnel Management were instructed not to process Biden personnel files? The transition team anticipated each of these problems and developed strategies to mitigate them.[8]

A transition team's planning for a contested election should begin by considering what it can do unilaterally to limit the damage the transition may cause. By focusing on the key people and initiatives that are necessary on Day One and running a shadow White House outside of the mainstream process, an incoming administration can still be fully functional even with no assistance from the outgoing administration.

To a large extent, appointments of key White House staff can still stay in motion during a contested election, albeit without the full security clearances that government access would provide. Outreach to third parties can also commence. Work on policy initiatives (such as legislation and executive orders) can continue, and the finished products can still be ready by Day One. The main downside to a contested election is incoming officials' lack of access to agency briefings, but a well-prepared Year Zero effort can still mitigate this by preparing substantive briefings from external material ahead of time and by hiring a mixture of experienced D.C. operatives, some of whom may have worked in previous administrations. A delay of a few weeks is frustrating but will not inhibit the full functioning of the White House on Day One.

Recommendations for Transition-Related Legislation

I set out below some thoughts on legislation that could assist planning for a contested election. These are outside the control of candidates but are included here for Congress to consider in the context of Year Zero.

The main problems surrounding the 2020 election can be split into two separate categories. The first consists of those concerning the certification of the Electoral College's votes, which is not a focus of this book and is being dealt with by Congress separately, for example, with the passing of the Electoral Count Reform and Presidential Transition Improvement Act in 2022.

The second and parallel set of weaknesses concerns the mechanics of the presidential transition that must happen while election results are being challenged. Two particular issues surrounding the transition process stand out and could be corrected as follows. First, federal law currently calls for the head of the General Services Administration (GSA) to "ascertain" the election results. This ascertainment is normally a pro forma activity that unlocks various resources for the incoming administration such as money and transition teams' access to agencies to start reviews. However, because President Trump contested the 2020 election, the head of the GSA felt she was obliged to delay ascertainment, causing considerable annoyance and frustration for the incoming administration. Ascertainment in the 2020 election was ultimately granted on November 23. This delay also happened in the 2000 election, although with less acrimony, as both parties were contesting the results. Because the head of GSA is a political appointee of the president, a worse situation than what happened in 2020 could arise in the future. An incumbent president who refuses to concede could pressure the GSA head to delay ascertainment even further. Or the president could fire the GSA head committed to ascertainment and substitute him or her with a more pliant official.

One solution would be for the law to be rewritten to trigger a "conditional ascertainment" in the case of a contested election. No political appointee would be able to exercise discretion over that step. The conditional ascertainment would give the incoming administration a series of transition-related rights and privileges (progressively increasing over time) that would allow them to carry out a successful transition to the best possible extent. If for some reason the election was not settled in their favor, they would return all material and be bound by confidentiality on the information given to them. There would be some redundant costs associated with funding two separate transition efforts, but this is a small amount for the country to pay for the "insurance" of a fully functioning government on January 20.

Another issue associated with a contested election is the high degree of overall discretionary cooperation that is in the hands of political appointees right up until inauguration. While the law says that they should cooperate, how they interpret that cooperation is to a large extent up to them, as they continue to run the government until January 20. Congress could address this in the future by establishing an independent entity specifically dedicated to managing the transition between election and inauguration, one that possibly would report to Congress. Civil servants inside the GSA and federal agencies would run the administrative aspects of the transition (as is currently the case), but they would report to the transition entity, not their politically appointed bosses. Political appointees would have no role, unless they volunteered one, and the incoming administration accepted it.

PLAN THE PREELECTION PERIOD TO BUILD THE ORGANIZATION NECESSARY TO TRANSITION

The *Romney Readiness Project 2012* book sets out a detailed playbook of how to run the preelection planning activities. A summary of the main points is set out below in this section.

There are two main phases prior to the election: preconvention and convention-through-election. The preconvention period takes place in the months leading up to the party convention where the candidate is nominated. In this phase, the infrastructure for the successful transition is built—the transition organization is designed, senior transition staff are appointed, a legal entity is set up, and personnel and administrative processes are designed. The convention-through-election phase constitutes roughly the seventy days between a party's convention and the election. Under the 2010 Pre-election Presidential Transition Act, the team can move into government-provided office space and receive GSA-enabled support immediately after the convention. This period is a time of significant growth in transition team staff (in the Romney case, from approximately 20 to more than 500).

Building a Team

The Year Zero team needs to scale to several hundreds of people by the election in time for the transition. As with all presidential campaigns, in the Romney case, even though the candidate eventually lost, the planning had to assume a win in order to be ready to govern. By Election Day there were some 500 people as part of the team. Some of those people were "badged"—having access to government-provided transition space—and officially working on tasks. Others were "virtual"—on standby and ready to be deployed immediately after the election. The successful Biden transition team had a similar number, with at least 500 people working on it on November 10, 2020.[9]

The best transition teams have a balance of operational people to manage the organization and its lightning-fast growth, alongside policy and personnel experts. A balanced top-notch transition team will, just like the White House itself, contain a mixture of D.C. insiders and outsiders. Some people volunteer to serve with a view to it being an audition for a permanent job, and some simply want to contribute to the country for a short period and then go back to their "day job." Individuals in both categories are welcome, but all must understand that a job on the transition team is no guarantee of a job in the administration. The service is welcome but carries with it no rights.

Finding and selecting the best transition staff is an important activity. There are many possible candidates willing to volunteer, but given their access to sensitive information, not everyone is a good fit. The transition planning team needs a personnel expert and a database of possible people to serve in the hundreds of roles that are needed for a successful transition. Organizations are generally supportive of giving people time off to volunteer. So, for example, in the recent Biden transition, employees of organizations such as Harvard University, Brookings Institute, CSIS, and Chan Zuckerberg Foundation served as volunteers.

Organizing the Team

Scaling up a transition team to the requisite size is challenging, to say the least. In the latter stage, dozens of people are being added each week, and each needs direction on what and how to perform. In order to coordinate the team, a well-conceived organizational structure needs to be implemented.

By Election Day, the number of project staff involved on the Romney transition team was as follows:

Department and agency review: 250
Presidential appointments: 124
Policy/legislative/other: 100
President-elect support: 31
   Total: 505

The transition team's leadership organized these teams around deliverables that were clearly outlined for them. Given the very fast ramp up and the short life span of the transition team, the number of people is not as important as the clarity of their responsibilities. For each of the units shown above, we created a "charter" that set out its overall objectives, responsibilities, and deadlines. These were then all compiled in a project management system that tightly managed the overall and individual lines of effort. The actual system used is not critical. What is important is that there is a system that is transparent to all involved and runs in a professional, comprehensive fashion.

Key for any transition team is building an organization capable of processing the huge number of applicants for administration employment. The team's target should be to clear some 1,500 appointments during the transition period. Achieving this high number requires expert planning and management. The first priority is to determine the number of appointments that the president-elect is interested in and capable of being directly involved with. For some positions he or she will want to interview two or three candidates and personally select the finalist. Realistically, during the transition this will cover only 50 to 75 positions, meaning the team can estimate the president will choose roughly one top-level staff member per day. These appointments are likely to be the most important to a functioning White House and those that have the closest connection to the president—assistants to the president in the White House and agency heads. The later section on a people pipeline shows a short list of likely positions that should be the president's main area of focus.

Concerning other positions, the president-elect should be happy to review the selection of approximately another 100 to 150 individuals. The ones where he or she reviews the decision will primarily be decided by the chief of staff or a member of the OPOTUS and are likely to be mostly the other commissioned officers and lower-level positions in the White House.

The great bulk of the other 8,000 appointments will have to be delegated. The head or the associate directors of the transition team's presidential personnel working group will determine most of these selections, receiving some input from the incoming agency heads (to the extent they have been identified). Since it will require months to confirm most agency heads in their roles, they will have to accept that a certain number of their reports will have been primarily chosen by the White House without their consultation in order to ensure a fast start. Speed of impact is the most important factor.

The transition team will also need to review the activities of numerous federal agencies as part of its work, and the resulting agency review teams make up the biggest number of people in the transition organization. In the Romney case, and in most recent actual transitions, they were organized around clusters of agencies with commonality, such as those with economic or national security functions.

Funding the Plan

The transition activities require funding separate from the campaign. The Year Zero team will need to forecast this funding and develop a plan to raise it. The transition entity can be established as a 501(c)4 under the rules of the Presidential Transition Act, allowing it to raise private funds, with a cap of $5,000 per person contributing. Generally, in the past the entity has been set up at or slightly before the time that the candidates have become the presumptive nominee of their party. This timing has varied over recent cycles. George W. Bush, John Kerry, and John McCain became the presumptive nominee in March of the election year, Mitt Romney and Joe Biden in April, Donald Trump in May, and Barack Obama and Hillary Clinton were the latest, in June.

Funding can be considered in three phases and derived from two sources. In the preconvention phase, only modest funds are needed to fund transition planning activities, and private sources can provide them. In the phase between the convention and the election, the campaign will need to expand transition planning activities significantly. Public funds and facilities become available to help do that, supplemented by private contributions. In the postelection phase, federal funding continues, as does private funding, which naturally becomes much easier to raise for a successful candidate.

As with presidential campaigns themselves, funding costs for transitions have increased dramatically in recent cycles. They are still modest in comparison to the campaign but are nevertheless substantial in their own right. Depending on the speed of scaling, the mix of paid and volunteer staff, and the amount of travel required (which can depend on where the transition activities are based), total private funding is likely to total in the $15 to 25 million range. Of this total, indicatively 5 to 10 percent is needed preconvention, 25 to 30 percent between the convention and the election, and the balance of 60 to 65 percent in the transition period itself.

CONCLUSION

The first two hundred days are perhaps the most important period of time in a presidency, with political capital the highest and the chance of passing meaningful policy the greatest. Would-be presidents should therefore use Year Zero to develop aspirational but pragmatic plans for achieving more than has ever been traditionally thought doable in the first two hundred days.

The first two hundred days start with reimagining Day One. Inauguration should be seen not just as a ceremonial celebration but as the first day of action, creating a wave of momentum. Planning then should work backward to ensure everything is ready for a Day One tsunami.

The first two hundred days of a second term are equally rich with opportunity. Rather than consolidate, an administration successful enough to earn reelection should see it as an opportunity to create a massive second wave of action.

Building a shadow White House is also crucial for any first-term presidential transition team, so that the core parts of the White House leadership are effectively already in place weeks ahead of the new president taking office. Assuming reelection, the second transition period can be the time to also make changes, so that Day One of the second term has a reinvigorated team in place that will carry the White House through the next four years.

Crises such as a contested election have the potential to derail smooth transition efforts and should be assumed to be an unfortunate result of the current polarized political environment. But a Year Zero team can still take unilateral steps to mitigate the complications of a contested election process and still be ready to govern on Day One.

9
TASK SIX
Build a Policy Pipeline

Start six months before the inauguration.

"I keep hitting hard because I know this honeymoon won't last. Every day I lose a little more political capital. That's why we have to keep at it, never letting up. One day soon . . . the critics and the snipers will move in and we will be at stalemate. We have to get all we can now, before the roof comes down."[1] So said President Lyndon Johnson to his aide Jack Valenti after the election of 1964. As a master politician, Johnson understood instinctively what is set out in this chapter: Year One is the most important year for passing the president's signature legislation.

The Year Zero team should be charged with building and filling the most important parts of the policy pipeline to achieve milestone victories, including a signature legislative victory in the first two hundred days and the objective of two pieces of legacy legislation in Year One.

Getting the first piece of major legislation passed in the initial two hundred days (i.e., before Congress's August recess) should be the highest priority for an incoming administration (outside of dealing with an unforeseen crisis). This legislative focus should be supplemented with executive orders and a regulatory approach that creates early momentum that in turn should lead to a second piece of significant legislation.

A similar approach should be taken to the first year of the second term. Assuming reelection, the incumbent president has a one-off opportunity in Year Five to cement his or her legacy.

LEGISLATION IS THE MOST IMPORTANT ITEM IN THE PIPELINE

The most significant promises a president makes on the campaign trail require legislation to fulfill. The window for passing legislation is small, and the political calculations leading to midterm elections can overwhelm the legislative calendar after Year One.

Recent practice has been to focus the early days of a presidency on issuing executive orders while slowly developing a legislative program. This approach is seemingly attractive because it leads to immediate activity without the need for congressional approval. Recent presidents (Obama, Trump, and Biden) signed dozens of executive orders in the first two hundred days. However, a proportion of these simply entailed overturning the past administration's equivalent executive orders, or were symbolic, carrying little policy weight. Few will be remembered over time as legacy achievements for the administration. So while executive orders are useful, the early months of the first year should be focused more on legislation, when presidents generally have the highest level of political capital they will enjoy during their presidency.

Assuming the president's party has performed well in the elections, it may also control both houses of Congress, or at least one of them. Even control of just one chamber in the first year will give the president the best chance of passing some legislation, albeit with support from members of the opposition party. All members of the House and a third of the members of the Senate are fresh from what has been for them a successful personal campaign, and they too have the highest reservoir of political capital that they can be expected to enjoy at any time in their terms. To the extent they want to get something done for the country, or for their own legacy, this is the best chance for it to happen.

The honeymoon quickly passes, and by the end of Year One, all House and one-third of Senate legislators turn at least one eye to their reelection in the midterms. As President Johnson said, "You've got to give it all you can that first year. Doesn't matter what kind of majority you come in with. You've got one year when they treat you right and before they start worrying about themselves."[2] In addition, crises can also happen at any time, derailing the best-laid plans. Unless success is achieved early, momentum swings against presidents and their power diminishes.

Incoming presidents should not rely on Congress to produce signature Year One legislation in isolation. They can save several months and significant debate by working with congressional members of their own party to draft proposals in advance of inauguration. The incoming president can and should drive the legislative agenda by immediately urging lawmakers to introduce that legislation and act on it.

HISTORICAL PERFORMANCE OF SIGNATURE YEAR ONE INITIATIVES

If not well planned and executed, Year One can be equally a year of disappointment and frustration. Several presidents have suffered defeats or delay on signature legislative items at the outset of their presidency. Bill Clinton could not get a healthcare bill passed in 1993. The Obama administration, too, spent months drafting and trying to pass the Affordable Care Act before it finally passed in his second year along highly partisan lines. Trump did not lead, but relied on Congress to lead, his initial signature legislation, the attempt to overturn what Republicans dubbed "Obamacare," and Capitol Hill Republicans spent six months trying to get consensus among themselves on the legislation including replacement. While the concept of overturning the Affordable Care Act was popular with Republicans, they lacked a viable alternative program to replace it—something that also could have been determined during the planning period in Year Zero. This process consumed virtually the whole first two-hundred-day window, and they finally gave up in July 2017, depriving the president of any early legacy-level legislative victory.

   In examining recent presidents' track record regarding their Year One legislation, two observations stand out. First, presidents have a poor record in getting legacy legislation passed. That record looks even worse when considering what they've been able to accomplish in the first six months. Clearly a number of laws passed, but when the filter is applied of what is truly major, even recognizing that determination involves a degree of subjectivity, the list becomes very small.

Richard Nixon

President Nixon had no major legislative victories in his first six months despite his knowledge of how to wield power in D.C. His main initial focus was the Vietnam War. His first major domestic legislative initiative, the Family Assistance Plan, was not unveiled until August of Year One and did not pass. He did have some victories, but they were late in Year One. In December, the Tax Reform Act, which increased the standard tax deduction, decreased the top marginal income tax rate and created the alternative minimum tax. He signed the National Environmental Policy Act (NEPA) on New Year's Day 1970, which required executive branch agencies to assess the environmental effects of their proposed actions and was the forerunner to the creation of the Environmental Protection Agency.

TABLE 2. Major legislation passed in Year One of recent presidencies

	First six months	Second six months
Nixon	—	Tax reform NEPA
Carter	—	—
Reagan	—	Tax reform Spending reform
George H. W. Bush	—	S&L relief
Clinton	—	Tax reform NAFTA
George W. Bush	Tax reform	Education reform Patriot Act
Obama	Economic relief	—
Trump	—	Tax reform
Biden	COVID-19 relief	Infrastructure investment

Jimmy Carter

President Carter passed several pieces of legislation in Year One, but few would be considered legacy. The Emergency Natural Gas Act in February gave Carter the authority to transfer surplus natural gas to shortage areas. The Reorganization Act in April gave him authority to create the Office of Personnel Management and the Federal Labor Relations Authority, but he abandoned the effort to create a Department of Natural Resources. A later act established the Department of Energy. Carter also rescinded federal funding for nineteen dams and water projects but ultimately was overridden by Congress in the appropriations process, creating lasting ill will between the two branches. A watered-down version of his signature energy bill was eventually passed in October of Year Two.

Ronald Reagan

President Reagan passed two major pieces of legislation in his first year, but neither until the middle of the first year. The Economic Recovery Act signed in August included a major cut in taxes. It built on an approach of the previous Republicans in Congress, which had been blocked by President Carter. The Omnibus Budget Reconciliation Act, signed at the same time, was the government spending side of his economic plan; it increased defense spending, offset by cutting a number of benefits programs. It ended a Carter-era public jobs program and cut many means-tested programs such as food stamps. In May, Reagan sent a letter to congressional leaders calling for Social Security reform, an initiative that was rejected.

George H. W. Bush

President Bush did not introduce any significant legislation in his first twelve months, other than a relief bill in response to the Savings and Loan (S&L) Crisis. His main focus was international affairs.

Bill Clinton

President Clinton passed the Family and Medical Leave Act (which had been vetoed twice by President Bush) in February 1993, which granted unpaid leave for qualified medical and family reasons. The Omnibus Budget Reconciliation Act was the first major reconciliation bill passed on party lines, and it increased taxes on personal and corporate incomes, increased the gas tax, and expanded the Earned Income Tax Credit. Clinton secured enactment of the Brady Bill ban on assault weapons in November. He also signed the North American Free Trade Agreement (NAFTA) in December 1992, which had been substantially negotiated during the Bush administration. On the failure side, Clinton proposed a financial package for inner-city programs that didn't pass the Senate, and he invested a lot of time and political capital in healthcare reform, which was unsuccessful.

George W. Bush

President Bush passed the Economic Growth and Tax Relief Reconciliation Act in June 2001, which was a $1.35 trillion (over ten years) tax cut that included rebates, a reduction in income tax, and cuts to capital gains and estate taxes. After the 9/11 terrorist attack, Bush signed the Patriot Act on October 26, 2001. The No Child Left Behind Act was passed right at the end of Year One in January 2002 and made federal funding conditional on students achieving measurable classroom achievement goals.

Barack Obama

President Obama passed the American Recovery and Reinvestment Act in February 2009, a $787 billion stimulus package in response to the financial crisis. In April he passed the Children's Health Insurance Program Reauthorization Act (which had been vetoed twice by Bush), expanding the program. Despite his large majority in Congress, he didn't pass anything else of major substance in the first year, with most of the focus centered on healthcare reform. This effort led to his signature achievement of the Affordable Care Act, but that took until Year Two to pass. In addition, the American Clean Energy and Security Act, which promoted cap-and-trade, was passed by the House in June of his first year but was never taken up by the Senate.

Donald Trump

President Trump's first major legislative initiative was the attempt to pass healthcare reform. The American Health Care Act passed the House in May but failed in the Senate in July. He was more successful with the Tax Cuts and Jobs Act, which included significant tax cuts, but that took until December 2017 to pass and required a reconciliation bill passed on party lines.

Joe Biden

President Biden passed the American Rescue Plan in March, an emergency package to mitigate economic damage from COVID-19. It was largely taken from the Health and Economic Recovery Omnibus Emergency Solutions Act introduced by congressional Democrats during the Trump administration in May 2020. He then passed the Infrastructure Investment and Jobs Act in November, which had originally proposed $2.2 trillion in new spending coupled with $1.75 trillion in tax increases. What eventually passed was a still-significant package of $550 billion in new spending. Build Back Better was initially proposed as a $3.85 trillion bill. The eventual Inflation Reduction Act ultimately passed in August of his second year.

Observations

Several observations stand out from the list above:

1. The list of accomplishments is modest for the world's most powerful government. Much of what was passed was important but secondary, and only a few have had sustainable long-term impact.
2. Most of the legislation was passed in the middle or late part of the first year. Very little was accomplished in the early months.

3. What has passed early has been mainly in response to a crisis (energy, financial, pandemic) or relates to legislation passed by Congress but vetoed by a previous president, making it already "prebaked."
4. The other main Year One legislative victories have been tax-related. Generally, these have been time-limited or impacted by changes from subsequent administrations.
5. Major healthcare reform has been a hill too steep to climb for several presidents.
6. A focus on international affairs distracted from the ability to pass legacy domestic legislation.

A similar analysis of Year Five of an administration (Year One of the second term) shows an even thinner list of legacy legislation passed. The second-term presidents Nixon, Reagan, Clinton, George W. Bush, and Obama passed few significant pieces of major legislation in their fifth year. Ironically, perhaps one of the most historic pieces was the War Powers Resolution in 1973, which was passed by Congress over a Nixon veto.

Preelection Approach

Presidents in the future can should aim to achieve better results by having draft legislation ready to present immediately. That, of course, is no guarantee of success, but it accelerates the timetable at a critical time—the early months when the president's situational power is likely at its strongest.

It also requires an act of bravery on the candidate's behalf. Being willing to publicly declare a first two-hundred-day legislative priority has some political risks but a lot of upside and should be sold as a positive by the candidate. Showing the degree of work going into preparing early legislation should be marketed to voters as a demonstration of competence and intelligent preparation. Also, the risks inherent in being transparent should be low if the legislation is truly signature, as it should be consistent with a central plank of the campaign. Assuming a number of citizens are voting based on that plank, they should welcome the demonstration of its likely implementation.

Conversely, trying to do too much or starting with the wrong priorities endangers the best chance to lock in a legacy achievement. Realistically, a president cannot expect to pass more than two pieces of transformational legislation in Year One, but two should be the target—one in the first two hundred days and one in the second half of the year.

The Year Zero team should decide on the legislative priority for the first two hundred days and begin building the necessary coalitions for successful passage. As with the current practice of executive orders, external think tanks and policy groups can be invited to help shape some of the drafting.

Additionally, candidates can stick to broad themes and principles without committing themselves to details. For example, on the Romney campaign, we captured the candidate's commitments in a document called "General Instructions—First 200 Days." It served as a guiding document for the policy teams working on the two-hundred-day plan and was split into broad themes such as "Revitalize the American Economy" and "Restore American Leadership."[3] These themes were then turned into a set of more detailed policy recommendations.

Adjusting to Year One Congress

The legislative approach also needs to be adaptable to the congressional structure. In the last fifty years, the president has mostly faced a divided Congress and has only had a filibuster-proof majority in the Senate twice. Presidents may campaign on transformative agendas, but their Year Zero team must consider scenarios that include bipartisan compromise to achieve an early victory and momentum. As the old saying goes, "Politicians campaign in poetry and govern in prose."

A deeper look into the historical makeup of Congress reveals an interesting trend. Figure 15 shows all the presidents since Roosevelt, and the Year One political composition of Congress. Three categories are offered:

Neither House nor Senate was controlled by the president's party.
There was a split—one controlled by the president's party, one by the other.
Both were controlled by the president's party.

Three distinct phases are apparent. In the first phase, all the presidents from Roosevelt to Johnson had in their first year the benefit of both chambers being controlled by their parties, and often with enough of a majority in the Senate to overcome the filibuster.

In the second phase, from the presidencies of Richard Nixon through George H. W. Bush, all presidents other than Democrat Jimmy Carter began with the president's party either controlling no chamber or controlling just one house of Congress in the first year.

Then, in the most recent phase (since the Clinton presidency), presidential terms have begun with the president's party controlling both houses of Congress in the first year. The reasons for these trends are manifold but mainly center around an enduring Democratic majority in the House from

	Neither	Split	Both	
Roosevelt			X	
Truman			X	
Eisenhower			X	I
Kennedy			X	
Johnson			X	
Nixon	X			
Ford	X			
Carter			X	II
Reagan		X		
H. W. Bush	X			
Clinton			X	
Bush			X	
Obama			X	III
Trump			X	
Biden			X	

FIGURE 15. First-Year Congress in modern presidencies

1954 to 1994; thereafter, contributing factors are the realignment of seats in southern states from Democratic to Republican control and, more recently, the level of a candidate's visibility in the media during the election helping with "coattail" voting.

Given the recent trend of achieving party alignment in Congress and the White House in the first year of a presidency, there might be a natural inclination to try to pass partisan legislation first, but this is very challenging. Although the president's party may control both chambers, the margins have become progressively smaller. The average first-year margin for Presidents Roosevelt and Kennedy was (by today's standards) an incredible 141 seats in the House and 25 seats in the Senate. Presidents Carter and Obama had a smaller but still-impressive average of 57 seats in the House and 10 in the Senate. By comparison, the most recent presidents, Trump and Biden, averaged just 13 seats in the House and 1 in the Senate.

Both Presidents George W. Bush and Biden had a fifty-fifty Senate, with the vice president casting the deciding vote when needed. Those presidents needed to lose just one vote to lose the majority—and this is exactly what happened to both. In May 2001, Senator Jim Jeffords of Vermont declared himself an independent and started caucusing with the Democrats as a protest to the Bush tax cut legislation. In 2021, Senator Joe Manchin of West Virginia, a Democrat, opposed Biden's Build Back Better legislation. Similarly, presidents facing small majorities in the House are even more susceptible to the presence of factions within parties derailing legislative efforts as a result of partisan politics.

George W. Bush was the first since Benjamin Harrison in 1888 to win the presidency with fewer votes than his rival candidate. Donald Trump repeated that in 2016. President Clinton was elected with just 43 percent of the vote, assisted to the presidency by the involvement of the independent candidate Ross Perot. A win at the Electoral College is still a win, but situational power relies to some extent on the strength of the public mandate.

Trying to pass purely party-line legislation in the first six months can result in a legislative quagmire. To the extent there is any hope of a major piece of president-proposed legislation securing bipartisan agreement, then the initial two-hundred-day period is the time to achieve it. Passing bipartisan legislation will generate some goodwill in an otherwise divided Congress, and early success of any kind builds power and momentum. Bipartisan legislation is also less likely to be challenged in court and more likely to succeed even if it is.

There are policy areas in which bipartisan legislation is possible even in the challenging environment in D.C. Having an industrial policy to compete with China, rebuilding the country's infrastructure, promoting the creation of middle-class jobs, and enacting comprehensive immigration reform all have some potential for progress as of this writing. This potential exists either because there are overlapping interests (e.g., industrial policy) or because each party wants their aspect of the policy implemented so strongly as to accept the addition of the other party's priorities (e.g., immigration reform). The No Child Left Behind Act of 2001 was successful because it gave both parties something they wanted—Republicans supported it because of mandatory student testing, and Democrats favored it because of increased education spending.

Achieving progress in this area will require compromise and all the president's skills and input. Politics has been described as the "art of the possible"—and presidents' ability to understand what is possible within the context they operate is critical. As George Edwards has noted, "Even those presidents who appeared to dominate Congress were actually facilitators rather than directors of change. They quite explicitly took advantage of opportunities in their environments and, working at the margins, successfully guided legislation through Congress."[4] To this end, not every desirable item must be included in a legislative package. Presidents can remember that other opportunities will exist to achieve subsidiary policy goals. To quote President Reagan, "Take seventy or eighty percent and then come back another day for the other twenty or thirty percent."[5]

Assuming the president can get one piece of signature legislation passed, the second piece of legacy legislation in Year One can either be bipartisan or more party-centric, depending on the context at the time and the power the president has accumulated (or lost) by then. It is also the time to consider using budget reconciliation as a tool. Reconciliation is a special procedure that overrules the filibuster, so certain legislation only requires fifty-plus votes in the Senate. However, a bill passed through reconciliation still requires a favorable majority in both houses, is limited to bills that have a revenue component, and can generally only be used once a year. It is a useful vehicle but not a silver bullet for all legislative priorities.

Dealing with Congress

Filling the legislative pipeline during Years Zero and One entails more than just proposing draft legislation—it involves a preelection and postelection strategy for dealing with Congress. Outreach should begin in Year Zero prior to the election with preliminary discussions with the members of the candidate's party on the campaign's priorities and how they will be fitted into a legislative calendar. Especially important will be identifying legislative allies who may be willing to introduce the future president's legislation in Congress, since presidents have no power of their own to do that. As the Year Zero team moves into the formal period of transition after the election, they can collaborate with members of an incoming Congress on the fine-tuning of drafted bills, planning the calendar, and clearing roadblocks.

As history has shown, some of the few pieces of early successful legislation are ones that have been passed by a previous Congress but vetoed by the previous president. The Year Zero team should work with Congress as early as possible to shape the legislative calendar of the incumbent Congress to draft and introduce bills even if they face a veto. This can save weeks of legislative time ironing out some of the major contentious details.

The administration needs a strategy for engagement with virtually all the 435 House and 100 Senate members, not just the party leaders. Such broad engagement recognizes the current reality of factions within each party. Clearly it is not realistic for the president to do all the outreach, so initially the Year Zero Leadership Team (Y0LT), and then the OPOTUS, needs to supplement and lead the work of legislative engagement. The strategy should only deploy the president for the most important discussions.

Draft signature legislation prepared as part of Year Zero efforts should be introduced as soon as practical after the inauguration. Negotiating with Congress and passing it should then be the president's number-one priority from Day One, unless there is a crisis. Everything else, in particular the ceremonial parts of the job, should be subservient to this goal. The early weeks and months are the time for the presidents to show they can deliver significant action, not just activity.

The time between commencement of the new Congress and the inauguration of the president represents a particular opportunity. By January 20, the new Congress will have been in session for almost three weeks (one result of changes brought in by the Twentieth Amendment is that they begin January 3). January 20 may be Day One for the president, but it is Congress's Day Eighteen, so they should have ironed out many of their own transition issues, be available for preliminary discussions with the president-elect before the inauguration, and be ready for legislative action thereafter.

EXECUTIVE ACTIONS ARE STILL IMPORTANT IN BUILDING EARLY MOMENTUM

While legislation should be the priority vehicle for securing achievements in Year One, executive actions (including executive orders, presidential memoranda, and presidential proclamations) are also useful during that time. But substance and longevity should be the determining filter for their issuance. Large numbers of ceremonial executive actions are a poor use of time and effort and distract the administration from its key results. Only a certain amount of policy can flow through the pipeline.

Some focus can be on overturning executive orders passed in the previous administration that are contrary to the current one's policy goals. However, this seldom advances the agenda significantly and is likely to result in a similar tit-for-tat when the next administration from the other party takes office.

New executive orders should be signed with the knowledge and expectation that a future administration is likely to overturn them. The so-called Mexico City policy was implemented by the Reagan administration to restrict federal funding to family planning clinics that provided abortion counseling or referrals. It was rescinded by President Clinton, reinstated by President George W. Bush, rescinded again by President Obama, reinstated by President Trump, and most recently rescinded yet again by President Biden. These actions were some of the first of each of the administrations, all occurring in January.

So, a reasonable question to ask is whether the impact of an executive order will be large enough and long enough to justify devoting precious resources and time. In simple terms, the executive orders that should be signed are those that score highly on the following simple formula: *Impact = speed of implementation × significance × likely longevity.* The administration's focus should therefore be on developing EOs that

- can be implemented very quickly, so there is a minimum of three years of impact, and/or
- have significant short-term impact; and/or
- have significant scale; and/or
- are bipartisan enough to likely be carried over by future administrations; and/or
- have little risk of being overturned legally; *and*
- in all cases have a well-developed plan, timetable, and dedicated resources to implement.

All first two-hundred-day executive orders should be predrafted and ready for implementation by Day One and then rolled out progressively along a well-orchestrated plan. They will still be subject to final legal clearance, but if the Year Zero work has been done well, these steps should be short and any hurdles manageable. Drafting tactics such as being concise, citing statutory authority in the preamble, avoiding novel concepts, and copying excerpts from executive orders previously approved by the Justice Department's Office of Legal Counsel (OLC) can lead to faster approval. Also structuring the executive orders to limit standing of groups likely to contest an order lowers the litigation risk.

When it comes to executive orders, less is more. Avoiding controversial orders initially can make sense so that bandwidth isn't taken up defending them and distracting the team from the more important legislation. Donald Trump's first executive order was a controversial and poorly drafted travel ban that opponents instantly challenged in court. Bill Clinton's ban on gays in the military distracted him from other agenda items. An administration will also have to prepare for the reality that executive orders are complicated and time-consuming, especially if they require any significant agency action. The fewer the number of executive orders, the more time there is to pursue other agency goals. Experts knowledgeable in the parts of government responsible for executing on an executive order should do a comprehensive review in Year Zero of their implementation plans. The organization of the Year Zero planning requires having these people recruited and on the team.

Executive orders whose primary purpose is as a messaging document should also be avoided in the first two hundred days, not because they take up agency time but because they use up scarce resources such as the policy councils or OLC review time. The OLC is very responsive but has limited bandwidth and has proved to be a bottleneck to overly ambitious numbers of executive orders.

The executive orders need to be approved both individually and collectively. Though different areas of the policy team will generate executive orders, the YOLT should consider the extent of overlap and decide which are the most worth doing. If one executive order can be implemented, but another one competes for the same resources, they crowd each other out, and neither gets implemented properly. That is the definition of ineffectiveness.

The president's role in the executive order process should be minimal, with his or her time saved for campaigning before the election and for legislation after it. He or she should have agreed on the main executive action priorities during Year Zero, and it is up to the YOLT initially and then the OPOTUS to deliver the product and oversee its implementation. The president could and should make any final decisions on issues that have arisen in the course of an order's drafting and agency and legal review, but that (plus the actual signing of the order and immediate "selling" to the extent appropriate) should be the extent of his or her involvement. If the executive orders have been chosen well, the impact for most of them should start to come through very quickly, meaning they can form one of the core planks of the president's Year Two strategy.

Executive orders in the second term take a slightly different approach. Clearly there is no need to spend any time on reversing any previous administration's executive orders, and the great bulk of the current administration's priorities should have already been carried out. For these reasons there should be even more emphasis on legislation in Year Five, with executive orders very targeted on niche issues or building on the policy momentum of those already passed.

Role of Think Tanks in Shaping Policy

External think tanks and specially created entities (normally structured as 501[c]4s) have in the past been very useful in creating executive orders and other policy ideas for campaigns. This is likely to continue and in fact should be encouraged: there are financial restrictions on what can be contributed to transition entities, but there are no restrictions on ideas. External entities (either long-established or recently set up for special purposes) have substantial resources, policy and other forms of expertise, and are one step removed from the candidate and the campaign, so they provide plausible deniability for products that land the campaign in hot water.

Both parties have been assisted in the past by outside entities contributing ideas and content on executive orders and other policy ideas. As far back as 1980, the Heritage Foundation produced their first "mandate for leadership" containing multiple policy proposals for reform. This was an influential document that President Reagan supposedly distributed at his first cabinet meeting. Heritage has consistently launched similar efforts aimed at presidential campaigns and at the time of writing has a major initiative for the 2024 cycle involving dozens of policy experts and previous administration officials. Special-purpose entities such as the America First Policy Institute have substantial transition-related activities, including generating proposed executive orders and lists of potential appointees. Similar efforts have existed on the Democratic Party side.

There are bipartisan entities, as well. Around the time of the 2000 election, historian and presidential expert Martha Kumar produced a series of essays that helped the Bush campaign during their abbreviated transition. This effort led to the bipartisan White House Transition Project, which produces high-quality research for the benefit of both parties.

Dealing with the Courts

Year Zero efforts should entail a comprehensive legal review of all pipeline policy ideas. As David A. Yalof has written, "the judiciary can so often make or break a president's policy agenda."[6] It is fruitless to begin work on policies that have little chance of withstanding legal challenges. Early executive orders must be strongly legally defensible—not just for the sake of securing policy victories but for building political momentum. The courts can derail or significantly slow down an administration's policy initiatives, taking the air out of a president's political balloon. For example, the Trump administration's rushed travel ban executive order was overturned in court and needed to be rewritten several times.

In addition to the White House Counsel's office, the Justice Department's Office of Legal Counsel (OLC), which was created in 1934, plays an essential role in evaluating government policy documents such as executive orders. They should be involved as early as possible and be a strong voice before any policy document is issued. If more billets can be created for staff in the OLC or the White House Counsel's office, that will help expedite the time-consuming legal review process.

Executive Agreements

Executive agreements (agreements made between the United States and one or more other countries) will roll out on a slower schedule than executive orders. Nevertheless, identifying which ones should take priority can be determined before Day One, along with a plan for early diplomatic engagement with the targeted countries. If executive orders are mostly a focus of activity in the first half of Year One, then executive agreements can be a focus of the second half. As with executive orders, the amount of presidential time committed should be minimal—a meeting and signing event with a foreign head of state should suffice. Staff should negotiate the terms, and any executive agreements that require significant negotiations at the head-of-state level should be left for Year Two onward.

Utilizing Old Laws

Laws seldom have an expiry date, so they remain available indefinitely. The Year Zero team should also look for old laws that allow new action, such as how the Trump administration used Section 232 of the Trade Expansion Act of 1962 and Section 301 of the Trade Act of 1974 to impose tariffs out of national security concerns.

The president enjoys considerable powers in the case of a legally defined national emergency. Before the 1976 National Emergencies Act (NEA), the president's powers to act during a national emergency were reflected in a patchwork of laws that allowed him to carry out a variety of actions, including the ability to seize property; control production, transportation, and communication; and institute martial law.

The passing of the NEA was an attempt to bring all of the powers together under one authority. President Ford stated that its purpose was to "reform the existing maze of statutes which [had] resulted from the states of emergency under which the country [had] been operating for over 40 years."[7] While the NEA produced a more orderly approach, it still gave the president considerable latitude to declare an emergency, and powers to use once it was declared. Most of the declared national emergencies since at least the late 1980s have concerned economic sanctions on American adversaries. Other national emergencies have been declared regarding export control regulations, arms control measures, and, in the case of President Trump, border security. A Brennan Center report released in December 2018 identifies 136 statutory powers at the president's disposal in a self-declared national emergency.[8]

Other acts that give the president extraordinary powers include the Defense Production Act of 1950 and the Stafford Act of 1988. The latter concerns disaster relief, whereas the former was implemented during the Korean War as a means of compelling private companies to adapt their business to meet the government's wartime needs. However, the Defense Production Act has been also used by recent presidents (Obama, Trump, and Biden) in nondefense emergency situations, most notably by President Trump to compel private companies to prioritize federal orders for medical supplies during the COVID-19 pandemic. President Biden also invoked it in April 2022 to add lithium, nickel, graphite, cobalt, and manganese to the list of items deemed critical for national defense, thus hoping to better secure a supply of critical minerals essential for the production of large-capacity batteries.

In cases where Congress is unhappy with the president's usage of an old statute, it can change the original legislation. However, given the state of polarization in Congress that modern presidents generally face, rewriting laws, even old ones, is now very difficult to do in anything other than exceptional circumstances.

THE POLICY PIPELINE SHOULD ENCOMPASS AGENCY ACTIONS

Year Zero planning should encompass what agencies can contribute as the delivery arm of many policy initiatives.

Every executive branch agency should have at most three goals defined by the president to be accomplished over the four-year administration period. Achievement of any more than three meaningful and long-lasting goals is unrealistic because of the difficulty of effecting change inside agencies, aligning the goals with the civil service, and ensuring there is a proper implementation plan. The goals can be new initiatives, but they must be realistic. To the extent that they require congressional support or funding, they need to be supported by a plan to achieve that. In some contexts that will require the goals to be bipartisan in nature. There should be two parts to the agency strategy: early regulatory initiatives, and long-term improvement of citizen services. In both cases, goals for the agency should be set during Year Zero, and the president should agree to them. That should be his or her only significant contribution, other than picking the people to execute the strategy.

An agency's secretary and other presidential appointees should be selected according to their personal alignment around those goals and be measured against nothing else except achieving them. They need to be passionate and expert about them, and be willing to fight through bureaucratic inertia, reasoning as to why goals cannot be achieved, delays in work processes, and other opponents of goal achievement. This is the perseverance and single-mindedness necessary to achieve change inside the agencies. White House support and bandwidth are limited, and it will be mainly up to agency leaders to deliver results.

Early Regulatory Initiatives

An approach similar to what is recommended regarding executive orders can be taken with respect to early regulatory initiatives. Proposed regulations can be drafted by outside entities, with a view toward a fast start by introducing them during the first two hundred days.

The Year Zero team should outline their policy goals and ask a selected group of think tanks and other knowledgeable bodies for all regulatory suggestions. It would then collate them for consideration during the transition period and then agree to a final set. The Year Zero team would also draft accompanying executive orders that the president would sign on Day One, directing the relevant agencies to take the draft regulations and publish them as proposed rules. The rules would still go through the normal regulatory process—including public comment and OIRA clearance—but this approach would significantly accelerate their adoption, cutting months out of the process, and minimizing agency inertia.

Early Senate-confirmed appointees and beachhead staff—in tandem with the agency and OMB Implementation Units—would be charged with ensuring that the process set out in the executive order was carried out (i.e., that the regulatory process is initiated speedily). This would be a major part of the beachhead team's responsibility in the first two hundred days.

One benefit of beginning the initiatives in Year Zero is that a wave of regulatory (or deregulatory) action can be introduced across the federal government. The size of the wave would collectively be massive, but per agency it will only amount to a manageable one or two. The White House decision-making process need not be a bottleneck, as all the prework has been done as part of Year Zero. However, as part of the work on the people pipeline, OIRA needs to be satisfactorily staffed to ensure that the resulting significant number of regulations can be processed after the review and comment period during Year One.

The regulatory initiatives strategy should also encompass stopping or, to the extent possible, overturning rules that are left over from the previous administration that are contrary to the incoming administration's policy framework. The Congressional Review Act (CRA) allows Congress to overturn regulations imposed in the previous sixty days, and federal law mandates a sixty-day delay for "major rules" before they take effect. An incoming administration can overturn late administration rules, in particular the "midnight" rules introduced at the last minute by the outgoing administration.

Long-Term Improvement of Citizen Services (Don't Fight the Administrative State—Make It Better)

Tens, and in some cases, hundreds of millions of Americans rely on the government for a multitude of basic services ranging from useful to life critical—whether it be Social Security payments, Medicare and Medicaid, veterans' health services, capital and advice to small businesses, student loans, Pell grants, research funding, air traffic control, providing weather information, nutrition assistance, farm assistance, access to national parks, or the vast regulatory framework that governs everyday life. Every citizen has at least one and in most cases multiple touch points with government. Therefore, the president should request that every citizen-facing agency have a goal of significantly improving its ability to deliver citizen services.

Presidential administrations have increasingly neglected to undertake major efforts to improve delivery of citizen services, either because the benefits of a short-term effort are believed to accrue to future administrations or because the task of making federal government processes more efficient is believed to be too burdensome. To the extent that improving delivery is tried at all, it is normally assigned a low priority relative to more visible executive actions. This approach is self-defeating. Without serious commitment or resources, any initiative of its kind is doomed to underperform.

If a president is ambitious enough to undertake reforms intended to boost the effectiveness of government in delivering citizen services, support from the civil service workforce inside federal agencies will be key. Unfortunately, virtually every president has viewed the civil service as a barrier to the implementation of his policies. President Carter said, "Before I became President, I realized and I was warned that dealing with the federal bureaucracy would be one of the worst problems I would have to face. It has been even worse than I had anticipated."[9]

Clearly there is significant inertia, and in any large organization there are bad actors. But some evidence suggests there is hope that positive change can be achieved—most civil servants are, in the words of John Brehm and Scott Gates, "principled agents."[10] Providing better citizen services is the reason that the most altruistic members of the federal workforce come to work every day. As the public policy scholar James Q. Wilson wrote, "What is surprising is not that bureaucrats sometimes can defy the president, but that they support his programs as much as they do. The reason is simple . . . bureaucrats want to do the right thing."[11] I take the optimistic, albeit realistic view of what can be done: my personal experience in the White House in dealing with career staff was generally extremely positive. For example, Mary Gibert, who served as the transition coordinator from the General Services Administration, was a consummate professional and very effectively carried out her duties in the 2020–21 transition under incredibly difficult circumstances. Other civil servants whom I dealt with in the initiatives such as the quest to modernize technology platforms were generally responsive, even if somewhat cautious.

Regardless of whether incoming presidents believe that the career staff are aligned with their agenda, it is in the presidents' interests to find a way to get the best from them. Presidents can help facilitate this by ensuring that the goals set for citizen services are aligned with the agency's core mission and apolitical to the greatest extent possible. Their program should not run directly counter to an agency's interests—the concept of "principled agent" only goes so far, and an agency has a high level of independence in the political system, despite being under presidential control. Asking an agency to do something it is not designed to do or will not do by virtue of the need to protect its own interests is a battle that the White House will lose unless it focuses huge energy and resources toward it. There is approximately a 100:1 ratio of civil servants to political appointees at every agency. They are focused exclusively on issues of importance to them, and they have direct relationships with Congress.

Delivering on initiatives designed to achieve major change through any federal agency will require a systematic approach spanning all four years. It is extremely hard to eliminate existing programs and start new ones (doing so always requires an expanded agency budget), so the focus should be on making existing lines of effort better. The White House's role should be limited, setting improvements in delivery of citizen services as a key agency goal, selecting political appointees who will execute on that improvement, and providing some central resource to help.

Presidents should include funding requests for each agency to achieve citizen services improvement as part of their initial budget request. The planning for this budgeting should be done as part of the Year Zero activities, and the amounts represented as an increase in the agency budget. Citizen services are largely bipartisan, and presidents should use some of their initial political capital to sell to Congress the benefits of improving programs. Congress can fund them from Year Two onward (that being the year that the initial federal budget will apply to), with the detailed planning done in Year One by the agency.

One example of an important area for improvement that could have bipartisan support is upgrading government technology. The federal government spends more than $100 billion per year on information technology, but most of it is years, or even decades, out of date. The upgrade of this technology has languished as a priority because of the lack of perceived political benefit but also because initiating changes in technology platforms is a cumbersome, time-consuming, and arduous ordeal. However, new advances in technology implementation such as cloud computing now mean that processes such as replacing legacy systems can be done in a much shorter time frame and at lower cost. Other advances, such as artificial intelligence, can be used to improve the government by combing through the vast regulatory maze to find conflicting or redundant regulations. A properly prioritized approach to upgrading internal technology systems, carried out alongside a parallel improvement of citizen-facing services, will lead to better delivery and financial savings.

These may seem like small victories compared to the higher-profile political fights in D.C. Collectively, however, they represent one of the biggest and most accessible opportunities available to any president. Well-executed plans of improvement in citizen services, established as Day One agency priorities, can deliver significant results within a president's four-year term. These real and tangible successes can then become part of the president's reelection campaign. If he or she can win reelection and continue the program, it can deliver meaningful change to the lives of ordinary citizens over eight years. This will be one of his or her most significant legacies.

CHANGE THE BUDGET FROM A "WISH LIST" TO ACTUAL PROPOSALS BACKED BY LEGISLATION

During the eighteenth and nineteenth centuries, Congress was the sole determinant of the federal budget. The few agencies that existed dealt directly and individually with Congress. The president's role was to accept and implement the budget, but he had little influence on its formulation. With the increasing size and complexity of the federal government, Congress found it progressively harder to manage this disaggregated approach. So, in 1921 Congress created the Bureau of the Budget (BOB) inside the Department of the Treasury with the purpose of creating and submitting a consolidated budget for the executive branch. Though Congress placed BOB in the Treasury so that it was still somewhat under their control, this also gave the president more of an opportunity to influence budget formulation. President Franklin Roosevelt moved BOB into the Executive Office of the President (EOP) in 1939 as part of a general reorganization but also to gain greater and more direct control over its output. Over time, BOB built up a professional staff and had a large informational advantage relative to the appropriations committees that received its output, and for several decades the president's budget submission drove the budget discussion. Congress nullified some of that advantage with the creation of the Congressional Budget Office in 1974, which returned more budgetary power to Capitol Hill.

Since the 1970s the budget process has become increasingly dysfunctional. Because of increasingly divergent views, Congress has not passed a budget on time (before the start of the fiscal year) since 1996. Often, there has been no budget passed at all, forcing the government to run on a series of continuing resolutions (that is, a continuation of the previous year's budget). The years 2013, 2018, and 2019 saw brief government shutdowns because of budget standoffs. While the president can propose a budget to Congress, and has every year, the submission has become increasingly irrelevant to the final yearly outlay of federal funds and is now more of a messaging document for communicating the president's policy (and political) priorities.

The president's power over the budget is also increasingly limited because of the growing percentage of federal outlays that have been committed to mandatory programs. Programs such as Medicare, Medicaid, and Social Security are automatically funded every year by statute, and the president has no power to change the funding levels. In addition, federal debt levels have risen dramatically in recent decades under all presidents due to large and persistent deficits. The resulting debt servicing in the form of interest payments is therefore taking up an increasingly greater share of the federal budget.

Only a relatively small part of the budget—about 30 percent—is subject to negotiation between the president and Congress.[12] And even then, defense, which makes up roughly half of that total, is virtually non-negotiable. So roughly 15 percent of the total budget is the subject of real debate.

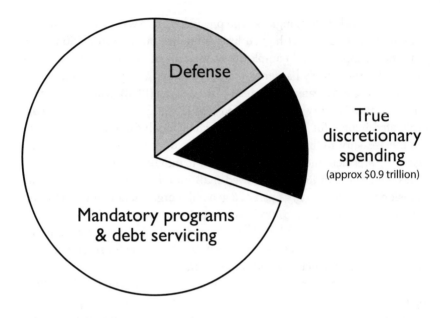

Total = $6.2 trillion

FIGURE 16. Discretionary spending
Source: Budget of the United States Government, Fiscal Year 2023, https://www.govinfo
.gov.

A budget corresponding to the policy pipeline reflecting available funding should be constructed during Year Zero. Typically, a president's initial
budget submission is due in mid-February, but all recent presidents have
missed that deadline. The last several presidents have chosen to present
a first-year document indicative of their priorities in mid-February with a
detailed budget following some months later (April or May). The approach
recommended here is that the budget submission should not only meet the
deadline but significantly exceed it. It should be submitted on Day One.
The Year Zero team can rely on a number of information sources to shape
the product, such as the previous year's presidential budget, Congressional
Budget Office publications, and the University of Pennsylvania's Budget
Model analysis tools. It should be possible to create a well-formed budget
even without OMB help well in advance of Election Day. For confidentiality,
multiple scenarios can be run against different policy settings to mask the
final actual budget.

The budget submitted should also avoid being a messaging document, full of a "wish list" of ideas, few of which will ever make it to the final appropriation given the constraints set out above. It should be targeted to support the specific policy initiatives that are intended to be introduced in Year One. The incoming administration's budget should be extremely focused on a small number of requests, letting the rest of the congressional budgeting process take its own course.

CONCLUSION

Any president is elected because voters are expecting him or her to enact a certain set of policies. Four years may seem like an ample amount of time for a president to deliver on what he or she promised, but crises, shifting priorities, midterm elections, and oppositional political forces compress the practical windows of opportunity.

Future presidents and their teams should therefore begin designing a policy program in Year Zero that can be implemented starting on Day One of the presidency. Pronouncements are not the priority. What is required are substantive, well-prepared pieces of legislation, executive orders, and agency actions with a targeted supporting budget.

The approach to the first year of the second term should be similar. This will be the best possible time to pass significant legacy legislation, and more targeted executive orders.

Year Zero is the time to make substantial progress on the work of drafting legislation, executive actions, coordinating with Congress, creating plans to improve the delivery of citizen services, and hammering out a budget that is more than a messaging exercise. These efforts will help secure significantly more achievements in the first years of both terms, thereby burnishing the president's political power and setting the platform for a legacy. In keeping with the philosophy of the Five-Year Presidency, presidential candidates should be willing (and in fact welcome the opportunity) to showcase their policy pipeline, in particular the legislation that will be introduced on Day One.

10
TASK SEVEN
Build a People Pipeline

Start six months before the inauguration.

John F. Kennedy observed, "I spent so much time getting to know people who could help me get elected that I didn't have time to get to know people who could help me, after I was elected, to be a good President."[1]

Few activities attract more attention in the early days of an administration than decisions on who is appointed to what role. Media and political insiders speculate on the candidates, and presidents-elect such as Donald Trump take advantage of the interest to make the appointments news events in their own right. Behind the theater is the much more substantive issue—picking the right people. The determinants of successful appointments can be set out well before the administration starts and can be structured to maximize the positive impact, and minimize the risks inherent in Kennedy's observation.

The job during Year Zero is to build the machinery capable of selecting thousands of the right people. The level of ambition to fill roles—especially those that do not require Senate confirmation—should be significantly higher than in the past. This is a herculean task. With this in mind, the Year Zero Leadership Team (YOLT) should contain, or appoint as one of their first hires, a head of personnel. This person will play a critical role in creating a pipeline of qualified candidates.

Presidents should carefully consider how they decide on the people who serve them, as they can substantially impact the success of their administration. Personnel choices carry asymmetric risk to the downside. Few people are individually critical to the success of an administration, but any one bad appointment can result in disproportionate problems. As President Carter found with Bert Lance, President Clinton with Zoe Baird, and President Trump with Michael Flynn, an early personnel scandal can consume energy and blunt the policy agenda.

UNDERSTAND THE APPOINTMENTS UNIVERSE

Between both full-time and part-time positions, presidents can appoint some 8,000 people to their administration. This is a large number but also needs to be seen in the context of the size of the U.S. federal workforce—about 4 million people including civilian and military personnel combined, plus several more million contractors. Political appointees thus represent only significantly less than 1 percent of federal employees, but, if chosen correctly, they exert a disproportionate influence as the most senior policymakers.

Of the 8,000 political appointees, approximately 1,000 require Senate confirmation to assume their posts. This is an increasingly arduous and lengthy process for the nominee. However, there are 7,000 who aren't subject to confirmation—that is, they are employed totally at the discretion of the president. Traditionally, the transition team does some preparatory work on these appointments before the election, but formal selection, background vetting, and security checks only really begin in earnest afterward, and they, too, must wait a lengthy time to begin work in their designated positions. A well-organized Year Zero team should aim to accelerate the process in order to get a significant proportion of these positions filled by Day Two Hundred, with the most important of them by Day One.

Because White House staff shape the initial agenda more than agency appointments and do not require Senate confirmation, they should be the personnel group the administration prioritizes. Cabinet secretaries and their top reports require Senate confirmation, and except for a few critical roles (secretary of state or treasury) their confirmation has progressively become a political pawn in a game of chess with the Senate. Year Zero planning should identify quality permanent candidates for all the roles but should also work on contingency plans for the event that those needed to steer the agency ship will not be in place for several months or, in some cases, more than a year.

Categories of Appointments

The first task for the Year Zero team is to identify all the positions that a president can fill, and by category. This is surprisingly challenging given several factors. Some categories (e.g., judges) depend on retirements for an appointment to become open. Other offices (e.g., White House Office commissioned staff) are governed by a budget limit, not a personnel limit, so the number of appointments will be determined by the total amount of staff salaries. Categorization can also be confusing because it is a matrix of a number of factors, such as whether a position is a fixed term or not, full-time or part-time, Senate-confirmed or not.

Presidential appointees (PAs) do not require Senate confirmation (they serve entirely at the discretion of the president, subject only to limits such as budgetary constraints or overall number by category). Presidential appointees with Senate confirmation (PASs), are, as the name suggests, nominated by the president but require Senate confirmation.

The president nominates all the senior and a number of junior staff in the White House. They are all PAs. They are supported by career staff such as Secret Service and military staff who carry over from administration to administration.

The Executive Office of the President (EOP) is the White House plus offices such as the Office of Management and Budget (OMB) and Office of Science and Technology Policy (OSTP). These latter offices are quite large and carry a mixture of PAS, PA, and career staff.

Agencies' most senior staff are PASs, the next levels are PAs, and thereafter the great bulk of people are career.

The White House, EOP, and agency roles are generally all full-time.

Boards and commissions are semi-autonomous entities where the president nominates just the directors. These roles are a mixture of PASs and PAs. Most of them are part-time. Some of these have extensive commitments and influence (e.g., the Board of the Federal Reserve); some are more ceremonial, albeit still prestigious (e.g., the Kennedy Center for Performing Arts).

List of Presidential Appointees

The following list sets out the various appointee totals by category with an explanation of each (they are also shown diagrammatically in figure 17):

White House
Commissioned officers occupy the most senior roles. These consist of approximately 25 assistants to the president, 25 deputy assistants to the president, and 50 to 75 special assistants to the president. All of these highly sought-after appointments receive a formal commission signed by the president and a title of "Honorable." There are approximately 600 more junior policy and support staff.

Agencies
The most senior roles (secretary, deputy secretary, general counsel, etc.) are Senate-confirmable and total some 800. Senior Executive Service (SES) officials are the next-most-senior group serving in agencies. They were created

as part of the Civil Reform Act of 1978 under President Jimmy Carter. They are intended to be a group of general-purpose high-performance leaders who can serve as a bridge between the top presidential appointees and the civil service. They number approximately 8,000 across the whole government, and 10 percent can be political appointees.

Schedule C appointees are the next (and lowest) level of political appointments. They must report to another political appointee and can range from relatively senior policy to more junior administrative staff. Their number is approximately 1,400, but this can vary considerably from administration to administration. "Beachhead" staff serve in temporary positions while the full-time positions are progressively filled.

Other Full-Time Roles

Other full-time roles eligible for presidential appointments are mainly ambassadorships and judgeships. There are almost 200 U.S. ambassadors. Of those, approximately one-third are political appointees, with the rest being career Foreign Service Officers. The countries that they are appointed to range from large (England, France, China) to small (Bahamas, Fiji). In some cases, appointees serve as ambassadors to organizations, not countries (the United Nations, the Organisation for Economic Co-operation and Development [OECD], the European Union). The politically appointed ambassadorships are highly sought after and generally are given to strong political or financial supporters of the president. They are subject to Senate confirmation, which can be very lengthy, given that confirming ambassadors is often a low priority in the great mix of Senate business. In the Biden administration, for example, there were still about forty ambassadors not confirmed as of March 31, 2023.

Judges for the Supreme Court, Appeals Courts, and District Courts all need to be appointed by the president and confirmed by the Senate. There are approximately 870 Article III judges (9 Supreme, 179 Appeals, 673 District, and 9 on the Court of International Trade). The number appointed in any one administration depends on vacancies caused mainly by promotion, retirement, or death, and typically can be up to 100 each year.

Other appointed roles that fall into a separate subcategory include U.S. Marshals, non–Article III judges, and appointments to international organizations.

Part-Time Roles

Advisory boards and commissions are large in number and vast in scope. Examples are the President's Council of Advisors on Science and Technology

Presidential appointments

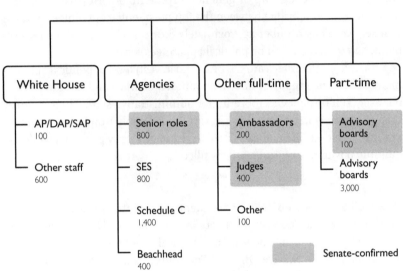

FIGURE 17. Presidential appointments

(PCAST), the President's Intelligence Advisory Board (PIAB), and the President's Commission on White House Fellowships. They are headed by people appointed mainly to part-time roles. They are generally appointed for a fixed term, so the number appointed in any period depends on the timing of the end of a previous term. The Biden administration called for all Trump nominees to resign regardless of whether or not their term had expired, so that caused a greater than normal number to be available.

BUILD A PIPELINE WITH AMBITIOUS TARGETS

The YOLT should design an overall appointments strategy, by category and time frame. The highest priority should be the commissioned officers and most of their direct staff in the White House. The great bulk of these appointments should be made during the transition period so that the White House is fully functioning at near-ideal staff levels on Day One. All remaining positions in the White House should be filled by the end of Day Two Hundred.

The senior roles in other offices of the EOP, such as OMB director or U.S. trade representative, require Senate confirmation, as do senior staff at federal agencies. The individuals holding these offices will require some time to be confirmed, given the logistics and politics of confirmation. Only the most senior are likely to be confirmed in the transition period or shortly thereafter, and a modest number beyond that in the first two hundred days. Most appointments will stretch out over the first two years, and potentially even longer. Given that slow schedule, the other EOP and agency roles are very important and should be filled as quickly as possible. These people can be in an "acting" capacity until the Senate-confirmed positions are filled. In addition, leveraging the beachhead positions, a concept explained below, can allow an administration to start its policy implementation immediately, without the delay associated with Senate confirmation.

Other part-time roles are not a priority and should be filled as necessary when resources can be freed up. Given their nature, a separate team should focus on them and have a constant approach to filling roles rather than a big push in the early months.

Table 3 shows a possible breakdown for the prioritization and timing of political appointments, by type. There are a number of roles that are the most critical to appoint during the transition period. These should be ranked by their importance to the president's agenda. Table 4 offers a possible list of the positions most necessary to have a functional White House and administration on Day One.

BUILD A PEOPLE STRATEGY FOR THE EXECUTIVE OFFICE OF THE PRESIDENT

During the transition, some 500 roles need to be filled at the White House and other EOP offices. Of these the senior commissioned officers (assistants to the president [APs] and deputy assistants to the president [DAPs]) are the most important and should be filled first. The president should take a personal interest in all the roughly 25 APs who will be his or her central advisory and implementation group. They should be chosen to fit the needs set out in the charters of the offices they will hold. It is a case of choosing "horses for courses," not choosing Thoroughbreds and then modifying the offices to suit them. The lessons of previous administrations, such as choosing a balance of D.C. insiders and newcomers, should be heeded.

DAPs should be mainly chosen by the OPOTUS with some input from the APs that they report to. This is the opposite of the approach that some administrations follow, where APs can choose and bring along their own staff. They should have an input, and in extreme circumstances a veto, but the OPOTUS is building an organization capable of delivering on the Year One agenda, not trying to optimize for APs' desires.

Below the DAP level, the OPOTUS in combination with the head of personnel should choose and appoint staff. Again, there should be input

TABLE 3. Timing of presidential appointments

Category	Type of appointees	Transition period	First 200 days	Thereafter	Total
White House					
Commissioned officers	PA	70	30	—	100
Other appointed staff	PA	430	170	—	600
Agencies					
Senior roles	PAS	10	150	640	800
SES	PA	390	300	110	800
Schedule C	PA	200	750	450	1,400
"Beachhead"	PA	400	—	—	400
Other full-time					
Ambassadors	PAS	—	20	180	200
Judges	PAS/PA	—	50	350	400
Other	PA	—	30	70	100
Subtotal full-time		1,500	1,500	1,800	4,800
Part-time					
Advisory boards	PAS	—	—	100	100
	PA	—	300	2,700	3,000
Subtotal part-time			300	2,800	3,100
Total		1,500	1,800	4,600	7,900

PA = presidential appointees
PAS = presidential appointees with Senate confirmation

but not control from APs and DAPs that lead the offices they will work in. Given the volume of roles that need to be filled, there will have to be a well-oiled appointment machine, and timely decisions made to ensure a fully functioning White House on Day One.

Of the other EOP offices, OMB is the most important, given its role in early policy and regulatory initiatives. Senate-confirmed positions such as the director, the deputy directors, and the head of the Office of Information and Regulatory Affairs (OIRA) should be high on the confirmation schedule. Non-Senate-confirmed appointments such as the 5 or more program associate directors (PADs) are critical to have on Day One. These often-overlooked roles should be given to high-performance individuals who will drive the early agenda in agencies. They should be supported by the creation and filling of a new role, the head of the Implementation Unit.

The second term is an excellent time to do a refresh of the senior staff

TABLE 4. Indicative top appointments

Wave 1a Top 25 priority White House/EOP roles	Wave 1b Top 25 priority Senate-confirmed roles
Chief of Staff*	Secretary of State[†]
Senior Adviser to the President*	Secretary of Treasury[†]
Counselor to the President*	Secretary of Homeland Security[†]
White House Counsel*	Attorney General[†]
National Security Adviser*	CIA Director[†]
Deputy National Security Adviser	Director of National Intelligence[†]
Presidential Personnel Director	OMB Director[†]
Director of National Economic Council	Secretary of Veterans Affairs[†]
Director of Domestic Policy Council	Secretary of HHS[†]
Staff Secretary	U.S. Trade Representative[†]
Press Secretary	Secretary of Energy[†]
Deputy Chief of Staff for Policy	Secretary of Commerce[†]
Deputy Chief of Staff for Operations	Secretary of Transportation[†]
Deputy Chief of Staff for Implementation	Secretary of Agriculture[†]
Deputy Chief of Staff for Communication	Ambassador to the United Nations[†]
Legislative Affairs Director	FEMA Administrator
Deputy Legislative Affairs Director—House	Council of Economic Adviser Chair
Deputy Legislative Affairs Director—Senate	OMB Deputy Director of Budget
Chief of Staff to the Vice President	OMB Deputy Director of Management
Chief of Staff to the First Lady	OIRA Administrator
OMB Program Associate Directors (×5)	Agency Deputy Secretaries (×5, subject to policy priorities)

*Possible OPOTUS member
[†]Cabinet-level appointment

of the White House. One hopes that by having a good OPOTUS structure and White House culture, most commissioned officers will have served the whole four years of the first term. But years in the White House can be like decades elsewhere, and there is a trade-off between experience and energy. Presidents, assisted by the OPOTUS, should do a complete review of the senior staff and make some hard choices. The same approach applies to cabinet members. The OPOTUS itself will need some turnover, although given its role, this should be managed in a more gradual fashion.

BUILD A PEOPLE STRATEGY TO RUN THE AGENCIES

The Senate is taking progressively longer to confirm nominees. In President Biden's first year, it took on average 103 days to confirm a nominee, almost three times the 36 days it took for a President Reagan appointee. This is not an anomaly for President Biden—the performance has been getting worse with every president.

The slow pace of Senate confirmations means that only a fraction of the individuals nominated to Senate-confirmable positions are in fact confirmed in the first year: around 15 percent of the roles by Day Two Hundred, around one-third of the roles by the end of the first year, and still only around two-thirds of the roles by the end of the second year. Furthermore, if the nominees are not confirmed by the end of the Senate session (essentially the end of the calendar year), the nominations get returned to the president. The Senate can allow nominations to carry over, but that requires a unanimous consent motion, so a controversial nominee may require resubmitting by the president, causing the process to start over again.

Every election cycle there is a call for a better and faster process. For example, the Partnership for Public Service has suggested converting a number of noncritical Senate-confirmed positions to nonconfirmed presidential appointments (i.e., eliminating the need for the Senate to use up its valuable time) and other technical process enhancements such as improving flow of "privileged nominations," many of which are part-time positions for boards and commissions, allowing them to bypass not just committees but floor time.

These calls are important and should be pursued, but given the polarized nature of Congress and the Senate's "advise and consent" role as provided for under the Constitution, giving up control is unlikely to happen, and Year Zero planning should not anticipate changes in the process. Therefore, the YOLT should have a plan that assumes that only a small proportion of the positions will be filled. The plan should have two parts: first, to maximize what confirmation capacity there is available and utilize it for the highest-value nominees, and, second, a parallel plan to run the agencies without many of the Senate-confirmable positions filled.

Maximize Confirmation Capacity

The Year Zero personnel team should perform detailed analysis to identify which Senate-confirmable positions are the most important in light of the administration's policy priorities. These may not necessarily be the most high-profile positions but, rather, the ones that are key to maximum impact. The initial focus of administration confirmation efforts is typically on cabinet secretaries and their core reports. In the most recent cycle, approximately 50 percent of the earliest PAS positions were located within the 15 cabinet agencies. However, there may be noncabinet roles within the EOP that are in fact more critical to the president's agenda than some cabinet secretaries. It is conceivable that the deputy director of OMB matters much more than the secretary of housing and urban development or the secretary of labor, depending on the policy agenda.

To increase confirmation capacity, the YOLT can encourage the Senate to expand resources for the initial waves of nominees. Procedural ideas, such as limiting time for debate on nominees, or expanding the number of workdays in the Senate calendar in the first two hundred days of a presidential year, should also be explored. It may be possible to batch clusters of PAS appointments for a single agency as part of the negotiations with the Senate. This is more likely in the politically important agencies such as defense, veterans' affairs, and intelligence-related agencies.

In all cases, the administration needs to incentivize the Senate to explore these ideas, especially if the Senate is controlled by the other party. One incentive is that until a president installs a Senate-confirmed nominee in a role, temporary political appointees with no Senate input are in charge. Also, the administration could consider negotiating with the Senate on the mix and sequencing of presidential appointments versus judges. The administration cares more about PAS appointments than judges in the first year. Judges are important but have a longer-term impact. Conversely, Senate members can care enormously about judges, and in particular federal circuit court of appeals judges from their states.

The Year Zero team should also focus on Senate-confirmed national security positions. The Intelligence Reform and Terrorism Prevention Act recommended that the Senate vote within thirty days on any national security positions nominated by an incoming administration by Inauguration Day. Few administrations have taken advantage of this imperative. The Partnership for Public Service found, "The administrations of Presidents Barack Obama, Donald Trump and Joe Biden were not able to nominate even half of top security positions needing Senate confirmation by the time they took office." They went on to note, "The issue does not center on the top-ranked, most visible positions. In fact, Cabinet secretaries and agency director positions are often nominated and confirmed on or near Day One of a new administration, demonstrating the confirmation process can work quickly. It is the other crucial levels of leadership—such as deputy secretaries and undersecretaries—that often take much longer to get through the nomination and confirmation process. Yet the 2004 law explicitly acknowledged the importance of roles beyond the Cabinet as it suggested new presidents nominate officials for roles 'through the level of undersecretary in cabinet departments.'"[2] This suggests that the issue is more on the campaign side, and hence a significant future Year Zero opportunity.

Running the Agencies without Senate-Confirmed Positions

The Year Zero team needs to ensure that each cabinet member has both a personnel plan that conforms to top presidential policy priorities and a realistic confirmation schedule. This means that several of them will have to accept having fewer core confirmed staff than they might hope for or expect.

Running the agencies without many Senate-confirmed officials can be mostly achieved through a combination of appointing "beachhead teams" and a fast start with Senior Executive Service (SES) and Schedule C appointments, none of which require confirmation. The incoming administration should be realistic about how much these skeleton teams can achieve in the first two hundred days, but the Year Zero team can still set goals and ensure alignment with the administration's plan. Issuing executive orders and draft regulations should be coordinated with the appointment of the beachhead teams to give them each a two-hundred-day plan of their own.

The beachhead concept was one that we developed during the Romney transition planning. President Trump later took up the concept and deployed more than 500 people in the beachhead program.

The term "beachhead" evokes the first wave of soldiers disembarking a troop transport to storm an enemy-held beach, à la the U.S. invasion force on D-Day—perhaps a little provocative for what is normally a peaceful activity. Beachhead staffers are those who have some level of preclearance to start on Day One of an administration and thus allow the administration to start its policy implementation immediately. They are appointed under Temporary Transition Schedule C authority for up to 120 days, although agencies can extend that for another 120. This action ensures that beachhead staffers can be in their jobs past the two-hundred-day mark, by which time it can be hoped that some of the Senate-confirmed positions will be filled. Beachhead team members can serve in other permanent positions after their beachhead service, sometimes in the same agency.

Additional flexibility can be achieved where the incoming administration plans for and places nominees for Senate-confirmed positions in temporary SES jobs while they wait for the Senate to vote on their nominations. They cannot serve in the positions for which they were nominated but can serve in an advisory role and offer input on agency policies and programs.

An administration should initially focus on appointments of SES and

Schedule C roles that have a general management or oversight aspect to them, for example, a chief of staff or White House liaison. Filling the "principal deputy" at an agency with a beachhead/SES appointee can cover the responsibilities left open while the Senate-confirmed senior positions are awaiting appointment. In the swirl of transition from one administration to another, they are there to ensure that agency actions are consistent with administration policy, in particular any priorities determined in Year Zero such as new regulations initiated through the policy pipeline.

FILLING THE PIPELINE

Attracting Possible Employees

The Year Zero team should put little effort into identifying and attracting possible appointees before the party's conventions. Other than being an unnecessary distraction, it will also be difficult to get many people interested when there are still multiple possible nominees. Think tanks such as the Heritage Foundation are increasingly compiling lists of names well ahead of even the primary elections for any candidate to consider. The Year Zero team can rely on these efforts to start the initial flow into the pipeline if the candidate becomes the party's nominee. The YOLT's most necessary work before the convention should be to properly staff the personnel part of the transition team.

There is also no shortage of applicants for key positions after the final candidate from each party is confirmed at their respective conventions. A system should be set up inside the transition, or in conjunction with external entities, for all prospective candidates to fill in all their government required disclosure forms, get tax and legal advice on their personal situations, and do induction training before the election.

Consistent with the Five-Year Presidency philosophy, attracting people should be carried out earlier, more comprehensively, and more visibly. Given the ambitious targets set out for the number of appointments in the first two hundred days, the candidate and campaign should actively encourage people interested in working for the administration to start their personal paperwork process as soon as possible after the convention. Filling in the ethics forms is time-consuming and a necessity if people want to serve. Also, the divestment requirements are onerous, and many possible candidates drop out after they realize the financial hit they will have to take to serve the country. It is better to find that out early than to go down the track and have them pull out at the last moment.

No commitments, however, should be made to individuals preelection regarding an appointment—applying and getting the paperwork started should simply be a gate they need to go through in order to be considered for the early roles (which are generally the most sought after and important).

After the election there is generally a flood of applications, and the challenge is more in dealing with the volume through the pipeline, not filling it. The Year Zero team needs to have designed an effective mechanism for wading through applications and making all the appointments. There will always be some candidates who only want to join the process after the election, when they see the winner, but they should be conscious that this might put them at a timing disadvantage.

The Year Zero team focused on personnel can usefully act as a buffer for the president, who receives an avalanche of job requests from all quarters. President Carter noted that "the constant press of making lesser appointments was a real headache. . . . I would be inundated with recommendations from every conceivable source. Cabinet Officers, members of Congress, governors and other officials, my key political supporters around the nation, family and friends, would all rush forward with proposals and fight to the last minute for their candidates."[3] In order to perform this incredibly valuable role of selecting the best candidates, the selection team itself needs a system for filtering, one that the president can trust to handle requested favors with "fairness."

Training

Recognizing that incoming political appointees face unique challenges and requirements coming into federal service, the Presidential Transition Act allows GSA to expend $1 million of federal funds allocated for training new appointees. The Year Zero appointments team should plan the best way of utilizing this funding, including working with outside groups that have developed programs for new appointees.

Training that can be outsourced to outside groups should cover areas such as

overview of the federal government;
ethics rules, including issues such as required divestments;
the budget process; and
filling in statutory forms.

Training that can be more customized by the Year Zero team includes

the White House decision-making process;
how to input into policy;

how to implement decisions;
the role of honest broker versus advocate;
crisis management; and
cultural expectations.

Training incoming appointees is crucial to an effective administration. Building a strong culture of performance requires not just role modeling from the top but also induction and training. Other more technical skills can be fine-tuned as well. For example, anyone who wishes to play a role as an honest broker needs to be trained in how to run large meetings effectively. Running a good meeting that brings out the best in people is an art form in its own right, and surprisingly few people are good at it. While this may sound trivial, it is exceptionally important for making sure the best policy options are generated for complicated decisions. Meeting organizers also need to know how to control attendance. There is a trade-off between size and impact, and to the extent possible, all nonessential people should be excluded from meetings. Navigating the politics of who is invited and who isn't is difficult, and it is a key part of the honest broker's role.

Dealing with Campaign Staff

There should be a separate unit established in the Year Zero team to focus on the placement of campaign staff. Someone who has strong credibility among the campaign leadership should lead this unit. The creation of this unit will substantially decrease the potential tension between the campaign and governance teams, especially as the election comes closer. A perennial issue in transition phases is the penchant for campaign staff to worry that the planning staff are not recognizing the substantial commitment and efforts they have made on behalf of the candidate and are giving out jobs to newcomers instead of them. The mandate of the unit should be to ensure that every member of the campaign who wishes to work inside the administration has the opportunity to do so, subject to professional suitability and a background check. Most of them will likely find jobs inside federal agencies as Schedule C or SES appointees, which are important midlevel roles. Many of these roles need to be filled early in the administration.

Hiring from the Private Sector

Administrations should be creative in determining how to hire more people from the private sector. It is difficult for agencies to fill high-impact roles, especially when they are competing with the private sector for talented individuals. One way of addressing the logistical and budgetary constraints associated with creating new billets would be to utilize short-term programs populated with hires from the private sector, people with technical, operational, and project management skills. Agency teams could be a hybrid of external "hired guns" and internal senior civil servants.

Such an arrangement—part of a new national emphasis on public service that a candidate can promote during Year Zero—would allow people to come in on temporary "tours of duty" to work inside the government, focused on solving specific problems. This approach has been successfully used by the United States Digital Services (USDS), to name one entity. The USDS was created during the Obama presidency as a reaction to the Obamacare website issues. It created a cadre of tech experts able to be dedicated to high-value projects and was successful enough to continue to be supported by the subsequent Trump and Biden administrations.

The USDS experience has shown there are many people who are willing to serve their country by giving some of their time—as long as the projects they participate in are well-structured, supported by the agency concerned, and lead to real impact. To eliminate the barrier to public service that many high-achieving people must hurdle, the temporary staffers could retain their private sector compensation, as long as they only work on areas that do not conflict with their employer's priorities.

Doing research on additional legal authorities that an administration could use to import more private sector talent and use it as part of the personnel strategy is a valuable Year Zero activity. Some additional means that are worth exploring (in all cases subject to ensuring there are no issues such as conflicts of interest) are as follows:

Special government employees (SGEs): Since 1962, federal law has allowed for special government employees—defined as "an officer or employee . . . who is retained, designated, appointed, or employed by the government to perform temporary duties, with or without compensation, for not more than 130 days during any period of 365 consecutive days."[4] Granting an individual SGE status allows the federal government to make use of his or her technical expertise, often in niche areas of technical skills or policy knowledge. The Office of Government Ethics has stated that "SGEs were originally conceived as a 'hybrid' class, in recognition of the fact that the simple categories of 'employee' and 'non-employee' are no longer adequate to describe the multiplicity of ways in which modern government gets its work done."[5]

The National Defense Authorization Act of 2017 was amended in 2018 to add a Public-Private Talent Exchange (PPTE). This program allows for the temporary assignment of an employee to a private sector organization, or from such private sector organization to a Department of Defense (DoD) organization, for a period of up to six months. In 2022 the Office of the Director of National Intelligence introduced a PPTE of its own. More federal agencies could explore standing up their own PPTE programs.

The Intergovernmental Personnel Act Mobility Program, like the SGE designation, allows agencies to bring in outside expertise. According to the Office of Personnel Management (OPM), the program "provides for the temporary assignment of personnel between the Federal Government and state and local governments, colleges and universities, Indian tribal governments, federally funded research and development centers, and other eligible organizations."[6] OPM notes, "Agencies do not take full advantage of the IPA program which, if used strategically, can help agencies meet their needs for 'hard-to-fill' positions such as Information Technology."[7]

CHOOSE PEOPLE FOR GOAL ALIGNMENT FIRST, EXPERTISE SECOND, LOYALTY THIRD

A well-functioning personnel team should begin to vet top-level candidates in a systematic and comprehensive way during Year Zero. More than just the vetting of qualifications, which can be delegated to junior staff, the senior members of the team can focus on creating a vetting rubric that reflects the president's priorities as well as the White House architecture.

A traditional approach to building a White House staff often emphasizes loyalty as the primary selection criterion. That quality is clearly important but should not be the primary determinant of an individual's fitness for service. It is hard to find 8,000 people truly loyal to the president, and loyalty is difficult to test and measure. Sustaining that loyalty such that it trumps individual agendas and the pressure from other constituencies is also extremely difficult. Some of the worst presidential mistakes, such as the Iran-Contra scandal, have arisen because of overenthusiastic loyalists carrying out what they "thought the president wanted."

Loyalty may be an appropriate top filter for the members of the OPOTUS, who must be completely trusted to protect the president's interests. But most appointees are there to generate or implement a narrow set of policy options. Therefore, goal alignment and role competence are the better primary filters for choosing people to perform these activities. (Although it is still hard to beat the 1937 Brownlow Committee recommendation that presidential appointees should be "possessed of high competence, great physical vigor, and a passion for anonymity.")[8]

The president's Year Zero team should determine a goal or set of goals for each role. These goals can clearly be different for each role, and their definition should be a key part of Year Zero. Whether a person shares every other objective of the administration or has known the president for a short or long time is then broadly irrelevant. Choosing a person who cares deeply about achieving the goal that corresponds to each role is the best way of avoiding misalignment and ensuring sustainable performance. Given the short time they are in their roles, the lack of ability to integrate them into a well-defined culture, and the sheer scale of trying to manage a large, diverse entity, it is not realistic to assume they can be managed otherwise.

What is realistic is that if he or she believes in the goal and is committed to it, they will spend every day trying to achieve it. Results are what a president needs, and there are past examples of a goal-first approach proving useful to produce them. "The political strategy for policy promotion by which the 'Reagan revolution' was pushed through Congress in 1981 was devised and executed by hired hands who were latecomers, at most, to Reaganism," writes Paul J. Quirk.[9]

The next-most-important factor is expertise. Assuming the candidate believes in the goal of their role, he or she needs to have the ability and expertise to carry it out successfully. Expertise in this context can come in many forms. For some roles it is subject matter expertise. For example, a member of the National Economic Council overseeing technology policy should be an expert in that field. Organizational expertise is another characteristic. Being an honest broker or implementation expert can be the most important skill for a role. Functional expertise is also welcome. For example, a digital communications director should be the best in the country at that functional skill. Experience navigating Washington is also essential for some roles. Writes Quirk, "If there was a single root cause of the Carter administration's failure . . . it was the President's refusal to recruit people with successful experience in Washington politics for top advisory and political jobs in the White House."[10]

Loyalty is the third important factor, but it sits behind the others. Loyalists, especially from the campaign, need to be rewarded with good roles. But the first question that they should answer is, "What do you want to achieve?" not, "What job do you want?" They should be allocated where their expertise is best suited, and in the policy areas for which they have the most personal passion. For others (which are the bulk of the 8,000 appointees) the administration clearly does not want them undermining its agenda by being disloyal. However, if there is goal alignment between them and their role, the chances of this should be minimized. Many federal boards and commissions also feature part-time roles that can be used to reward loyalty. Not all loyalists seek the commitment of a full-time role, or the financial and other sacrifices that come with it.

Outside of the EOP, choosing primarily for goal alignment is even more important. Cabinet members can only be expected to carry out one or two major initiatives. They spend the great bulk of their time away from the White House, acting independently and making many decisions regarding their agencies which they are statutorily empowered to make. They should be selected based on their being people who believe passionately in the goals the White House chooses for their agencies, and their expertise in pursuing them.

Lower-level agency appointments can also be made with the predominant agency goals in mind. Their loyalty to the president is even less important than that of White House staffers as long as they demonstrate loyalty to the goal. Their selection process can be much more efficient if the White House doesn't try to control every appointment by imposing loyalty tests, which are extremely hard to determine and even harder to enforce. The agency head can have input into the appointment, with the White House setting the goals.

START CULTURE BUILDING IN YEAR ZERO

An organization's culture is the set of unwritten rules, procedures, values, and norms that drive behavior. One of the few advantages of the White House having near 100 percent turnover when a new administration takes the reins is that the president can build the culture that he or she wants. One of the key roles of the Y0LT and then the OPOTUS is to build that culture within the EOP on behalf of the president. Cultural norms—which should key off the president's personality, priorities, and work style—should be agreed to during Year Zero, explicitly set out, and enforced by the OPOTUS.

While presidents' actions can reinforce the culture, they should not take a lot of their time focusing on internal culture-building. Presidents shouldn't be expected to be the guardian of anything other than the positive aspects of the culture. They should hand out praise, appear in photo opportunities with staff, and generally provide affirmation, but the OPOTUS should shield them from the negative energy of the "dirty work" activities, such as reprimands or internal disciplinary measures. Their energy should be elsewhere.

Motivation

The window of opportunity for an administration to achieve change only exists for a short time, so effectiveness is more important than collegiality. While it is obviously important and desirable for people to enjoy the experience of public service, it is more important that they are driven by purpose and a desire to achieve the president's agenda. It is not difficult to find people of this type for the White House; staff are normally very mission-driven and motivated. They work long hours and are poorly paid compared to similarly difficult jobs in the private sector. Their primary reward comes from the ability to achieve impact.

Thus, the cornerstone of culture is in fact good process and structural design. Staff most of all need clear pathways to achieving a personal impact.

Communication and coordination play a role in making this happen. Generally, after the morning senior staff meeting, the assistants to the president present go to their respective offices for a debrief and communicate the priorities and cadence of the day. Communication flows outward from the center. Other communication is achieved through formal and informal groupings across the White House. One of the most sought-after informal gatherings was a regular meeting of deputy assistants to the president that I held to swap notes on their work and discuss upcoming events. Attendance was optional, but the meeting was always full as it built camaraderie and allowed them to do their job better.

The OPOTUS has a role in building and reinforcing the positive aspects of culture. It should promote good behaviors and recognize them publicly. Other than impact, the most important and visible rewards mainly concern the president, so examples of rewards include occasionally being able to sit in meetings in the Oval Office, having a photo with the president at the Resolute Desk, traveling on Air Force One, or receiving an invitation to sit in on an important public event—these are costless but very well-received rewards for staff of all levels.

Task Conflict versus Personality Conflict

In his book *Think Again*, Adam Grant distinguishes between task conflict and relationship conflict. Relationship conflict is "personal, emotional clashes that are filled not just with friction, but also with animosity." Task conflict, however, is "clashes about ideas and opinions."[11] Relationship conflict is negative and destructive, but task conflict can be positive if it is directed in the right fashion.

Grant shows that relationship conflict often marks low-performing teams: "It took months for many of the teams to make real headway on their relationship issues, and by the time they did manage to debate key decisions, it was often too late to rethink their directions."[12] Inside the White House, relationship conflict can be a major drag on effectiveness. The

White House doesn't have the luxury of devoting time to letting relationship conflicts play out, and issues that arise from it can be fatal to good decision-making. Task conflict, by contrast, is a positive force, in particular when creativity or innovation is necessary. Grant shows that high performance teams demonstrated plenty of task conflict but low relationship conflict.

It is the role of the YOLT to select, and of the OPOTUS to manage, people who can engage in task conflict without generating relationship conflicts. Regardless of how talented they are, or what their relationship is to the president, the presence of individuals who engage in relationship conflicts is toxic. Keeping them out of the fold should be non-negotiable and one of the most important "red lines" that an OPOTUS must enforce. The culture should be intolerant to anyone demonstrating this behavior, and there should be a mechanism for dealing with anyone who does, including, eventually, dismissal. Conversely, task conflict should be encouraged and promoted, in particular during the option generation process. This is a key part of the honest broker's role.

Dealing with Bad Actors

Personality conflict is inevitable to some extent in an organization such as the White House, which is full of strong personalities and egos no matter who is president. But the OPOTUS can minimize personality conflict if they choose people according to goal alignment, delineate lines of responsibility as much as possible, empower true honest brokers to run an effective set of processes, and enforce norms to prevent people from straying outside their lanes. Standardizing the structure and process of the White House will help with these duties. The more people understand their own role to be unambiguous, and the more they understand the procedural norms governing the organization, the less they will be tempted to veer outside of their remits.

The task of enforcing these norms again highlights why the concept of the OPOTUS is important. It is impossible for one person to police the whole EOP. Chiefs of staff have tried to be ever-present, but they are limited in how much bandwidth they can devote to enforcing norms. The strength of a team is also necessary to ensure the president doesn't unconsciously or consciously undermine the norms. For example, if the president tolerates personality conflict, it will be impossible for a chief of staff to extinguish it. But the collective power of the OPOTUS team has a chance to overcome it.

There is nothing more corrosive or destructive to culture than poor behavior, and, if tolerated, eventually it will hurt the president. No structure or process design survives bad actors. The power to minimize destructive behavior can be enhanced considerably with the power of dismissal. Presidents have generally hated firing people and, short of truly egregious offenses, seldom do it for behavior that detracts from the culture he or she wishes to instill. The OPOTUS should collectively ask the president for power to dismiss any staff member and be ruthless in its application.

Other causes for dismissal should include continual "end running" (operating outside of established procedures), leaking (to the extent that it is provable), poor treatment of junior staff, and promotion of a personal agenda. Leaks will never be eliminated entirely, nor are they a new phenomenon: Reagan's chief of staff Donald Regan recalled, "In the Reagan Administration the leak was raised to the status of art form. Everything . . . appeared in the newspapers and on the networks with the least possible delay."[13] It is unrealistic to expect that leaks can be eliminated entirely, but they can be minimized by having people be part of an honest broker process and by limiting them to just the debate on ideas, not on the final decision.

On end runs, people are clever and will find ways of getting to the president if they really want to. On many occasions I heard an end runner claim something like, "The president called me and told me to report back directly to him." Sometimes this is true, and indeed if the president wants to directly reach out to someone, he or she obviously can (and in fact it should be encouraged for information seeking). But the rule should be that the reply comes back through the OPOTUS, not directly. This will help preserve situational awareness for senior staffers and help the OPOTUS know what actions to take to support the president. Exceptional circumstances can happen, but if the lack of visibility on the president's conversations becomes a habit, the whole system will start to collapse.

One of the most difficult people to dismiss is the chief of staff. Traditionally this has been something presidents have struggled with and have not done it quickly enough because of the emotional toll of carrying it out. The president can delegate to the chief of staff most other dismissals, but not that one! Whether it was Eisenhower with Sherman Adams, Nixon with Bob Haldeman, Reagan with Donald Regan, or George H. W. Bush with John Sununu, presidents lost crucial time and capacity to effect change by hanging in too long with a chief of staff. The OPOTUS can play a crucial role by having it as part of their mandate to be able to collectively ask for the chief of staff to be dismissed, and then have the collective strength to make it happen when its necessity becomes obvious.

Mistakes in appointments can be minimized by good Year One vetting and interviewing. However, a fast start with a great number of appointments means there will still be errors made. Learning how to rectify mistakes is a fast-response skill that the senior leadership of the White House needs to develop and role-model. Everyone serves at the pleasure of the president and is there for him or her, not themselves. Eliminating some of the inevitable bad actors early and publicly may cause some short-term angst, but it will be extremely beneficial in the long term. This may sound draconian, but time is short, and no one in the White House is indispensable. It is better to cut people out early than tolerate them. Dismissals should be celebrated as showing that the system is working, not failing.

CONCLUSION

Consistent with the Five-Year Presidency philosophy, candidates' efforts at assembling a strong and sizeable team quickly should be received as a positive signal of their ability to govern.

The mass of thousands of individuals whom the president can expect to appoint to roles of various kinds can be the difference between an agenda that is well executed or one that isn't. Contrary to an oft-used phrase, people should not be policy, but they are critical in developing and implementing it.

Year Zero should be the time to build the machinery capable of appointing a very large number of the best appointees. By focusing on appointments that are full-time but not Senate-confirmed, and by setting out goals for each of those roles, the administration can reap a huge momentum that starts on Day One.

Candidates for appointments should be encouraged to start the application process as soon as possible after the convention. This is considerably earlier and more visible than the traditional approach. No appointments will be made until after the election, but eliminating a bureaucratic bottleneck and minimizing the number of people who pull out at the last moment when faced with the difficulties of joining the government will save crucial weeks in getting a fully functioning team in the first two hundred days.

Developing a positive and effective culture begins in Year Zero, is championed by the president, and is fostered by the OPOTUS. Goal alignment, expertise, and loyalty—in that order—should be the key factors in selecting for staff. Thereafter, having the structure and set of processes designed in Year Zero that give staff the opportunity to have impact is not only going to build the best culture for them but will guarantee a significantly more effective White House. Some decisions are forced on presidents. Some require compromise. Few are totally under their control, but personnel largely is. Presidents can choose whomever they want to serve, whenever they want, and using whatever criteria they want. The only exception to this rule is those appointments that require Senate confirmation, where presidents are partially constrained. Core White House staff—as well as most other political appointees—do not require this approval and serve entirely at the president's pleasure. They should take advantage of this rare example of unilateral power.

CONCLUSION

The best way to save democracy is to make government more effective. Regardless of which political party runs it, the White House must be seen as the most effective governing unit in the world. And the best way for the public to *see* it as that is for it to actually *be* the most effective governing unit in the world.

All organizations go through evolutions. This is true of the White House, which has evolved from a small family office to a midsized organization sitting on top of the most powerful government the world has seen. Its evolution included the creation and development of the Executive Office of the President (EOP) in an attempt to provide support for the president. But the Executive Office of the President remains fundamentally a personality-driven entity—not just the personality of presidents but of the staff that surround them.

It is time for the entity to evolve again to institutionalize that support through a highly efficient organization that is set up to maximize the impact of the person at its center. "The President (still) needs help," to rephrase the 1939 Brownlow Committee report, just help of a larger and more comprehensive nature and stretched out over five years.

The scale of the task is significant. John F. Kennedy said after his first year, "The problems are more difficult than I had imagined them to be. The responsibilities placed on the United States are greater than I imagined them to be, and there are greater limitations upon our ability to bring about a favorable result than I had imagined them to be."[1]

Since that time the challenge has only become larger. Terry Moe observed in his essay "The Politicized Presidency," "Barring some fundamental and unforeseen change in American institutions, the gap between expectations and capacity will continue to characterize the presidency."[2] My hope is that the ideas of the Five-Year Presidency can help close that gap. To do so, I have urged a set of prescriptions that impact the preparation and operations of the White House and, consequently, how it executes its mission.

Some of the ideas put forth in the book are evolutionary, simply extending what is already happening; others are totally new. Some are very simple and practical; others will be challenging to implement. Some will be intuitive, others perhaps counterintuitive. Some are binary (either do something or don't do it); others can be implemented to a greater or lesser extent along a spectrum. Some are linked to each other; others are stand-alone. What they do collectively is represent an ambitious new paradigm for thinking about the *how* of government—in particular, the need for a Five-Year Presidency.

SUMMARY OF PROPOSALS

The main suggestions from the book are summarized and set out below, clustered within the tasks to which they relate:

Overall

Proposal 1: Consider the presidency to be a five-year journey, beginning with a conscious set of activities to build an effective White House, starting a year before the inauguration (Year Zero). Aim to be 100 percent more effective in Year One.

Proposal 2: Measure the drapes. Start earlier, do more, and be more visible. Showcase your efforts. Make it a basis for voter selection.

Proposal 3: Take the same approach to the second term. The last year of the first term becomes a new Year Zero, with an aim of totally refreshing and reinvigorating the White House.

Proposal 4: Organize your efforts around seven tasks, ordered as shown in figure 18.

Task 1: Assemble a Year Zero Leadership Team

Proposal 5: Create a joint governance team that oversees both the campaign and Year Zero operations.

Proposal 6: Get the right people on the bus first. Choose a Year Zero Leadership Team, give it a formal status, and do it all earlier than is usual—approximately one year ahead of the election.

Proposal 7: Populate the Year Zero team with people who demonstrate not only political and policy skills but also managerial ones.

Proposal 8: The chief of staff's responsibilities have become too expansive

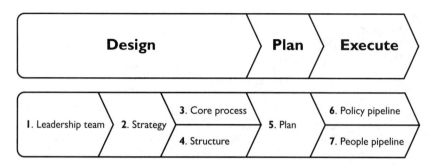

FIGURE 18. Year Zero: Phases and tasks

for any one person to handle. Consider morphing the chief of staff's role/ office into a new entity—the Office of the President of the United States (OPOTUS)—that collectively shares those duties.

Proposal 9: Use Year Zero to test whether members of the Year Zero Leadership Team can work together in a way that will allow them to become the OPOTUS. Set the expectation that the chief of staff and other members serve the same duration as the president—all four years.

Task 2: Develop a Strategy and Operating Model

Proposal 10: Study and learn the lessons from previous White Houses before embarking on any organization design. Use a multidisciplinary group and approach.

Proposal 11: Conduct again for the second term, including a review of the first-term successes and mistakes.

Proposal 12: Define in Year Zero a desired legacy for the administration and use that legacy to frame the strategy, operating model, yearly priorities, and Year One agenda in that order.

Proposal 13: Design the operating model to be a synchronized combination of structure, core processes, and people.

Proposal 14: Consider reprioritizing activities, in particular ceremonial, diplomatic, and media events, to make Year One a year of achieving results, not selling them.

Task 3: Design Core Processes to Achieve Action

Proposal 15: Make the core process of presidential decision-making and its implementation the basis for all design, in particular structure and people selection.

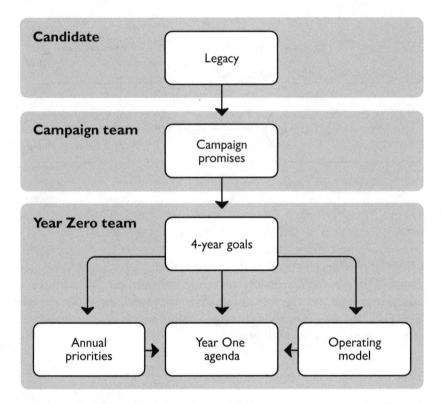

FIGURE 19. Building a legacy, one year at a time

Proposal 16: Define all the activities in the decision-making process along a map that provides clarity and direction for all involved.

Proposal 17: Allocate the roles of the main participants along the lines depicted in figure 7 (p. 131).

Proposal 18: Minimize the president's involvement in option generation and implementation, but allow him or her to access formal and informal information flows to assist with decisions.

Proposal 19: Design the system to be flexible enough to add "fluid" processes to the more structured approach, when necessary, notably when dealing with crises.

Proposal 20: Be ruthless in identifying priorities. All of them should be determined top-down, with any bottom-up ideas eliminated.

Proposal 21: The decision-making process should follow a multiple advocacy model run by a strong honest broker. Other participants can (and should) be advocates for options, but they cannot be in charge of running the process.

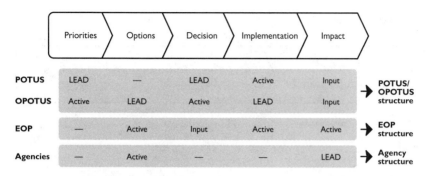

FIGURE 20. Decision process drives structure

Task 4: Design a Coherent White House Structure

Proposal 22: Use a consistent and evergreen approach to White House organizational design that corresponds to the core decision process.

Proposal 23: Customize the OPOTUS structure to suit the behavioral and decision-making characteristics of the president. Create a "translation layer" between it and the rest of the EOP to shield the president from daily workings and to ensure he or she receives the output in a customized fashion.

Proposal 24: Standardize to the extent possible all other roles and responsibilities in the EOP. Document these in a set of charters. Provide clarity, not bureaucracy.

Proposal 25: Carry out a "clean-sheet" design of offices including allocation of resources based around Year One priorities. Select the office leadership around the office design; don't design the office for the person.

Proposal 26: Clarify and document the nature of the reporting relationship between the president, the chief of staff/OPOTUS, and the White House staff. Also do the same for the cabinet.

Proposal 27: Clarify and document the nature of the reporting relationship of "shadow staffs"—staffers who perform the same functions inside different offices—within the EOP.

Proposal 28: Create a unit inside the White House responsible for overseeing the implementation of decisions and link it to ones created within federal agencies.

Proposal 29: Reconsider the idea of a spokes-of-the-wheel management approach, updated for the scale of the modern EOP but made possible with the other ideas set out here.

Plan backward:

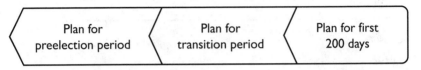

FIGURE 21. Planning for the first two hundred days

Task 5: Plan for the First Two Hundred Days

Proposal 30: Start by identifying goals for the first two hundred days and then work backward to plan the activities needed to achieve them.

Proposal 31: Reimagine Day One of the administration to not just be a day outlining a vision but also to simultaneously launch one piece of legacy legislation, a draft budget, priority executive orders, and agency goals.

Proposal 32: Assume the possibility of a contested election and make plans to accomplish transition preparations without assistance from the sitting administration. Plan for other crises over the transition period.

Proposal 33: (suggestion for Congress) Pass legislation to allow a conditional ascertainment that gives campaigns early resources and access even in the event of a contested election.

Proposal 34: (suggestion for Congress) Consider establishing an independent entity to govern the mechanics of presidential transitions.

Proposal 35: Build a large, well-organized, and well-funded transition organization, building and developing on best practices from previous cycles.

Proposal 36: Build and operate a shadow White House during the transition so that by Inauguration Day all that changes is their location.

Task 6: Build a Policy Pipeline

Proposal 37: Have the primary focus of Year One be to pass legacy legislation, with one piece passed in the first two hundred days and a second by year's end. Work with members of Congress before the election to prepare for engagement from Day One. Be equally aspirational with the first year of the second term.

Proposal 38: Be prepared to make the initial legacy legislation bipartisan, dependent on the election result.

Proposal 39: Study historical legislation for ideas that can be used for current initiatives.

Proposal 40: As a secondary activity, supplement legislation with executive orders prepared during the preelection period. Put an emphasis on those that create major impact, can be quickly implemented, and are long-lasting.
Proposal 41: Encourage external think tanks and other entities to provide draft executive orders and legislative ideas during the preelection period.
Proposal 42: Prepare in Year Zero at least one regulatory initiative for each agency to pursue in the first two hundred days. Choose beachhead members with a view to this being their main initial task.
Proposal 43: Task every agency to also produce a plan in the first two hundred days for significantly improving citizen services over the course of the four-year administration.
Proposal 44: Deliver a draft budget on Day One that is not a wish list but, rather, a series of actual proposals that support the legislative and regulatory rollout plan.

Task 7: Build a People Pipeline

Proposal 45: Build an aspirational plan for installing presidential appointees during the first two hundred days—some 1,500 roles filled on Day One and more than 3,000 by Day Two Hundred.
Proposal 46: To achieve the targets, prioritize the installment of White House staff and agency beachhead teams over Senate-confirmed positions.
Proposal 47: Work with the Senate to streamline and speed up confirmations where possible. Build a parallel strategy to run the agencies for a lengthy period without confirmed appointees.
Proposal 48: Structure the transition personnel team around clusters of agencies. Have separate units inside the transition team to focus on placing campaign staff and attracting nontraditional candidates. Build new pathways for private sector and other candidates to come in on short-term assignments.
Proposal 49: Choose people for goal alignment first, expertise second, loyalty third.
Proposal 50: Start building the culture of impact in Year Zero, in particular the promotion of idea-generating task conflict and eliminating people who generate personal conflict.

PUTTING THE PROPOSALS INTO PRACTICE

Putting the proposals into practice requires a commitment from prospective presidential candidates and incumbents considering a second term. As the former fight to gain a foothold in their party's nomination race, the thought of planning for governance will probably seem a light-year away, not a year. However, candidates can start slowly and build up their Year Zero efforts. First and foremost, they just need to "get the right people on the bus" in the early months, when the field of candidates is broad and resources are scarce. That can be a small team, and those people can do research as set out here, which is not an expensive operation.

Also, it is possible that external entities will be doing some of the work on behalf of multiple candidates and handing over work products as the field narrows, or even as late as the convention. By phasing in the workload and taking advantage of the knowledge in this book and from other sources, the initial Year Zero operations can be very manageable.

I have tried to be realistic in assessing the practicality of the proposals, focusing in particular on ones that are largely or totally inside the control of a candidate and president-elect. There is no point in putting forward ideas that cannot be implemented or that rely significantly on the relinquishing of shared control by players who may have other objectives and incentives. Any structural suggestions also must be considered in the context of how people tend to behave inside an organization. That is especially true in the case of the White House, where large egos and personalities wield a tremendous amount of power. My suggestions don't try to ignore human nature; they promote it by letting people be advocates for policy they are passionate about and giving them effective pathways to action. People who make it to the White House are talented and clever and will work around the rules if they want to and are able to. Therefore, any system is only as good as how well it is implemented and must allow for some degree of flexibility and "exceptions to the rule." Perfection is not the objective, because it is not attainable. The goal is to make the White House—the core executive governing unit at the national level—the best that it can be.

I don't expect that every one of the proposals will be acceptable or of interest to a candidate. In the past, candidates have been reluctant to be seen to be doing too much planning for governing the White House for risk of being criticized for "measuring the drapes." Succumbing to this fear is wrongheaded. A strong candidate should be totally transparent about the amount and comprehensiveness of his or her planning—thereby conveying how he or she is treating the presidency with the seriousness it deserves and showing that he or she has the management skills necessary to run a complicated organization.

They need to showcase them, making visible what has previously been largely invisible. They need to be bold, for example by publicly announcing the team in charge of their Year Zero activities, allowing media access to some of the nonsensitive planning, encouraging people to sign up and start their paperwork as possible appointees as early as straight after the convention, announcing on the campaign trail their intended Day One legislation, and generally highlighting preparations as they occur.

It is not just candidates who need to believe and recognize the importance of Year Zero but also the people around them. In the Romney transition we took a very low profile. Now I believe the Year Zero Leadership Team can be more public, albeit limiting themselves to talking about the "how" and not the "what."

However, I do not expect candidates to suddenly become expert managers or the voting public to make a wholesale change in their basis of candidate selection. No recent successful candidate has campaigned purely on managerial competence. What I do think is realistic is threefold.

First, for candidates to act in their self-interest and realize that a successful presidency requires more than a passing interest in Year Zero preparation and therefore to commit to the importance of planning. If they choose the right people and empower them, the machinery of an effective government can be built for them.

Second, by simply showcasing how effective a governing machine is being built, they can add another feather to their presidential candidacy bow. They can still campaign primarily on their policy platform and media skills but demonstrate that they are also a more complete candidate, thoughtful and capable enough to build a Year Zero apparatus.

Third, for voters to also act in their self-interest and realize that the ability of candidates to deliver on campaign promises requires more than rhetoric. Managerial expertise may not be criterion number one for a vote, but it should be *a* criterion, and perhaps the difference in an "all other things being equal" selection.

LOOKING FORWARD

The topic of the "best" way of setting up and running the White House, the most important governing unit in the world, is a vast and critical one. Each presidential cycle brings new and interesting developments on the topic. There is no one "correct" answer for every White House, and different perspectives are integral to building a better institution.

Ultimately, I believe the concept of the Five-Year Presidency can lead to more significant legislation for the country, fewer but more effective and longer-lasting executive actions, and a better delivery of basic citizen services. I hope readers challenge the ideas set out here, build upon them, and perhaps develop their own. My ideas are not intended to be helpful exclusively to one political party or another—they are applicable to all seeking the highest office. And they apply equally to incumbents looking to cement their legacy in a second term. The goal remains simply a more effective White House that can deliver results for the American people.

The size of the prize is even more considerable than it may first appear. In the private sector, effective planning can marginally improve an organization; in the White House, it can make the first year up to 100 percent more effective, since the administration won't have to waste much of the first six months learning to govern and making mistakes. Achieving two pieces of legacy legislation in the first year sounds like a modest goal, but it represents (at least) twice as much as virtually all recent presidents have achieved.

Similarly, the ability to get real action in Years Three and Four of an administration depends enormously on the results of the midterm elections. Achieving a good outcome in the midterms, fueled by demonstrating real results in the first two years, compared to losing one or both of the chambers, can easily be the difference between continuing with a legacy program versus having to rely on more modest executive actions.

Furthermore, the same problems and opportunities that exist in the American system apply to a greater or lesser extent to democracies across the world. Functioning political institutions are essential elsewhere, too. As Samuel Huntington noted, "The more complex and heterogeneous the society, the more the achievement and maintenance of political community becomes dependent on the workings of political institutions."[3]

Many of the concepts set out in this book therefore also can be applied in other countries. Clearly there are many differences in the electoral systems of countries, and every country has a different way of establishing governments, transitioning between them, and running their political system. But every government has a core governing unit, and effective government requires a conscious and systematic commitment to its design. That design is best done before the all-consuming activity of governing begins.

Defining what that core governing unit is, and considering how to best design and run it, and when to do that, is a key task for any leader. In taking up that mission, he or she doesn't need to be an expert in organizational design, political science, or history—he or she just needs to believe in the importance of doing it and summon the political courage to follow through, even if it is new ground. In this regard, as with any challenge, no presidential words are as inspiring to me as those of Theodore Roosevelt:

It is not the critic who counts; not the man who points out how the strong man stumbles, or where the doer of deeds could have done them better. The credit belongs to the man who is actually in the arena, whose face is marred by dust and sweat and blood . . . who at the best knows in the end the triumph of high achievement, and who at the worst, if he fails, at least fails while daring greatly, so that his place shall never be with those cold and timid souls who neither know victory nor defeat.[4]

Acknowledgments

Writing a book has been on my list of challenges for more than a decade. I'm delighted it is on a topic that I care deeply about, but I couldn't have achieved it without the support of numerous people.

I'd like to first recognize both David Marchick and Josh Bolten for their roles during the tumultuous transition of 2020–21. Without their friendship and moral support, I would not have made it to the finish line, and this book might still be just an idea.

On the book itself, thanks go to all the people who helped me and made the drafts better. Professor Karthik Ramanna ran the fellowship program at Oxford University, where I did a lot of the research, and provided very useful guidance on the overall approach. Lisa Queen, Brian Sweeney, and Brad Smith all showed belief in the early concept, offering lots of great suggestions along the way. David Wilezol was a wonderful partner who took the drafts and gave them much better flow and readability. John Miller helped with an earlier short article version on the topic. Theo Merkel helped with the legislative section, Jaden Evans with the references, Robert Gabriel with the diagrams and some of the research, and Doug Hoelscher with some of the detail on the ideas. Professor Charles Cameron of Princeton University gave me excellent feedback on the later drafts. Nadine Zimmerli of the University of Virginia Press shepherded it through the publishing process and assisted me as a first-time writer.

Thanks also to all the people I served with in government. Working together in the most challenging environment imaginable forges lifetime friendships, and I count myself lucky to have been with such fine colleagues.

And, most of all, thanks to my wife, Renee, and my children for believing in me and going on this journey with me, first to the White House, and then to the world of writing.

Notes

INTRODUCTION

1. Ronald Reagan, "Inaugural Address 1981," January 20, 1981.
2. Francis Fukuyama, *The End of History and the Last Man* (Harlow, UK: Penguin, 2012).
3. "Few Think Our Democracy Is Working Well These Days," Associated Press–NORC, October 19, 2022, https://apnorc.org/projects/few-think-our-democracy-is-working-well-these-days/.
4. Andrew Heywood, *Politics*, 5th ed. (New York: Bloomsbury Academic, 2019), 119.
5. James Madison, "Federalist No. 51," in *The Federalist Papers*, ed. Clinton Rossiter (New York: Signet Classics, 1999), 319.
6. U.S. Office of Personnel Management, "Executive Branch Civilian Employment since 1940," https://www.opm.gov/policy-data-oversight/data-analysis-documentation/federal-employment-reports/historical-tables/executive-branch-civilian-employment-since-1940/.
7. *Federal Workforce Statistics Sources: OPM and OMB* (Washington, DC: Congressional Research Service, 2022), 6, https://sgp.fas.org/crs/misc/R43590.pdf.
8. Raymond Moley, *After Seven Years* (New York: Harper, 1939), 128, quoted in Stephen Hess and James P. Pfiffner, *Organizing the Presidency*, 4th ed. (Washington, DC: Brookings Institution Press, 2021), 8.
9. The Executive Office of the President, *Congressional Budget Submission Fiscal Year 2023* (Washington, DC: The White House, March 2022), https://www.whitehouse.gov/wp-content/uploads/2022/03/FY-2023-EOP-Budget-Submission.pdf.
10. GovInfo.gov, "Budget of the United States Government, Fiscal Year 2023," 119, https://www.govinfo.gov/content/pkg/BUDGET-2023-BUD/pdf/BUDGET-2023-BUD-26.pdf.
11. Quoted in James P. Pfiffner, "Can the President Manage the Government?," in *The Managerial Presidency*, ed. Pfiffner (College Station: Texas A&M University Press, 1999), 3.
12. See Heywood, *Politics*, 86.
13. Megan Brenan, "Americans' Trust in Government Remains Low," Gallup, September 30, 2021, https://news.gallup.com/poll/355124/americans-trust-government-remains-low.aspx.

14. NBC News Survey conducted October 14–18, 2022, https://www.documentcloud.org/documents/23171526-220699-nbc-news-october-poll-v3.

15. John Campbell, *Margaret Thatcher: Grocer's Daughter to Iron Lady* (New York: Vintage, 2011), 93.

16. I cowrote, with Daniel Kroese and Clark Campbell, a report on our experiences in the book *Romney Readiness Project 2012: Retrospective and Lessons Learned* (self-pub., 2013), Amazon.

17. Stephen Hess and James P. Pfiffner, *Organizing the Presidency*, 4th ed. (Washington, DC: Brookings Institution Press, 2021), 2.

1. PRESIDENTIAL POWER AND IMPACT

1. Edward M. Kennedy, "Senate Floor Speech Made in Response to the Announcement of Bork's Nomination," July 1, 1987, Cong. Rec. S18518–19, 100th Cong., 1st Sess. 133 Cong. Rec. S 9188, vol. 133, no. 110.

2. Seminal books include Woodrow Wilson's *Congressional Government in the United States* and Edward Corwin's *The President: Office and Powers*.

3. William Howard Taft, *Our Chief Magistrate and His Powers* (New York: Columbia University Press, 1916), 139–40.

4. Thomas Jefferson, "First Inaugural Address," delivered in Washington, DC, March 4, 1801, https://avalon.law.yale.edu/19th_century/jefinau1.asp.

5. Theodore Roosevelt, *An Autobiography of Theodore Roosevelt*, ed. Stephen Brennan (New York: Skyhorse, 2011), 304–10.

6. Abraham Lincoln, "Abraham Lincoln Papers: Series 1. General Correspondence. 1833 to 1916: Abraham Lincoln to Albert G. Hodges," April 4, 1864, retrieved from the Library of Congress, https://www.loc.gov/resource/mal.3207700/?sp=2&r=-0.071,-0.032,0.691,0.366,0.

7. John Locke, *Two Treatises of Government*, new edition corrected, section 160 (London: Whitmore, Fenn et al., 1821), 328.

8. John W. Dean, *Broken Government: How Republican Rule Destroyed the Legislative, Executive, and Judicial Branches* (New York: Viking, 2007), 102.

9. Richard Neustadt, *Presidential Power and the Modern Presidents*, 2nd ed. (New York: Macmillan, 1990), ix.

10. Ibid., x.

11. Ibid., 11, 40.

12. Bill Simmons, "President Obama and Bill Simmons: The GQ Interview," *GQ*, November 17, 2015, https://www.gq.com/story/president-obama-bill-simmons-interview-gq-men-of-the-year.

13. James David Barber, *The Presidential Character: Predicting Performance in the White House* (Englewood Cliffs, NJ: Prentice-Hall, 1985).

14. Paul Quirk, "Resolved, Presidential Successes and Failure Are Better Explained by Political Time and the Strength of Governing Coalitions Than by a President's Character and Leadership Qualities," in *Debating the Presidency: Conflicting Perspectives on the American Executive*, ed. Richard J. Ellis and Michael Nelson (Thousand Oaks, CA: Sage, 2021), 126.

15. Ibid., 122.

16. Woodrow Wilson, *Constitutional Government in the United States* (New York: Columbia University Press, 1908), 70.

17. Adam Raphael, "Mrs. T Looks out of Touch," *Observer,* March 11, 1984, ref. QuoteInvestigator.com, March 20, 2023, https://quoteinvestigator.com/2020/08 /31/events/#f+438302+1+1.

18. Stephen Skowronek, "What Time Is It? A New President Might Want to Wear Two Watches, to Track Both Secular and Political time," First Year 2017, Miller Center of Public Affairs, October 15, 2015, 1, http://firstyear2017.org/essay/what-time-is -it.html.

19. Susan Cornwell, "Like Bush, Obama Asserts Prerogatives When Signing Laws," Reuters, January 6, 2012, https://www.reuters.com/article/us-obama -congress-signing/like-bush-obama-asserts-prerogatives-when-signing-laws -idUSTRE8051WQ20120106.

20. House Committee on Government Operations Staff, 85th Cong., 1st Sess., Executive Orders and Proclamations: Study of a Use of Presidential Powers, quoted in Vivian S. Chu and Todd Garvey, *Executive Orders: Issuance, Modification, and Revocation* (Washington, DC: Congressional Research Service, 2014), 1, https://sgp.fas .org/crs/misc/RS20846.pdf.

21. James Bennet, "True to Form, Clinton Shifts Energies back to U.S. Focus," *New York Times,* July 5, 1998, quoted in Andrew Rudalevige, "The Presidency and Unilateral Power," in *The Presidency and the Political System,* ed. Michael Nelson (Thousand Oaks, CA: Sage, 2021), 564.

22. Rudalevige, "The Presidency and Unilateral Power," in *The Presidency and the Political System,* ed. Nelson, 564.

23. Jennifer Epstein, "Obama's Pen and Phone Strategy," *Politico,* January 14, 2014, https://www.politico.com/story/2014/01/obama-state-of-the-union-2014 -strategy-102151.

24. U.S. Department of Homeland Security, "About Us," February 28, 2023, https://www.dhs.gov/about-dhs.

25. Tom Temin, "Smallest Federal Agency Looks after the Biggest Creatures on Earth," Federal News Network, May 21, 2021, https://federalnewsnetwork.com /people/2021/05/smallest-federal-agency-looks-after-the-biggest-creatures-on -earth/.

26. Clyde Wayne Crews Jr., "How Many Federal Agencies Exist? We Can't Drain the Swamp until We Know," *Forbes,* July 5, 2017, https://www.forbes.com /sites/waynecrews/2017/07/05/how-many-federal-agencies-exist-we-cant-drain-the -swamp-until-we-know/?sh=5f43a42d1aa2.

27. Rudalevige, "The Presidency and Unilateral Power," 569–70.

28. M. S. Eccles, *Beckoning Frontiers* (New York: Knopf, 1952), 336.

29. Executive Order 12291 of February 17, 1981, hosted at the U.S. National Archives, https://www.archives.gov/federal-register/codification/executive-order /12291.html.

30. Eric Katz, "Agencies with Career Leaders Have More Satisfied Employees Than Those Led by Politicals, Report Finds," *Government Executive,* February 24, 2022, https://www.govexec.com/management/2022/02/agencies-career-leaders -have-more-satisfied-employees-those-led-politicals-report-finds/362398/.

31. U.S. Bureau of Labor Statistics, "Employee Tenure in 2022," September 22, 2022, https://www.bls.gov/news.release/pdf/tenure.pdf.

32. *Humphrey's Executor v. United States,* 295 U.S. 602 (1935), accessed via Justia, https://supreme.justia.com/cases/federal/us/295/602/.

33. Alexis de Tocqueville, *Democracy in America*, trans. Arthur Goldhammer (New York: Library of America, 2004), quoted in *Debating the Presidency: Conflicting Perspectives on the American Executive*, ed. Richard J. Ellis and Michael Nelson (Thousand Oaks, CA: Sage, 2021), 179.

34. U.S. Congress, Senate, *Joint Resolution to authorize the use of United States Armed Forces against those responsible for the recent attacks launched against the United States*, 115 STAT 224, 107th Cong., September 18, 2001, https://www.congress.gov /107/plaws/publ40/PLAW-107publ40.pdf.

35. Rudalevige, "The Presidency and Unilateral Power," 579.

36. Office of the Under Secretary of Defense (Comptroller), *National Defense Budget Estimates for FY 2023*, 276–77, https://comptroller.defense.gov/Portals/45 /Documents/defbudget/FY2023/FY23_Green_Book.pdf.

37. Performance.gov, "Department of Defense."

38. Eric Katz, "USPS Plans to Slash 50,000 Positions in Coming Years to Reach 'Break Even' Point," *Government Executive*, July 28, 2022, https://www.govexec.com /workforce/2022/07/usps-plans-slash-50000-positions-coming-years-reach-break -even-point/375096/.

39. Jonathan Masters and Will Merrow, "How Much Aid Has the U.S. Sent Ukraine? Here Are Six Charts," Council on Foreign Relations blog post, February 23, 2023, https://www.cfr.org/article/how-much-aid-has-us-sent-ukraine-here-are-six -charts.

40. Ben Bradlee, *Conversations with Kennedy* (New York: Norton, 1984), 128.

41. George C. Edwards III, Kenneth R. Mayer, and Stephen J. Wayne, *Presidential Leadership: Politics and Policy Making*, 11th ed. (Lanham, MD: Rowman and Littlefield, 2020), 175.

42. Michael Baruch Grossman and Martha Joynt Kumar, "Carter, Reagan, and the Media: Have the Rules Really Changed or the Poles of the Spectrum of Success?" (paper presented at the Annual Meeting of the American Political Science Association, New York, September 3–6, 1981), 8, quoted in Edwards, Mayer, and Wayne, *Presidential Leadership*, 175.

43. Ronald Reagan, *An American Life* (New York: Simon & Schuster, 1990), 459, 471, quoted in Edwards, Mayer, and Wayne, *Presidential Leadership*, 165.

44. Jean Yi, "Why Biden's First State of the Union Might Not Change Much," *FiveThirtyEight*, March 1, 2022, https://fivethirtyeight.com/features/why-bidens -first-state-of-the-union-might-not-change-much/.

45. Neustadt, *Presidential Power and the Modern* Presidents, xx.

2. THE MODERN WHITE HOUSE

1. Joseph Alsop, *FDR, 1882–1945: A Centenary Remembrance* (New York: Washington Square Press: 1982), 92–93, quoted in Stephen Hess and James P. Pfiffner, *Organizing the Presidency*, 4th ed. (Washington, DC: Brookings Institution Press, 2021), 2.

2. Harold C. Relyea, *The Executive Office of the President: An Historical Overview* (Washington, DC: Congressional Research Service, 2008), 6, https://sgp.fas.org /crs/misc/98-606.pdf.

3. Office of the Under Secretary of Defense (Comptroller), *National Defense Budget*

Estimates for FY 2023, 294, https://comptroller.defense.gov/Portals/45/Documents/defbudget/FY2023/FY23_Green_Book.pdf.

4. Relyea, *The Executive Office of the President: An Historical Overview*, 11.

5. The Executive Office of the President, *Congressional Budget Submission for Fiscal Year 2023* (Washington, DC: The White House, March 2022), https://www.whitehouse.gov/wp-content/uploads/2022/03/FY-2023-EOP-Budget-Submission.pdf.

6. White House Office of Management and Budget, "Table 1.1—Summary of Receipts, Outlays, and Surpluses or Deficits: 1789–2028," https://www.whitehouse.gov/omb/budget/historical-tables/.

7. "John Adams to Abigail Adams, 19 December 1793," Founders Online, National Archives, https://founders.archives.gov/documents/Adams/04-09-02-0278. [Original source: The Adams Papers, *Adams Family Correspondence*, vol. 9, *January 1790–December 1793*, ed. C. James Taylor, Margaret A. Hogan, Karen N. Barzilay, Gregg L. Lint, Hobson Woodward, Mary T. Claffey, Robert F. Karachuk, and Sara B. Sikes (Cambridge, MA: Harvard University Press, 2009), 476–77.]

8. Tony Horwitz, "The Vice Presidents That History Forgot," *Smithsonian Magazine*, July 2012, https://www.smithsonianmag.com/history/the-vice-presidents-that-history-forgot-137851151/.

9. National Security Act of 1947, Chapter 343; 61 Stat. 496; Sec. 101 (b) 1, approved July 26, 1947, https://www.govinfo.gov/content/pkg/COMPS-1493/uslm/COMPS-1493.xml.

10. *Report of the President's Special Review Board*, February 26, 1987, 1, https://archive.org/details/TowerCommission/President%27s%20Special%20Review%20Board%20%28%22Tower%20Commission%22%29/page/n7/mode/2up.

11. "Executive Order 13228 of October 8, 2001, Establishing the Office of Homeland Security and the Homeland Security Council," Code of Federal Regulations, title 3 (2001): 796–802, http://www.gpo.gov/fdsys/pkg/CFR-2002-title3-vol1/pdf/CFR-2002-title3-vol1-eo13228.pdf.

12. U.S. Department of Homeland Security, *Presidential Homeland Security Directive-5*, February 28, 2003, https://www.dhs.gov/sites/default/files/publications/Homeland%20Security%20Presidential%20Directive%205.pdf.

13. Partnership for Public Service, Center for Presidential Transition, "Senate Confirmation Process Slows to a Crawl," https://presidentialtransition.org/wp-content/uploads/sites/6/2020/01/Senate-Confirmations-Issue-Brief.pdf.

14. Eric Katz, "Agencies with Career Leaders Have More Satisfied Employees Than Those Led by Politicals, Report Finds," *Government Executive*, February 24, 2022, https://www.govexec.com/management/2022/02/agencies-career-leaders-have-more-satisfied-employees-those-led-politicals-report-finds/362398/.

15. Department of Justice, "About Us," https://www.justice.gov/about#:~:text=the%20taxpayers'%20dollars.-,Organization,and%20more%20than%20115%2C000%20employees.

3. YEAR ZERO

1. *The Candidate*, dir. Robert Redford (Warner Brothers, 1972).

2. Chris Liddell, Daniel Kroese, and Clark Campbell, *The Romney Readiness Project 2012: Retrospective and Lessons Learned* (self-pub., 2013), Amazon, 10.

3. Partnership for Public Service Center for Presidential Transition, "Presidential Transition Act Summary," March 10, 2020, https://presidentialtransition.org/publications/presidential-transition-act-summary/.

4. Executive Order 13176 of November 27, 2000, "Facilitation of a Presidential Transition," hosted at the UC Santa Barbara American Presidency Project, https://www.presidency.ucsb.edu/documents/executive-order-13176-facilitation-presidential-transition.

5. Partnership for Public Service Center for the Presidential Transition, "Two Decades Later: How Lessons from the 9/11 Commission Report Can Help Us Improve the Political Appointment Process and Protect our National Security," September 9, 2021, https://presidentialtransition.org/blog/lessons-from-the-9-11-commission-report/.

6. Ibid.

7. U.S. Congress, Senate, Intelligence Reform and Terrorism Prevention Act of 2004, S. 2845, 108th Cong., December 17, 2004, https://www.govinfo.gov/content/pkg/PLAW-108publ458/pdf/PLAW-108publ458.pdf.

8. George W. Bush, *Decision Points* (New York: Broadway Paperbacks, 2010), 467.

9. Executive Order 13476 of October 9, 2008, "Facilitation of a Presidential Transition," https://irp.fas.org/offdocs/eo/eo-13476.htm.

10. U.S. Congress, Senate, *Presidential Transition Enhancement Act of 2019*, S. 394, March 3, 2020, https://www.congress.gov/bill/116th-congress/senate-bill/394.

11. David Marchick, *The Peaceful Transfer of Power: An Oral History of America's Presidential Transitions* (Charlottesville: University of Virginia Press, 2022), 153.

12. Liddell, Kroese, and Campbell, *Romney Readiness Project 2012*, 13.

13. Marchick, *The Peaceful Transfer of Power*, 72.

14. Leavitt quoted in Liddell, Kroese, and Campbell, *Romney Readiness Project 2012*, 10.

4. TASK ONE: ASSEMBLE A YEAR ZERO LEADERSHIP TEAM

1. James C. Collins, *Good to Great: Why Some Companies Make the Leap and Others Don't* (New York: HarperBusiness, 2001).

2. John P. Burke, "Lessons from Past Presidential Transitions: Organization, Management, and Decision Making," in *The White House World: Transitions, Organization, and Office Operations*, ed. Martha Joynt Kumar and Terry Sullivan (College Station: Texas A&M University Press, 2003), 33.

3. President George W. Bush White House, "History of the National Security Council, 1947–1997," https://georgewbush-whitehouse.archives.gov/nsc/history.html.

4. David Cohen, Charles E. Walcott, Shirley Anne Warshaw, and Stephen J. Wayne, *Reports 2009–21: The Chief of Staff*, The White House Transition Project (2008), 4, www.whitehousetransitionproject.org/wp-content/uploads/2016/03/WHTP-2009-21-Chief-of-Staff.pdf.

5. TASK TWO: DEVELOP A STRATEGY AND OPERATING MODEL

1. Jack Nelson and Robert Donovan, "The Education of a President," *Los Angeles Sunday Times Magazine*, August 1, 1993, 14, quoted in John P. Burke, "The Institu-

tional Presidency," in *The Presidency and the Political System*, ed. Michael Nelson (Thousand Oaks, CA: Sage, 2021), 443.

2. Livy, *The Early History of Rome: Books I–V of The History of Rome from Its Foundation* (Harmondsworth, UK: Penguin, 1971).

3. Mike Allen, "Scoop: Inside Biden's Private Chat with Historians," *Axios*, March 25, 2021, https://www.axios.com/2021/03/25/biden-historians-meeting-filibuster.

4. As quoted in Martha Joynt Kumar, *Before the Oath: How George W. Bush and Barack Obama Managed a Transfer of Power* (Baltimore, MD: Johns Hopkins University Press, 2015), 15.

5. "Washington Wire," *New Republic* (December 15, 1952), 3, quoted in Stephen Hess and James P. Pfiffner, *Organizing the Presidency*, 4th ed. (Washington, DC: Brookings Institution Press, 2021), 42.

6. Arthur Schlesinger, *A Thousand Days*, 680–82, quoted in Hess and Pfiffner, *Organizing the Presidency*, 67.

7. "The White House Staff vs. the Cabinet: Hugh Sidey Interviews Bill Moyers," *Washington Monthly*, February 1969, 78, quoted in Hess and Pfiffner, *Organizing the Presidency*, 67.

8. Joseph A. Califano Jr., *Governing America: An Insider's Report from the White House and the Cabinet* (New York: Simon & Schuster, 1981), 403, quoted in Hess and Pfiffner, *Organizing the Presidency*, 124.

9. Martha Joynt Kumar, Statement prepared for the House Subcommittee on Government Operations hearing titled "The Elements of Presidential Transitions," December 10, 2020, https://www.whitehousetransitionproject.org/wp-content/uploads/2020/12/Statement-to-Govt-Ops-2020-12-10.pdf.

10. Hess and Pfiffner, *Organizing the Presidency*, 162.

11. John P. Burke, "The Bush Transition in Historical Context," *Political Science*, March 2002, 24, quoted in Hess and Pfiffner, *Organizing the Presidency*, 170.

12. "Top Government Posts Remain Open," Brookings Institution press release, March 1, 2002, quoted in Hess and Pfiffner, *Organizing the Presidency*, 175.

13. David Marchick, *The Peaceful Transfer of Power: An Oral History of America's Presidential Transitions* (Charlottesville: University of Virginia Press, 2022), 119.

14. Ibid., 115–16.

15. Paul J. Quirk, "Presidential Competence," in *The Presidency and the Political System*, ed. Nelson, 167.

16. Ibid., 168.

17. Arthur Schlesinger, *A Thousand Days* (New York: Houghton Mifflin, 1965), 688, quoted in Hess and Pfiffner, *Organizing the Presidency*, 65.

18. Earl Mazo and Stephen Hess, *Nixon: A Political Portrait* (New York: Harper and Row, 1986), 314–15, quoted in Hess and Pfiffner, *Organizing the Presidency*, 89.

19. Scott Detrow, "Obama Warns Trump against Relying on Executive Power," National Public Radio, December 19, 2016, https://www.npr.org/2016/12/19/505860058/obama-warns-trump-against-relying-on-executive-power.

20. Michael Nelson, Jeffery L. Chidester, and Stefanie Georgakis Abbott, *Crucible: The President's First Year* (Charlottesville: University of Virginia Press, 2018), 94.

21. Scott Keller and Mary Meaney, "Successfully Transitioning to New Leadership Roles," McKinsey & Company, May 23, 2018, https://www.mckinsey.com/capabilities/people-and-organizational-performance/our-insights/successfully-transitioning-to-new-leadership-roles.

22. Richard Allen, "The Man Who Won the Cold War," *Hoover Digest*, no. 1 (2000), https://web.archive.org/web/20110501052925/http:/www.hoover.org/publications/hoover-digest/article/7398.

23. Woodrow Wilson, *Constitutional Government in the United States* (New York: Columbia University Press, 1908), 56.

24. Paul J. Quirk, "Resolved: Presidential Success and Failure Are Better Explained by Political Time and the Strength of Governing Coalitions Than by a President's Character and Leadership Qualities," in *Debating the Presidency: Conflicting Perspectives on the American Executive*, ed. Richard J. Ellis and Michael Nelson (Thousand Oaks, CA: Sage, 2021), 124.

25. Samuel Kernell, *Going Public: New Strategies of Presidential Leadership* (Washington, DC: CQ Press, 2006), 3.

26. George C. Edwards III, Kenneth R. Mayer, and Stephen J. Wayne, *Presidential Leadership: Politics and Policy Making*, 11th ed. (Lanham, MD: Rowman and Littlefield, 2020), 139.

6. TASK THREE: DESIGN CORE PROCESSES TO ACHIEVE ACTION

1. "Bush: 'I'm the Decider' on Rumsfeld," CNN.com, April 18, 2006, https://www.cnn.com/2006/POLITICS/04/18/rumsfeld/.

2. Jimmy Carter, *Keeping Faith: Memoirs of a President* (New York: Bantam, 1982), 57, quoted in Stephen Hess and James P. Pfiffner, *Organizing the Presidency*, 4th ed. (Washington, DC: Brookings Institution Press, 2021), 124.

3. As quoted in "Cover Story: Reagan on Decision-Making, Planning, Gorbachev, and More," *Fortune*, September 15, 1986.

4. Scott Faulkner, "Personnel Is Policy," *Washington Examiner*, February 2, 2016, https://www.washingtonexaminer.com/personnel-is-policy.

5. John P. Burke, *Honest Broker? The National Security Adviser and Presidential Decision Making* (College Station: Texas A&M University Press, 2009).

6. Roger B. Porter, *Presidential Decision Making: The Economic Policy Board* (Cambridge: Cambridge University Press, 1982), 242.

7. Karla J. Nieting et al., "Oral History Roundtables: The Role of the National Security Adviser" (Center for International Studies at Maryland and the Brookings Institution, 1999), quoted in Burke, *Honest Broker?*, 4.

8. Gen. Brent Scowcroft, telephone interview by John P. Burke, November 15, 2007, quoted in Burke, *Honest Broker?*, 7.

9. Condoleezza Rice, *No Higher Honor* (New York: Crown, 2011), 506–7, quoted in George C. Edwards III, Kenneth R. Mayer, and Stephen J. Wayne, *Presidential Leadership: Politics and Policy Making*, 11th ed. (Lanham, MD: Rowman and Littlefield, 2020), 269.

10. Ted Sorenson, *Decision-Making in the White House* (New York: Columbia University Press, 1963), 62, quoted in Edwards, Mayer, and Wayne, *Presidential Leadership*, 251.

11. Gerald Ford, *A Time to Heal: The Autobiography of Gerald Ford* (New York: Harper and Row, 1979), 187–88, quoted in Edwards, Mayer, and Wayne, *Presidential Leadership*, 259.

12. Robert M. Gates, *Duty* (New York: Knopf, 2014), 300, quoted in Edwards, Mayer, and Wayne, *Presidential Leadership*, 53.

13. Richard Neustadt, *Presidential Power and the Modern Presidents* (New York: Macmillan, 1990), 129.

14. Arthur M. Schlesinger Jr., *The Age of Roosevelt*, vol. 2: *The Coming of the New Deal* (Boston: Houghton Mifflin, 1959), 522–23, quoted in Neustadt, *Presidential Power and the Modern Presidents*, 131.

15. Quirk, "Presidential Competence," quoted in *The Presidency and the Political System*, ed. Nelson, 165.

16. Matthew J. Dickinson, "Resolved: Presidential Power Is the Power to Persuade," in *Debating the Presidency: Conflicting Perspectives on the American Executive*, ed. Richard J. Ellis and Michael Nelson (Thousand Oaks, CA: Sage, 2021), 135.

17. Schlesinger, *Roosevelt*, vol. 2, 528, quoted in Neustadt, *Presidential Power and the Modern Presidents*, 133.

18. Neustadt, *Presidential Power and the Modern Presidents*, 10, emphasis in the original.

19. Doris Kearns, *Lyndon Johnson and the American Dream* (New York: Harper & Row, 1976), 226, quoted in Edwards, Mayer, and Wayne, *Presidential Leadership*, 333.

7. TASK FOUR: DESIGN A COHERENT WHITE HOUSE STRUCTURE

1. Dwight D. Eisenhower, *The White House Years: Mandate for Change, 1953–1956* (New York: Doubleday, 1963), 114, quoted in Stephen Hess and James P. Pfiffner, *Organizing the Presidency*, 4th ed. (Washington, DC: Brookings Institution Press, 2021), 55.

2. Chris Whipple, *The Gatekeepers: How the White House Chiefs of Staff Define Every Presidency* (New York: Broadway, 2018), 75.

3. Samuel Kernell and Samuel L. Popkin, *Chief of Staff: Twenty-Five Years of Managing the Presidency* (Berkeley: University of California Press, 2022), 71.

4. James P. Pfiffner, ed., *The Managerial Presidency* (College Station: Texas A&M University Press, 1999), 11.

5. George C. Edwards III, Kenneth R. Mayer, and Stephen J. Wayne, *Presidential Leadership: Politics and Policy Making*, 11th ed. (Lanham, MD: Rowman and Littlefield, 2020), xix.

6. Henry Mintzberg, *The Structuring of Organizations* (New York: Prentice-Hall, 1979), 198.

7. Hal G. Rainey, *Understanding and Managing Public Organizations* (New York: Wiley and Sons, 2014), 40.

8. Mike Deaver, personal interview by Colin Campbell, May 3, 1983, Washington DC, quoted in Samuel Kernell, "The Evolution of the White House Staff," in *The Managerial Presidency*, ed. Pfiffner, 47.

9. Terry M. Moe, "The Politicized Presidency," in *The New Direction in American Politics*, ed. John Chubb and Paul Peterson (Washington, DC: Brookings Institution Press, 1985), 235.

10. Richard Neustadt, *Presidential Power and the Modern Presidents* (New York: Macmillan, 1990), 82.

11. Herbert Brownell, *Advising Ike: The Memoirs of Attorney General Herbert Brownell*, with John P. Burke (Lawrence: University of Kansas Press, 1993), 294, quoted in Burke, "The Institutional Presidency," in *Presidency and the Political System*, ed. Michael Nelson (Thousand Oaks, CA: Sage, 2021), 445.

8. TASK FIVE: PLAN FOR THE FIRST TWO HUNDRED DAYS

1. David Marchick, *The Peaceful Transfer of Power: An Oral History of America's Presidential Transitions* (Charlottesville: University of Virginia Press, 2022), 163.

2. Chris Liddell, Daniel Kroese, and Clark Campbell, *The Romney Readiness Project 2012: Retrospective and Lessons Learned* (self-pub., 2013), Amazon, 18.

3. Dwight D. Eisenhower, "Address Given by Dwight D. Eisenhower, Republican Nominee for President," Detroit, Michigan, October 24, 1952.

4. Samuel Kernell, *Going Public: New Strategies of Presidential Leadership* (Washington, DC: CQ Press, 2006), 17.

5. Robert A. Dahl and Charles E. Lindblom, *Politics, Economics, and Welfare*, quoted in Kernell, *Going Public*, 17.

6. Testimony of Fred Fielding to the U.S. Senate Subcommittee on Oversight of Government Management, The Federal Workforce, and the District of Columbia, September 14, 2004, 54, https://www.google.com/books/edition/The_9_11_Commission_Human_Capital_Recomm/lEfo3yW99QQC?hl=en&gbpv=1.

7. Martha Joynt Kumar, "Joseph Biden's Effective Presidential Transition: 'Started Early, Went Big,'" *Presidential Studies Quarterly*, September 2021, 1–27, https://www.whitehousetransitionproject.org/wp-content/uploads/2021/08/Kumar-BTransition-Start-Early-Go-Big.pdf.

8. Marchick, *The Peaceful Transfer of Power*, 165.

9. Lisa Rein, "These Are the Experts Who Will Lead Biden's Transition at Federal Agencies," *Washington Post*, November 10, 2020, https://www.washingtonpost.com/politics/biden-transition-team-federal-agencies/2020/11/10/6b4b6388-237f-11eb-a688-5298ad5d580a_story.html.

9. TASK SIX: BUILD A POLICY PIPELINE

1. Jack Valenti, *A Very Human President* (New York: Norton, 1975), 96, quoted in George C. Edwards, "Director or Facilitator? Presidential Policy Control of Congress," in *The Managerial Presidency*, ed. James Pfiffner (College Station: Texas A&M University Press, 1999), 296.

2. Harry McPherson, *A Political Education* (Boston: Little, Brown, 1972), 268, quoted in Roger B. Porter, "The President and the National Agenda," in *The Managerial Presidency*, ed. Pfiffner, 324.

3. Chris Liddell, David Kroese, and Clark Campbell, *Romney Readiness Project 2012: Retrospective and Lessons Learned* (self-pub., 2013), Amazon, 77.

4. Edwards, "Director or Facilitator?," in *The Managerial Presidency*, ed. Pfiffner, 297.

5. Martin Anderson, *Revolution* (San Diego, CA: Harcourt Brace Jovanovich, 1988), 85, in Stephen Hess and James P. Pfiffner, *Organizing the Presidency*, 4th ed. (Washington, DC: Brookings Institution Press, 2021), 136.

6. David A. Yalof, "The Presidency and the Judiciary," in *The Presidency and the Political System*, ed. Michael Nelson (Thousand Oaks, CA: Sage, 2021), 540.

7. President Gerald Ford, "Statement on Signing the National Emergencies Act," September 14, 1976, hosted at the UC Santa Barbara American Presidency Project, https://www.presidency.ucsb.edu/documents/statement-signing-the-national-emergencies-act.

8. Elizabeth Goitien, "Trump's Hidden Powers," Brennan Center, December 5,

2018, https://www.brennancenter.org/our-work/analysis-opinion/trumps-hidden -powers.

9. Haynes Johnson, "Tests," *Washington Post,* April 30, 1978, quoted in Nicholas Henry, *Public Administration and Public Affairs* (London: Taylor and Francis, 2015), 22.

10. John Brehm and Scott Gates, *Working, Shirking, and Sabotage: Bureaucratic Responses to a Democratic Republic* (Ann Arbor: University of Michigan Press, 1997), 202, quoted in Edwards, Mayer, and Wayne, *Presidential Leadership,* 309.

11. James Q. Wilson, *Bureaucracy: What Government Agencies Do and Why They Do It* (New York: Basic, 1989), 275, quoted in Edwards, Mayer, and Wayne, *Presidential Leadership,* 309.

12. The Center on Budget and Policy Priorities, "Policy Basics, Introduction to the Federal Budget Process," February 2, 2023, https://www.cbpp.org/research/federal -budget/introduction-to-the-federal-budget-process#:~:text=Basic%20Budget %20Spending%20and%20Revenue%20Categories&text=Spending.,on%20debt %20(see%20chart).

10. TASK SEVEN: BUILD A PEOPLE PIPELINE

1. Kenneth P. O'Donnell and David F. Powers, *Johnny, We Hardly Knew Ye: Memories of John Fitzgerald Kennedy* (New York: Pocket Books, 1972), 270, quoted in George C. Edwards III, Kenneth R. Mayer, and Stephen J. Wayne, *Presidential Leadership: Politics and Policy Making,* 11th ed. (Lanham, MD: Rowman and Littlefield, 2020), 313.

2. Carlos Galina, Paul Hitlin, and Mary-Courtney Murphy, "Slow Nominations and Confirmations Pose a Threat to National Security," Partnership for Public Service Center for Presidential Transition, May 24, 2022.

3. Jimmy Carter, *Keeping Faith: Memoirs of a President* (New York: Bantam, 1982), 61.

4. Charles S. Clark, "Clinton Email Fracas Raises Question: What Is a 'Special Government Employee?,'" *Government Executive,* September 4, 2015, https://www .govexec.com/oversight/2015/09/clinton-email-fracas-raises-question-what-special -government-employee/120362/.

5. Ibid.

6. U.S. Office of Personnel Management, "Intergovernment Personnel Act," https://www.opm.gov/policy-data-oversight/hiring-information/intergovernment -personnel-act/.

7. Ibid.

8. Richard J. Ellis, *Presidential Lightning Rods: The Politics of Blame Avoidance* (Lawrence: University of Kansas Press, 2021), 100.

9. Paul J. Quirk, "Presidential Competence," quoted in *The Presidency and the Political System,* ed. Michael Nelson (Thousand Oaks, CA: Sage, 2021), 168.

10. Ibid., 167.

11. Adam Grant, *Think Again* (New York: Penguin, 2021), 78.

12. Ibid.

13. Donald T. Regan, *For the Record: From Wall Street to Washington* (San Diego, CA: Harcourt Brace Jovanovich, 1988), xiv, quoted in Edwards, Mayer, and Wayne, *Presidential Leadership,* 191.

CONCLUSION

1. John F. Kennedy, "After Two Years—A Conversation with the President," American Broadcasting Company, December 17, 1962.

2. Terry M. Moe, "The Politicized Presidency," in *The Managerial Presidency*, ed. James Pfiffner (College Station: Texas A&M University Press, 1999), 158.

3. Quoted in Samuel P. Huntington, *Political Order in Changing Societies* (New Haven, CT: Yale University Press, 2006), 9.

4. Theodore Roosevelt, "Citizenship in a Republic," speech given at the Sorbonne, Paris, France, April 23, 1910.

Index

Page numbers followed by f or t indicate figures and tables.

staff in temporary roles, 191, 201, 202f, 203, 204t, 206, 208–9, 227; briefings of president-elect, 163, 167–68; budgetary expansion for, 3; citizen services, improvement of, 104, 129, 151, 161, 190, 192–94, 197, 227, 229; creation and number of, 22; in decision-making process, 149–51; "detailing" people to serve in White House, 56; formal and long-standing, 150; formal and short-lived, 150; growth of and rising expenditures of, 3, 4f, 39; implementation role, 22–25, 58, 112, 127–28, 131, 131f, 139, 151–52; independent agencies, 22, 25; informal and long-standing, 150; informal and short-lived, 150; interagency disputes, 152; policy pipeline to include, 190–94; program associate directors (PADs), 204; reporting relationships, 150–53; reviews by transition teams, 164, 171–72; rule-making authority of, 22, 24; running without Senate-confirmed officials, 206, 208–9, 227; senior political appointments, 151, 191, 202, 202f, 204t; strategic plans, 100; succession plans as part of transition, 65; in White House structure, 138f, 139, 225f. See also cabinet; federal employees; regulations
federal budget. See budget
Federal Communications Commission (FCC), 22, 25
federal employees: civil servants, 23–24, 54; increase in, 3–4; political appointees, 23, 25, 29–31, 54. See also civil servants; federal agencies
federal government: operational effectiveness of, 6–7; trust in, 3, 5, 9, 39, 108, 148. See also specific branches, agencies, and officials
Federalist: No. 51, 3; No. 74, 33
federal judgeships: appointment of, 31–32, 199, 201, 202f, 204t; legacy effect of appointments, 50; lifetime tenure, 32; number of, 201; Senate

confirmation of, 31, 32, 207; White House Counsel's role, 49–50. See also Supreme Court, U.S.
Federal Labor Relations Authority, 177
federal land restrictions, 22
Federal Reserve, 22, 25, 149, 200
Federal Trade Commission (FTC), 22, 25
Fielding, Fred, 165
filibuster, 16, 32, 184
filibuster-proof majority, 181
financial crisis: 2008–9, 4, 178–79; in first year of presidency, 16
first ladies: chief of staff to, 205t; role in OPOTUS, 82
first one hundred days as meaningful milestone, 158–59
first two hundred days (Task Five), 68, 69, 69f, 157–73, 223f, 226; achieving results as priority in, 161, 173, 226; congressional dealings in, 161–62; consulting with outsiders for fresh perspectives, 227; contested election, plan for, 166–68; crisis management planning, 165–69, 173; Day One as signal moment for, 162, 173; executive orders issued in, 175, 186–87, 227; inaugural speech giving detailed goals and plans for, 162; legislation preparation preelection enabling introduction in, 180, 181, 227; passing signature legislation in, 174; planning eight months before the inauguration (Year Zero), 157–58, 159f, 160, 226f; presidential appointments, 164, 167, 199, 202–3, 204t, 206, 227; priority choices for, 159–61, 187; of second term, 160, 173; shadow White House, 165–67, 173; transformational plan, 158–62, 159f, 226f; transition period used to plan, 162–69; working backward to plan for achieving goals, 99, 159, 159f, 173, 226, 226f. See also transition teams
501(c)(4) nonprofit organization to privately fund transition activities, 75, 172, 188

7, 60; 2016, on Trump's transition
team, 7, 60; 2018–21, Trump's deputy chief of staff, 7–8, 113–14, 118–19,
124, 133–34; 2020–21, White House
officer in charge of Trump-Biden
presidential transition, 10, 84, 157–
58; American Technology Council
chaired by, 145–46; meetings with
deputy assistants to the president,
216; *The Romney Readiness Project 2012: Retrospective and Lessons
Learned* (with Campbell and Kroese), 66, 67, 86, 158–59, 165, 169
Lighthizer, Robert, 124
Lincoln, Abraham: amnesty for Civil
War soldiers, 33; financial crisis and,
16; personal assistants and advisers
of, 77–78; on policy setting, 100;
presidential power and, 13; state
secession after election of 1860, 157;
transition of 1861, 61
Lindblom, Charles E., 161
line-item veto, 19
Livy, 85
lobbying: of federal agencies, 30; by
the president, 12, 18–19
Locke, John, 13
loyalty as hiring criteria, 213–15, 219, 227

Macmillan, Harold, 16
Madison, James, on federal govern-
ment, 3
Manchin, Joe, 183
Manhattan Project, 87
Marchick, David: *The Peaceful Transfer
of Power*, 66, 86, 167
Marine Mammal Commission, 22
Mayer, Kenneth: *Presidential Leadership*
(with Edwards and Wayne), 86
McConnell, Mitch, 32
McIntyre, Marvin, 37
McLarty, Mack, 92, 136
McNamara, Robert, 89, 150
media: anonymity of senior staff with,
82; backgrounding, 82; coverage
frustrations, 33–34; outreach in Year
One, 105–6; policy promotion by
president and, 148

Medicaid, 195
Medicare, 195
Meese, Ed, 80, 91
meetings: of incoming and outgoing
presidents on Inauguration Day,
62; number of advisers meeting
with president at one time, 125, 211;
presidential meetings with foreign
leaders, 105, 108; training on how to
run, 211
memorandum of understanding with
GSA, 64, 65
midterm elections: achieving results
tied to, 104, 230; limiting possibility
of legislation, 106, 175; presidential
campaigns' start following, 67, 72;
unfavorable to incumbents, 107;
Zero Year approach's effect on,
68, 70
military: aid, 28–29; force, use of, 18,
27–28; size of, 4, 28
Mintzberg, Henry, 141
mistakes, 98, 165–66, 218–19, 230
Mnuchin, Steve, 124
Moe, Terry, 5, 147, 221
Mondale, Walter, 40–41
Montreal Protocol on Substances
That Deplete the Ozone Layer
(2022), 27
Moyers, Bill, 89
Murphy's Law, 100

NASA, 22, 25
National Defense Authorization Act of
2017, 212
National Economic Council (NEC):
competence of members, 214;
creation of, 46, 47; Economic
Policy Board as forerunner to, 90;
presidential appointment, 205t; as
primary interface for private sector,
154, 155f; role of, 46, 112; staff, 145;
structure of, 134–36; West Wing
office, 53
national emergencies, declaration of,
18, 189–90
National Emergencies Act of 1976
(NEA), 189–90

MILLER CENTER STUDIES ON THE PRESIDENCY

The Presidency and the American State: Leadership and Decision Making in the Adams, Grant, and Taft Administrations
Stephen J. Rockwell

Mourning the Presidents: Loss and Legacy in American Culture
Lindsay M. Chervinsky and Matthew R. Costello, editors

The Peaceful Transfer of Power: An Oral History of America's Presidential Transitions
David Marchick and Alexander Tippett, with A. J. Wilson

Averting Doomsday: Arms Control during the Nixon Presidency
Patrick J. Garrity and Erin R. Mahan

The Presidency: Facing Constitutional Crossroads
Michael Nelson and Barbara A. Perry, editors

Trump: The First Two Years
Michael Nelson

Broken Government: Bridging the Partisan Divide
William J. Antholis and Larry J. Sabato, editors

Race: The American Cauldron
Douglas A. Blackmon, editor

Communication: Getting the Message Across
Nicole Hemmer, editor

American Dreams: Opportunity and Upward Mobility
Guian McKee and Cristina Lopez-Gottardi Chao, editors

Immigration: Struggling over Borders
Sidney M. Milkis and David Leblang, editors

Crucible: The President's First Year
Michael Nelson, Jeffrey L. Chidester, and Stefanie Georgakis Abbott, editors

The Dangerous First Year: National Security at the Start of a New Presidency
William I. Hitchcock and Melvyn P. Leffler, editors

The War Bells Have Rung: The LBJ Tapes and the Americanization of the Vietnam War
George C. Herring